The Holocaust in Literature for Youth

A Guide and Resource Book

Edward T. Sullivan

The Scarecrow Press, Inc.
Lanham, Maryland, and London
1999

SCARECROW PRESS, INC.

Published in the United States of America
by Scarecrow Press, Inc.
4720 Boston Way
Lanham, Maryland 20706

4 Pleydell Gardens, Folkestone
Kent CT20 2DN, England

British Library Cataloguing in Publication Information Available

Library of Congress Cataloging-in-Publication Data

Sullivan, Edward T.
    The Holocaust in literature for youth : a guide and resource
book / Edward T. Sullivan.
        p. cm.
    Includes bibliographical references and indexes.
    ISBN 0-8108-3607-6 (cloth : alk. paper)
    1. Holocaust, Jewish (1939-1945)--Bibliography. 2. Holocaust,
Jewish (1939-1945)--Juvenile literature--Bibliography. 3. Holocaust, Jewish
(1939-1945)--Study and teaching--Bibliography. I. Title.
Z6374.H6 S85 1999
D804.3 016.94053'18--dc21   98-48768
                                                          CIP

♾™ The paper used in this publication meets the minimum requirements of
American National Standard for Information Sciences—Permanence of
Paper for Printed Library Materials, ANSI Z39.48–1984.
Manufactured in the United States of America.

CONTENTS

Acknowledgments   v
Foreword   vii
Introduction   1
About the Bibliographies   9

1. Anthologies   11
2. Autobiography and Biography   13
3. Drama   41
4. Fiction   45
5. Nonfiction   71
6. Picture Books   105
7. Poetry and Songs   109
8. Reference   115
9. Making Connections   119

Appendices
A. Professional Resources for Educators   143
B. Electronic Holocaust Resources   163
C. International Directory of Holocaust Memorials,   181
    Museums, Organizations, and Other Institutions
D. Booktalks, Classroom Activities, and Lesson Plans   207
E. Building a Core Holocaust Collection in Your School   223
    Library

Author Index   227
Geographic Index   235
Grade Index   237
Subject Index   241
Title Index   245

About the Author   261

Acknowledgments

There are a number of people to whom I owe thanks for their help with putting this book together. To the staffs of The New York Public Library Center for the Humanities Jewish Division and of The United States Holocaust Memorial Museum Resource Centers, I thank you for your invaluable assistance. Thank you to Marc Aronson of Henry Holt Books for Young Readers, Leslie Barban of the Richland County Public Library System, and Beryl Eber and Nancy Zink of The New York Public Library for your important contributions to the book. I must also thank Dr. Jinx Watson of The University of Tennessee School of Information Sciences for your many helpful suggestions. To my patient and supportive wife, Judy, thank you for doing all of that tedious proofreading.

Foreword

Creating Holocaust Literature for Young People:
An Editor's Perspective

Marc Aronson

I have now worked on five books that are connected to the Holocaust. The experiences they recount include a Gentile gay teenager in Poland who was imprisoned by the Nazis once they found out about his affair with a German soldier (*Damned Strong Love* by Lutz Van Dijk); five teenagers who kept diaries until they were taken to camps and killed (*We Are Witnesses* by Jacob Boas); a French teenager who became increasingly active in the Resistance, losing her sister in the process (*Spyglass* by Helene Deschamps); the diary a teenager kept in Auschwitz and Plazow (*The Beautiful Days of My Youth* by Ana Novac) and a diary of a young woman who began the war in her late teens kept in Theresienstadt (*We're Alive and Life Goes On* by Eva Roubickova).

Working on these books, I had to read and reread the texts over and over and over again. Every single time I did not want to do it. I didn't want to go where I knew the words were taking me. I didn't want to see the camps, hear the agonies of cattle cars, smell the charnel house smoke. Most of all, I did not want to care for people I knew were going to suffer, and in most cases die, horribly. I had to steel myself to pick up the pages in order to make corrections, or check proofs, or write copy.

And, each and every time, a moment in the book would catch me off guard. Then, instead of being numb I'd be angry—at the world, at the Germans, at God, even at the Jews. Everything in my daily life would seem silly, pointless, all so easy. Then, I had to face the theological questions: How could this evil have happened, and so recently, and to people like me, done by people who could also have been me? I would get plunged into a kind of reckoning that almost never comes any other way. Reading about the Holocaust stops the world. The events are incomprehensible, which is why we must keep trying to comprehend them. Reading about the camps forces you to decide what it means to be human.

Any good book on the Holocaust will challenge you in that way. But as the books added up, I started to learn something else about the genocide: People's experiences during those terrible days were astonishingly varied, as varied as people can be. The real story of Holocaust is not just death and loss, it is love, bravery, courage, theft, greed, cowardice: every sin and every grace was there in the camps. Moshe Flinker in *We Are Witnesses* understood the Holocaust as a sign of the end of time. He wanted things to get worse, so that God would arrive. Yitzhak Rudashevski, in the same book, devoted himself to reading and culture, until he tried to join a partisan group to fight.

It was one kind of experience to move from Moshe's world to Yitzhak's. It was quite another to read *We're Alive and Life Goes On* just after publishing *The Beautiful Days of My Youth*. In Auschwitz, Ana Novac wrote a bitter, ironic, composed diary about life in a surreal place where guards whipped prisoners with lizards. She only managed to preserve fragments, and even these were palimpsests of memory that she wrote and rewrote, translated and retranslated over time. Her diary reads exactly like a hand held camera, shooting newsreels in hell. One page is a punch in the stomach as you see real evil, with no filter. And the next is absurd. The pages are relentless, and the only hope is to survive in any way and at any cost.

Eva Roubickova, in Theresienstadt, wrote about flirting with boys and stealing vegetables from the camp garden to bring to her father. Her diary is so different from Ana's that you almost cannot use any single world to describe both experiences. She was growing vegetables when Ana was starving for a crust of bread. And yet beneath the surface of the model camp's almost normalcy there was exactly the same perversion of humanity, and the same challenge to the human spirit. Daily, people were shipped out of Theresienstadt, never to return. And at each "selection" there were impossible choices: should I give up my life to accompany a loved-one to her doom? How can I? How can I not?

Every camp was a test it was impossible to pass. So people tried everything. We are now so fortunate to be able to read their records, and see ourselves. If every book on the camps tests our humanity, it also displays the variety of human reactions. That is one of the great losses of other tragedies such as the Middle Passage. There, we can only talk about collective experience. We don't have all of these separate voices clamoring to tell their corner of the story. That leaves the Holocaust both to indict us, and to speak for us. No books ask more of us, or are more important.

I hope that Ed Sullivan's book will encourage librarians and teachers, students and parents, to read widely, so that they see the many different stories of the Holocaust, all of which are ours. We should read these books not only to understand the past and to rededicate ourselves to shaping a better future, but also because they show us who we are, and ever more shall be so. What more could you ask of a book?

Marc Aronson, Ph.D. is a senior editor of Henry Holt Books for Young People and the author of Art Attack: A Short Cultural History of the Avant-Garde

Introduction

More than fifty years have passed since the concentration and death camps were liberated by the Allied forces in Europe and the world discovered the horrific atrocities human beings were capable of perpetrating upon one another. Fortunately for humankind, these monstrous acts are still remembered and, interestingly, it seems as if we now make more of an effort than ever before to remember. There are many people responsible for keeping this darkest moment in history alive. Most significant are those who survived the Holocaust and chose to share their experiences in classrooms and in recorded and written testimonies. As those living witnesses to history pass on, we have to concern ourselves with who will carry on their story. There are those who have built memorials, monuments, and museums to keep the memory alive. There are people like filmmaker Steven Spielberg who, with his film *Schindler's List*, vividly brought that part of history to life for people who were born long after it occurred and might otherwise know little or nothing of it. Most important are educators, who have recognized the importance and necessity of Holocaust education.

Requiring the Holocaust be taught on all grade levels, many states have developed and implemented detailed curriculum standards for Holocaust education. Many more states are in the process of following suit or have plans to, guaranteeing that the Holocaust will be a standard subject of study nationwide.

Remembering the Holocaust will prevent it from ever happening again—that is the hope of the survivors who have borne witness, as it is the hope of all who want to keep it alive through education, memorials, and other means. In discussions of the Holocaust, Carlos Santayana's words are often invoked: "Those who forget the past are condemned to repeat it." That statement has proven itself true time and time again. The truth of it is justification enough for Holocaust education.

We have seen far too many examples of what can happen when the past is forgotten. Consider how many genocides there have been since the Holocaust: millions of Cambodians slaughtered under the Pol Pot Khmer Rouge regime; "ethnic cleansing" in the former Yugoslavia; the Hutu and Tutsi ethnic factions massacring one another in Rwanda; the attempted annihilation of the Kurdish population living in northern Iraq; and widespread, government sanctioned massacres in Algeria of one religious sect are just a few of many to consider. How many millions of people have died and continue to die from ethnic, racial, and religious conflicts in East Timor, India, Israel, Lebanon, Nigeria, Northern Ireland, South Africa, the former Soviet Union and Sri Lanka? Remembering the Holocaust has certainly not ended anti-Semitism. Not a day goes by without a report of the vandalism of a synagogue, a Jewish cemetery, or the home or business of a Jew in the United States. What is most profoundly disturbing is that the perpetrators of these acts are often among the youngest members of our society

Neo-Nazi and other white supremacist organizations prey upon alienated, angry, impressionable youth. They tap into the anger and ignorance of these young people and teach them how to hate. They fill the voids in their lives with it; hate gives their lives a sense of direction and purpose. It is not at all unlike what Hitler and his young Nazi party accomplished in Germany in the late 1920s. Germany, a nation devastated by economic depression and humiliated from its defeat in World War I, was ripe to fall under the spell of someone who could give the disenfranchised a scapegoat. Hitler gave them the Jews. The Jews were blamed for all of Germany's ills. Hating the Jews gave people something to be passionate about again. This is what our dispirited, disaffected youth succumb to in the United States. They fall prey to hatemongerers who offer them Jews, Blacks, Hispanics, Asians, homosexuals, and any other "non-Aryan" as their scapegoats. Hate gives meaning to their lives. Amongst their fellow hatemongerers, they feel a sense of belonging. One reads about or hears of consistent reports of Neo-Nazi "skinheads" or some other gang terrorizing some individual or group. Consider the recent rash of arsons of black churches across the South and the racially motivated attacks in Denver as two of many examples. Even more frightening to contemplate is that these acts are not committed by common thugs, by "bad seeds," or a few sociopathic anomalies of the human race. They are otherwise normal children who were never taught compassion, never taught tolerance and respect, never given love, and never given a sense of belonging.

A considerably more dangerous enemy we have to worry about is those historical revisionists who would have us believe that there was no Holocaust. Those of us who know better can dismiss these lunatics and their utterly preposterous assertions, but what about all the people who do not know better? I am thinking specifically of children and teenagers. When they come across the publications of these factions on the World Wide Web (which are quite extensive), they will not recognize what they read for the nonsense it is because they do not know the truth. The revisionists are far more dangerous than any sort of other belligerent hatemongerers like skinheads and neo-Nazis, because they dress their hate in reason. Unlike militant hate organizations, revisionists are educated enough to recognize that subtlety and the appearance of reason are far more powerful weapons against impressionable minds. The tone of revisionist documents is remarkably reasonable, restrained, and superficially, even appears objective. Revisionist documents are typically full of footnotes and extensive bibliographies, giving the impression that what one is reading is the result of careful, thoughtful research. Anyone who knows little or nothing of the truth about the Holocaust could easily be swayed by such lies. My fear is that the youngest members of our society, our most impressionable, are the most likely victims of these insidious attempts to obscure and pervert the truth.

To counter these efforts, we must educate in a comprehensive, consistent, diligent and, most important, meaningful and relevant manner. Holocaust education must be much, much more than the study of people, places, and events. It must go far beyond the superficial highlights of history textbooks. For Holocaust education to be truly effective, it must go beyond the study of those ten years in Europe when six million Jews in Europe and millions of other people were slaughtered under the direction of Adolf Hitler and his Nazi regime. Studying those events is merely the beginning of Holocaust education. Holocaust education can only be meaningful when we look at those events in the greater context of human experience.

The Holocaust was not the first mass genocide of an entire people, nor was it the first instance of the wholesale persecution of Jews. When Hitler rose to power and began implementing his slow stranglehold on Europe's Jews, did they remember the enslavement in Egypt or oppression under the Roman Empire? Did they remember the Spanish Inquisition or pogroms in Russia and Eastern Europe? What about the untold numbers of Africans who perished in the Middle Passage on their way to enslavement? As for mass genocide, did they forget what the Turks did to the Armenians during World War I, or what the United States government did to its indigenous peoples? Forgotten was a history spanning thousands of years of the human race committing one barbaric act after another. If these horrors were remembered, would Germany and the rest of the world ever have allowed Hitler to come to power? The Holocaust stands out from other genocides in history for a multitude of reasons. Most obvious is that no other genocide before or since has been perpetrated on such a grand scale. Jews and other "enemies of the state" had been persecuted from the moment Hitler seized power in 1933, but the wholesale, systematic killing of Jews was not begun until the early 1940s. The Wannsee Conference, held in 1942, was where the architects of the Final Solution actually planned the elaborate infrastructure that enabled them to exterminate human beings at an unprecedented rate on an unprecedented scale. The majority of the six million Jews and millions of other people exterminated occurred within the short time frame of only three years from 1942 to 1945. Hitler came very close to achieving his goal of a Jew-free Europe. No one, thank God, has ever preceded or surpassed the Nazi's efficiency in organized, wholesale murder. The sheer magnitude of the event ensured that it would be remembered long after it occurred. The Nazis were also scrupulously efficient about keeping records, and their failure to destroy a good deal of them before they were captured has left us with plenty of documentary evidence. There is also the fact that the Holocaust occurred in the midst of a global conflict. It ended when the war ended, and so all the world was present to bear witness. One must also consider the scores of Holocaust survivors who have devoted their lives to ensuring the memory stays alive by speaking to audiences, and writing and recording their experiences for posterity. More has been written about the Holocaust than any other genocide. There is a vast canon of Holocaust literature written for readers of all ages. The Holocaust has also served as the subject for innumerable motion picture and television productions. Across the country are hundreds of educational centers, libraries, memorials, and museums dedicated to keeping the memory alive.

Despite its preeminence for all those reasons, the Holocaust alone cannot be the sole content of Holocaust education. To make it truly meaningful and relevant, it must be studied in respect to other genocides in the context of the whole of human experience. There are some Jews who strenuously disagree with this notion. There is the belief that examining the Holocaust as only one of many genocides somehow trivializes its importance. I find that position totally without foundation. Of what benefit can it be to anyone to study the Holocaust as an isolated event? We do not live in a vacuum, and the Holocaust did not occur in one. I can think of no greater disservice than to lead a student to think otherwise. Another perception shared among some Jews is that the Holocaust should be studied as a uniquely Jewish experience. That notion is absurdly wrongheaded. Those who would deny the murders of Gypsies, homosexuals, the mentally and physically handicapped, Jehovah's Witnesses, political enemies, and millions of other non-Jews are as dangerous as the revisionists who deny the Holocaust.

The primary goal of Holocaust education is not, and should not be, teaching students about the Holocaust. The Holocaust is merely the means, not the end, of Holocaust education. The goal should be to teach the student about him or herself. Specifically, it should be about hate, the hate that is within all of us, and the hateful acts of which we are capable. We can do that only if we look at many instances of genocide, prejudice, and persecution. If we teach students only about the Holocaust and do not connect it to similar events at other times in history in different parts of the world, then they are left with the impression that the Holocaust was an isolated moment in history when some members of humanity went mad. We must be very, very careful never to convey that dangerous impression. We must look at hate as a human condition, common to all, which must be confronted and subdued. Albert Camus said: "The truth is that every intelligent man, as you know, dreams of being a gangster and of ruling over society by force alone." Once we accept that about ourselves, and remember it, and never forget it, and teach our children to know and remember and never forget it, maybe then we will not have to worry about there ever being another Holocaust. Teaching young people about the Holocaust, and the genocides that came before and after it, are the best means we have of teaching those important lessons.

If this book accomplishes nothing else, I want it to make teachers aware that there is a lot more to the Holocaust than Anne Frank's *Diary of a Young Girl*. If students read any Holocaust literature at all in their entire elementary and secondary education, it is that book. I am, by no means, disparaging the work. It is rightfully regarded as a classic and should be read. I find it disturbing, however, that that book alone will be the only exposure students will have to Holocaust literature. In addition to a few boldfaced facts in a history book, it is likely to be all that students graduating from high school will know of the Holocaust. I find that idea most disturbing. No wonder neo-Nazi groups are having such an easy time recruiting young people. Frank's *Diary of a Young Girl* offers little insight into the catastrophic proportions of the Holocaust and does little to convey the unspeakable horrors people suffered. The book is more a coming of age story of precocious young adolescent than an insightful look into the horrors of the Holocaust. Because Anne Frank has become an international icon, a symbol of what was lost in the Holocaust, students and teachers alike mistakenly think that reading her diary will tell one all one needs to know about the Holocaust. The sad truth is that Frank's story is only one of millions of stories from the Holocaust. Her experience is not representative of all the other people who suffered and perished. All that we need to know about the Holocaust will not be learned from reading *Diary of a Young Girl*. It's a good place to begin, perhaps, but it is only one small glimpse of a much larger picture. To see that picture, teachers must expose students to the many other personal narratives, novels, poems, and other works from the vast canon of Holocaust literature.

The purpose of this book is to provide classroom teachers, public and school librarians, and any other person concerned with educating young people about the Holocaust, a practical, comprehensive resource guide that will refer them to all of the literature available for children and young adults on the subject. In addition to books about the Holocaust, there is a section called "Making Connections," which lists works pertaining to themes, and other genocides and historical events that can easily be tied into any study of the Holocaust. As I said, it is not sufficient to study the Holocaust alone. It is the connections we make that will make Holocaust education meaningful and relevant. I have, by no means, cited all of the connections one can make to the Holocaust, but there are several here to give you a place to begin. Of course, I strongly urge you to make your own connections and, even more important, encourage your students to do so.

To complement the literature are a number of other resources: a listing of Internet and other electronic resources for educators and their students; a directory of museums and other educational organizations that can provide you with further information and support; and extensive references of professional resources educators on all levels can use to help them shape their curriculum and teaching strategies. A final feature is a collection of booktalks, classroom activities, and lesson plans educators can utilize in their entirety, or use as foundations

for strategies of his or her own.
There are many excellent bibliographic resources already available on Holocaust literature for educators so why, one might ask, create another? Many of these bibliographic resources on the Holocaust do not address literature for children and young adults, and those that do are far from comprehensive. The purpose of this publication is to fill that void, to offer a comprehensive look at Holocaust literature for youth. All Holocaust literature for youth—good, mediocre, and poor—is included here to reveal the full scope of this important genre. One should remember that for all the excellent Holocaust literature available for young people, there is plenty that is bad, too. There are plenty of books for all ages that are too didactic, too sensational, that try to evade the horrible truths, and some that are just poorly written. In addition to annotations for all the works listed in the bibliographies, I have offered some critical commentary on many of them as well. Please do not take my opinions of these works as gospels. Read and compare what reviewers have said about them and, of course, see for yourself. All I ask is that you consider carefully the literature you recommend to young people. You want them to have not only accuracy, but quality as well.

About the Bibliographies

Every attempt has been made to offer educators a comprehensive resource guide to the Holocaust literature available for children and young adults. These bibliographies include literature for youth of all ages, from the earliest elementary school grades through senior high. Because this is such a wide audience, one will find children's and young adult literature, as well as adult literature that has potential appeal for older teenage readers.

One should remember that although the term "young adult" is commonly defined as ages 12-18 in librarianship, the literature published in the category of young adult is typically for the age range 10-14. Few books are written and published specifically for older teens. Judging what adult titles will have appeal for older teens is tricky business but, for the older members of the young adult audience, I have included numerous adult titles that I believe will be of some interest to them.

Determining a range of grade levels for these materials is largely an arbitrary task. Librarians and teachers should view these ranges as merely a suggested guideline. Before assigning or recommending a work to a student or class, one should consider the abilities, interests, and motivations of that person or group. One will find all of the bibliographic information one will need to locate a particular work (i.e. author, title, publisher, date and place of publication). The ISBN, if available, is also included. When possible, this information has been verified through *Books in Print*. One should note, however, that not all books were currently in print. Because books go in and out (and in again) of print with such rapidity, it was decided not to include that information in the bibliography. For books that have gone through several publishers, the most recent data for hardcover and/or paperback publication is offered. In some cases, I have made some mention of a work's publication history.

Books have been arranged in the following categories: Anthologies, Autobiography and Biography, Drama, Fiction, Picture Books, and Poetry, Reference, and Songs. Making Connections is a concluding category featuring a collection of bibliographies of books on subjects educators can use to approach the Holocaust in broader contexts. Each book is assigned a number and is indexed by author, geographic location, subject, and title. All entries are annotated and, when possible, a brief evaluative comment is also offered.

Anthologies

One will find listed in this section collections of autobiographical works (in whole or in part), poetry, short stories, and works of art by several different authors. There are a number of titles, I chose not to include here: *Plays of the Holocaust*, *Shadows of the Holocaust*, and *So Young to Die*, all cited in "Drama;" *Blood to Remember*, *Ghosts of the Holocaust*, *Holocaust Poetry*, *I Never Saw Another Butterfly*, *Oral History and the Holocaust*, *Peace and War*, and *Young Voices from the Ghetto*, all cited in "Poetry;" and *We Are Here* and *Yes We Sang!* both cited in "Songs." Works listed here are typically found in the nonfiction section of a library, but I wanted to distinguish these books from other works of nonfiction.

001 Frielander, Albert, ed. *Out of the Whirlwind: A Reader of Holocaust Literature*. Illus. Jacob Landau. New York: Schocken, 1976. 536 pp.
Gr. 9-12. A thematically arranged collection of selections from longer Holocaust works and complete shorter pieces. Among the distinguished authors represented are Leo Baeck, Bruno Bettelheim, Anne Frank, Rolf Hochhuth, Primo Levi, and Elie Wiesel. Illustrated with black-and-white drawings. Originally published by the Union of American Hebrew Congregations in New York in 1968.

002 Glatstein, Jacob, et al., eds. *Anthology of Holocaust Literature*. New York: Atheneum, 1977. 412 pp. (pbk. 0-689-70343-0) $11.95
Gr. 9-12. A thematically arranged collection of sixty-five selections from personal Holocaust narratives, all by victims and eyewitnesses. Includes a glossary and biographies of the contributors.

003 Grafstein, Jerry S., ed. *Beyond Imagination: Canadians Write About the Holocaust*. Toronto: McClelland and Stewart, 1995. 265 pp. (hc. 0-7710-3506-3) $29.95
Gr. 9-12. An anthology of short fiction and nonfiction pieces from Canadian authors and historians. Includes brief biographical sketches of the contributors.

004 Holliday, Laurel, ed. *Children in the Holocaust and World War II: Their Secret Diaries.* New York: Pocket, 1995. 409 pp. (hc. 0-671-52054-7) $20.00; (pbk. 0-671-52055-5) $ 12.00
Gr. 7-12. An outstanding collection of the diaries of twenty-three children, ranging in age from eleven to eighteen, telling of their Holocaust experiences. Countries represented include: Austria, Belgium, Czechoslovakia, Denmark, England, Germany, Holland, Hungary, Lithuania, Poland, and Russia. This is an extraordinary collection of personal narratives of young people who experienced the Holocaust. A must for any collection.

005 Langer, Lawrence L. *Art from the Ashes: A Holocaust Anthology.* New York: Oxford UP, 1995. 689 pp. (hc. 0-19-507559-5) $30.00; (pbk. 0-19-507732-6) $23.00
Gr. 9-12. A rich anthology of excerpts of novels, drama, journal and diary excerpts, paintings, personal narratives, poetry, and short stories. The paintings are represented only in black-and-white. An amazing, invaluable collection of important works.

006 Rochman, Hazel and Darlene Z. McCampbell. *Bearing Witness: Stories of the Holocaust.* New York: Orchard, 1995. 135 pp. (hc. 0-531-09488-X) $15.95
Gr. 7-12. An anthology of excerpts from major works of Holocaust literature offering a multifaceted view from a variety of perspectives. An outstanding sampler, well suited for classroom use. Includes a bibliography.

007 *Survivors Speak Out.* Jerusalem: Geffen, 1990. 96 pp. (pbk. 965-229-041-6)
Gr. 9-12. Concentration camp survivors express their experiences in poetry, prose narrative, or short story.

008 Teichman, Milton and Sharon Leder. *Truth and Lamentation: Stories and Poems on the Holocaust.* Urbana: U of Illinois P, 1994. 526 pp. (hc. 0-252-020-28-6) $39.95; (pbk. 0-252-06335-X) $17.95
Gr. 9-12. Another excellent anthology of Holocaust literature, this one international in scope and comprised of poetry and short stories. Includes brief biographical sketches of the authors and a bibliography.

Autobiography and Biography

One will find in this section books by people telling of his or her own life or experiences, and books about individuals by other people. I have included autobiographies and biographies of rescuers, perpetrators, resisters, survivors, and victims. One will also find works by and about people who have other unique personal connections to the Holocaust. There may be some disagreement among my fellow librarians over some of the works I chose to include in this section. For instance, Anne Frank's *Diary of a Young Girl* can be found in a nonfiction section with other history books, or in the biography section of a library. In some cases, one can find the book in both sections of the library. How materials are cataloged and classified can sometimes be an arbitrary matter, and so it is in the case of some works cited here.

009 Adelson, Alan, ed. *The Diary of Dawid Sierakowiak: Five
     Notebooks from the Lodz Ghetto*. Trans. Kamil Turowski. New
     York: Oxford UP, 1996. 271 pp. (hc. 0-19-510450-1) $27.50

Gr. 9-12. Dawid Sierakowiak was fifteen when the Nazis occupied Poland. Dawid and his family were among the 200,000 Jews living in the Lodz area at the time of the occupation who were forced into a sealed ghetto. From June 1939 to his death in April 1943, Dawid faithfully kept a diary that filled five notebooks. In intimate, revealing prose, the young author offers detailed accounts of the relentless daily horrors he faced: struggling to obtain food; battling hunger and illness; trying to rationalize the madness surrounding him; fighting cold, disease, and exhaustion; and coping with the constant threats of deportation. Dawid's last diary entry is dated April 15, 1943. A few days later, he succumbed to what was known as "ghetto disease," a lethal combination of tuberculosis, exhaustion, and starvation. This diary is one of the most detailed and revealing personal accounts of the Holocaust one will find. Includes many captioned black-and-white photographs depicting life in the Lodz Ghetto, a map of the city and ghetto, and footnotes throughout the text putting Dawid's observations in historical context. Engrossing and profoundly moving, this book is a necessary addition to any middle or secondary school and public library young adult collection.

010 Adler, David A. *A Child of the Warsaw Ghetto*. Illus. Karen Ritz.
New York: Holiday House, 1995. 32 pp. (hc. 0-8234-1160-5)
$15.95
Gr. 2-4. A picture book biography of Froim Baum, born in 1936 and
orphaned shortly after the Nazi invasion of Poland in 1939. Baum lived
in Janusz Korczak's orphanage in the Warsaw Ghetto until the ghetto's
liquidation, and then was sent to Dachau where he managed to survive
until liberation. An excellent read aloud book. Illustrated with
thoughtful, expressive pastel drawings.

011 —. *A Picture Book of Anne Frank*. Illus. Karen Ritz. New
York: Holiday House, 1993. 29 pp. (hc. 0-8234-1003-X) $15.95;
(pbk. 0-8234-1078-1) $6.95
Gr. 2-5. The story of Anne Frank's life and death is told for young
readers. Adler manages to say a great deal in this brief but most
informative book. Ritz's vivid, realistic drawings have a photographic
quality. This is an excellent introduction to Anne Frank's story for
elementary school students. Includes a historical note from the author
and a list of important dates in Anne's life.

012 Admur, Richard. *Anne Frank*. New York: Chelsea House, 1993.
111 pp. (hc. (0-7910-1641-2) $18.95; (pbk. 0-7910-1645-5)
Gr. 4-8. From *The Chelsea House Library of Biography*. The life of
Anne Frank, her fate, and her legacy are recounted for readers not yet
ready to tackle Anne's own diary. Generously illustrated with black-
and-white photographs, it also includes a chronology, suggestions for
further reading, a list of all the languages the book has been translated
into, and a subject index.

013 Appel, Benjamin. *Hitler: From Power to Ruin*. New York:
Grosset & Dunlap, 1964.
Gr. 4-8. A biography of Hitler for younger readers covering his life in
obscurity, his rise to power, and his downfall and suicide. Includes
black-and-white photographs.

014 Appleman-Jurman, Alicia. *Alicia: My Story*. New York: Bantam,
1990. 448 pp. (pbk. 0-553-28218-2) $6.99
Gr. 9-12. In this personal narrative, the author tells how she, at the age
of thirteen, saved the lives of many people from the Nazis. An
outstanding autobiography of a heroic person.

015 Arnothy, Christine. *I Am Fifteen and I Don't Want to Die*. New

York: Scholastic, 1986. 128 pp. (pbk. 0-590-44630-4) $3.50
Gr. 7-12. Fifteen-year-old Christine and her family are caught in the middle of war-torn Budapest with the German army on one side and the Russians on the other. Though Christine is not Jewish, she and her family share a hiding place with a Jewish man who believes his yellow star will protect him when the Russians come. In fact, his yellow star gets him shot by the Russians.

016 Atkinson, Linda. *In Kindling Flame: The Story of Hannah Senesh, 1921-1944.* New York: Beech Tree, 1992. 214 pp. (0-688-11689-2) $4.95
Gr. 7-12. A biography of Hannah Senesh, the young Jewish heroine, whose work trying to help Hungarian Jews made her a martyr and inspiration. An exceptional biography of a fascinating person. Includes black-and-white photographs, suggestions for further reading, and a subject index.

017 Auerbacher, Inge. *I Am a Star: Child of the Holocaust.* Illus. Israel Bernbaum. New York: Puffin. 1993. 87 pp. (pbk. 0-14-036401-3) $4.99
Gr. 3-7. The author remembers her childhood in Germany, several years of which were spent in a concentration camp. Includes several poems by the author.

018 Ayer, Eleanor H. *The Importance of Adolf Hitler.* San Diego: Lucent, 1996. 128 pp. (hc. 1-56006-072-7) $17.96
Gr. 5-10. A biography of Hitler from his early life in Austria to his suicide at the end of World War II. The author looks at Hitler's place in history and what impact his actions had upon the world of his time and will continue to have upon future generations. A well-researched, sometimes intriguing biography. Includes black-and-white photographs, notes, suggestions for further reading, and a subject index. From *The Importance Of* series.

019 Baldwin, Margaret. *The Boy Who Saved the Children.* New York: Julian Messner, 1981. 62 pp. (hc. 0-671-43603-1); (pbk. 0-671-49470- 8) $4.95
Gr. 3-6. Adapted from Ben Edelbaum's *Growing Up in the Holocaust* (an adult book not cited here) for younger readers. Illustrated with black-and-white photographs.

020 Banet, Chana Marcus. *They Called Me Frau Anna.* New York:

C.I.S., 1990. 331 pp. (hc. 1-56062-0293) $17.95
Gr. 9-12. A personal narrative of how, in Poland, a young Jewish
mother, struggled to save herself and two children from the Nazis.

021 Bar Oni, Bryna. *The Vapor*. Chicago: Visual Impact, 1976. 127
pp. (hc. 0-913426-03-2)
Gr. 7-12. Bryna's story begins in 1937 where she enjoys her life as a
twelve-year-old girl in a small Polish town. Her life is shattered two
years later when the Nazis come and unleash their terror.

022 Bartoszewski, Wladyslaw. *The Warsaw Ghetto: A Christian's
Testimony*. Trans. Stephen G. Cappellari. Boston: Beacon Press,
1987. 117 pp. (hc. 0-8070-5602-2) $14.95
Gr. 7-12. A Catholic-Polish historian and journalist, Bartoszewski
serves as a liaison between the Jewish leadership in the Warsaw Ghetto
and the Polish underground. A fascinating personal narrative by one of
only a few Christian Poles who helped Polish Jews during the
Holocaust. Illustrated with black-and-white photographs. Includes a
subject index. Translated from the German.

023 Bauman, Janina. *Winter in the Morning: A Young Girl's Life in
the Warsaw Ghetto and Beyond, 1939-1945*. New York: Macmillan,
1986. 195 pp. (hc. 0-02-902530-3) $16.95
Gr. 7-12. Based on the diaries she kept as a teenager, Janina Bauman
recounts what life was like for her living in the Warsaw Ghetto. A
pampered daughter of a prosperous Jewish family, Janina's sheltered,
comfortable life was shattered when the Nazis came and her family was
forced into the ghetto. She vividly recounts the awful, brutal, hand-to-
mouth existence she endured. An excellent personal narrative.

024 Benisch, Pearl. *To Vanquish the Dragon*. New York: Feldheim,
1991. 451 pp. (hc. 0-87306-570-0) $20.95; (pbk. 0-87306-571-9)
$16.95
Gr. 11-12. Amidst the horrors and ordeals of the Nazi occupation of
Krakow, Poland, a group of religious girls, the daughters of Beth Jacob,
hold firm in their faith in the Torah. An inspiring personal story of faith
and the will to survive. Includes a glossary.

025 Bernheim, Mark. *Father of the Orphans: The Story of Janusz
Korczak*. New York: Dutton, 1989. 160 pp. (hc. 0-525-67265-6)
$15.95
Gr. 5-12. A biography of the Polish pediatrician, author, educator,

founder of orphanages, and champion of children's rights, who cared for the orphans in the Warsaw Ghetto and stayed with them all the way to the gas chambers of Treblinka. A moving and inspiring portrait of a kind, selfless man who was a point of light in one of history's darkest moments. Includes a foreword by Katherine Paterson, black-and-white photographs, and a subject index. From the *Jewish Biography Series*.

026 Bernstein, Sara Tuvel. *The Seamstress: A Memoir of Survival.*
New York: Putnam, 1997. 353 pp. (hc. 0-399-14322-X) $25.95
Gr. 9-12. The author tells of how, when she was a teenager, her life in a Romanian mountain village was suddenly destroyed when the Nazis came. She, her younger sister, and two friends were sent to the Ravensbruck concentration camp in Germany. In vivid and dramatic prose, she tells of how they tried to help each other survive their terrible ordeal. Includes a subject index.

027 Bierman, John. *Righteous Gentile: The Story of Raoul*
Wallenberg, Missing Hero of the Holocaust. New York: Penguin,
1995. 221 pp. (pbk. 0-14-024664-9) $11.95
Gr. 9-12. In this revised edition of his 1981 bestseller, to mark the fiftieth anniversary of Wallenberg's disappearance, Bierman brings up to date the case of the missing diplomat. A well researched, detailed account. Includes black-and-white photographs and a bibliography.

028 Bitton-Jackson, Livia. *Elli: Coming of Age in the Holocaust.* New
York: Times, 1980. 248 pp. (hc. 0-8129-0882-1)
Gr. 9-12. In this first-person true account, the author tells of how, at the age of thirteen, her life was shattered when the Nazis deported her and the rest of her village to concentration camps. Miraculously, she survived the ordeal to tell her story.

029 —. *I Have Lived a Thousand Years: Growing Up in the*
Holocaust. New York: Simon & Schuster, 1997. 224 pp.
(hc. 0-689-81022-9) $17.00
Gr. 5-10. In 1944, Elli Friedmann, a thirteen-year-old Hungarian Jew is deported with her family to Auschwitz. The author is chillingly effective in depicting the horrors of the concentration camp, but her narrative is awkward at times. Despite its flaws, this is a notable Holocaust narrative. Includes a Holocaust chronology and glossary. This book is adapted especially for younger readers from the author's *Elli: Coming of Age in the Holocaust.*

030 Breznitz, Shlomo. *Memory Fields*. New York: Knopf, 1993. 179
pp. (hc. 0-679-40403-1) $21.00
Gr. 11-12. The author describes what life was like for him and his sister
in a Catholic orphanage in Czechoslovakia when his parents sent them
there just before they were deported to Auschwitz.

031 Brown, Gene. *Anne Frank: Child of the Holocaust*. New York:
Blackbirch Press, 1991. 64 pp. (hc. 1-5671-1030-4) $15.95;
(pbk. 1-5671-1049-5) $7.95
Gr. 2-4. A biography for young readers about Anne Frank and the
Holocaust. The text is straightforward and informative. Illustrated
throughout with black-and-white photographs. Includes a glossary,
suggestions for further reading, and a subject index.

032 Buchignani, Walter. *Tell No One Who You Are: The Hidden
Childhood of Regine Miller*. Montreal: Tundra, 1994. 185 pp.
(hc. 0-88776-286-7) $17.95
Gr. 5-8. When the Germans invade Belgium, ten-year-old Regine
Miller is sent into hiding by her father and lives out the war with four
different families while hiding her Jewish identity. This is a vivid,
moving personal account of one of thousands of hidden children. The
author met Regine Miller at the First International Gathering of Hidden
Children in New York City in 1991, which was attended by 1,600
people from twenty-eight countries.

033 Butterworth, Emma Macalick. *As the Waltz Was Ending*. New
York: Four Winds Press, 1982. 187 pp. (hc. 0-590-07835-6)
Gr. 5-10. The author discusses how her ballet career with the Vienna
State Opera was interrupted by the Nazi occupation and how she later
had to fight for her life during the Russian occupation.

034 Deschamps, Helene. *Spyglass: An Autobiography*. Ed. Karyn
Monget. New York: Holt, 1995. 308 pp. (hc. 0-8050-3536-2)
$16.95
Gr. 7-12. Seventeen-year-old Helene joins the French Resistance,
working as a spy in Vichy and gathering information for the Allies. A
remarkable story of a young heroine. Includes a subject index and
black-and-white photographs.

035 Deutschkron, Inge. *Outcast: A Jewish Girl in Wartime Berlin*.
Trans. Jean Steinberg. New York: Fromm International Publishing
Corp., 1989. 262 pp. (hc. 0-880-64116-9) $18.95

Gr. 7-12. The author describes her constant struggle to survive in wartime Berlin, living along with her mother as "non-Jews." A vivid, detailed personal narrative. Translated from the German.

036 Dribben, Judith. *A Girl Called Judith Strick*. Toronto: Cowles, 1970. 340 pp. (hc. 0-011-3970-0)
Gr. 9-12. An autobiography of a seventeen-year-old Jewish girl who was a spy and active in the resistance movement in the Ukraine. She eventually escaped safely to Israel. Includes black-and-white photographs and a foreword by Golda Meir.

037 Drucker, Olga Levy. *Kindertransport*. New York: Holt, 1992. 146 pp. (hc. 0-8050-1711-9) $14.95; (pbk. 0-8050-4251-2) $7.95
Gr. 4-8. The author describes how her life changed when Hitler came to power; she was sent off to live in England by her parents after the *Kristallnacht* and did not see them again until she immigrated to the United States in 1945. An exceptionally powerful personal narrative.

038 Edelstein, Dov Beril. *Worlds Torn Asunder*. Hoboken, NJ: KTAV, 1984. (hc. 0-88125-040-6) $12.95
Gr. 9-12. Edelstein, a devout Hasidic Jew from the town of Szatimar, Hungary, was sent to Auschwitz when he was seventeen. This exceptionally well-written account of his experiences in the camp is told from a strong spiritual perspective. Profoundly moving. Includes black-and-white photographs.

039 Edvardson, Cordelia. *Burned Child Seeks the Fire: A Memoir*. Trans. Joel Agee. New York: Beacon, 1997. (hc. 0-8070-7094-7) $18.00
Gr. 9-12. The personal narrative of a woman who was imprisoned in the Theresienstadt (Terezin) concentration camp in Czechoslovakia.

040 Eisner, Jack. *The Survivor of the Holocaust*. New York: Kensington, 1996. 302 pp. (pbk. 1-575-66104-7) $11.00
Gr. 9-12. Teenager Jack Eisner takes part in ghetto uprisings and manages to survive imprisonment in the camps.

041 Emmerich, Elisabeth with Robert Hull. *My Childhood in Nazi Germany*. New York: Watts, 1992. 96 pp. (hc. 0-531-18429-3) $13.90
Gr. 4-8. The author describes her daily life as a child in Nazi Germany and describes how the war affected her personal relationships and

changed where she lived.

042 Epstein, Rachel. *Anne Frank*. New York: Watts, 1997. 63 pp.
      (hc. 0-531-20298-4) $21.00
Gr. 3-6. From the *First Books: Biographies Series*, this is a concise,
serviceable biography, focusing on the Frank family's years in hiding.
Includes black-and-white, archival photographs, a full color map of
World War II Europe, and a diagram of the Secret Annex. There is a
subject index, a list of suggested further reading, and Internet sites are
also recommended. This is an appropriate biography to give to students
interested in Anne's life, but not yet old enough to appreciate her own
diary.

043 Fenelon, Fania. *Playing for Time*. Syracuse, NY: Syracuse
      University Press, 1997. 304 pp. (pbk. 0-815-60494-7) $17.95
Gr. 9-12. A Jewish woman survives the Holocaust because she is part
of a Nazi organized orchestra. Originally published by Berkley in 1976.

044 Ferson-Osten, Renee. *Don't They Know the World Stopped
      Breathing? Reminiscences of a French Child During the Holocaust
      Years*. New York: Shapolsky, 1991. 259 pp. (hc. 1-56171-019-9)
      $16.95
Gr. 9-12. A personal narrative of how, as a young girl living in France
during the Holocaust, the author hid in a convent after her parents were
deported by the Nazis. Includes black-and-white photographs.

045 Fisch, Robert O. *Light from a Yellow Star: A Lesson of Love from
      the Holocaust*. University of Minnesota: Frederick R. Weisman Art
      Museum, 1994. 40 pp. (hc. 1-885116-00-4) $14.95;
      (pbk. 0-964489-60-0) $9.95
Gr. 7-12. A moving remembrance in words and paintings by a
Hungarian Holocaust survivor. A brief narrative relating a moment
from the author's experience is preceded by a translation from a
gravestone in the memorial concentration camp cemetery in Budapest.
The narratives are followed by one of the author's Holocaust paintings.

046 Flinker, Moshe. *Young Moshe's Diary: The Spiritual Torment of a
      Jewish Boy in Nazi Europe*. New York: Anti-Defamation League
      of B'nai B'rith, 1985. 126 pp. (hc. 0-68674-948-0) $6.00
Gr. 5-12. Moshe Flinker, a teenager who perished in Auschwitz, left
behind books in which he described his innermost thoughts in the days
prior to his deportation. An intensely religious Jew, Moshe wrestles

with the spiritual questions of persecution. These are amazingly insightful, thoughtful observations from such a young man. A profoundly moving work that should be compared and contrasted to Anne Frank's *Diary* and Elie Wiesel's *Night.*

047 Frank, Anne. *The Diary of a Young Girl: The Definitive Edition.*
Ed. Otto H. Frank and Mirjam Pressler. Trans. Susan Massotty. '
New York: Doubleday, 1995. 340 pp. (hc. 0-385-47378-8) $25.00
Gr. 7-12. This edition of Anne's diary contains diary entries that had been omitted from the previous editions. Since the publication of this book, however, several more pages have been discovered. No addition with those additional pages has yet been published. This is also a new translation. *The Diary of a Young Girl* is also available from Bantam in paperback in its original edition (0-553-29698-1). The paperback edition includes an introduction by Eleanor Roosevelt.

Historical Background on Anne Frank's *The Diary of a Young Girl*:
The diary was first published in Holland in 1947 as *Het Achterhuis* (*The Secret Annex*). It was published in the United States in 1952 as *Anne Frank: The Diary of a Young Girl.* Since the 1950s, there had been accusations that the diary was fake, that something so well written could not have come from a young girl. These rumors were dispelled when a thorough examination of the late Otto Frank's papers proved beyond doubt the diary's authenticity. The results of the examination were published in Holland in 1986 as *The Diaries of Anne Frank.* It was published in the United States in 1988 as *The Diary of Anne Frank: The Critical Edition.* Since the publication of *The Diary of a Young Girl: The Definitive Edition* in 1995, several more pages of the diary were discovered rendering this edition not truly definitive. To date, no edition has been published including those recently discovered pages.

048 Friedman, Ina R. *Flying Against the Wind: The Story of a Young Woman Who Defied the Nazis.* Brookline, MA: Lodgepole, 1995. 202 pp. (pbk. 1-886721-00-9) $11.95
Gr. 5-10. A biography of Cato Bontjes van Beek, a young German girl who actively worked against the Nazis and was executed for her brave efforts. An inspiring story illustrated with black-and-white photographs. Includes chronologies of world events and Cato's life, a glossary, a bibliography of books on resistance in Germany, and a subject index.

049 Fry, Varian. *Assignment Rescue: An Autobiography*. New York:
Scholastic, 1993. 192 pp. (pbk. 0-590-46970-3) $3.50
Gr. 7-10. Varian Fry, an American citizen living in France, saves
thousands of people from Nazi concentration and death camps through
his extraordinary resourcefulness. Includes black-and-white
photographs.

050 Ganor, Solly. *Light One Candle: A Survivor's Tale from Lithuania
to Jerusalem*. New York: Kodansha, 1995. 353 pp.
(hc. 1-56836-098-3) $25.00
Gr. 9-12. This survivor of the ghetto in Kaunas, Lithuania, and the
death march from Dachau waited fifty years before telling his story.
Ganor writes vividly and honestly of his happy days growing up in his
native Lithuania before the war and the horrors he suffered and
witnessed when the war came to him. After World War II, Ganor went
to Palestine to fight in Israel's War for Independence. An extremely
emotional and memorable personal narrative.

051 Geve, Thomas. *Guns and Barbed Wire: A Child Survives the
Holocaust*. Chicago: Academy, 1987. 220 pp. (hc. 0-89733-261-X)
$18.95
Gr. 9-12. The author spent a total of twenty-two months in the
Auschwitz and Buchenwald concentration camps and vividly describes
his experiences there in this stunning personal narrative. Geve
effectively conveys the feeling of hope, which enabled young Jewish
prisoners to survive.

052 Gies, Miep with Alison Leslie Gold. *Anne Frank Remembered:
The Story of the Woman Who Helped to Hide the Frank Family*.
New York: Touchstone, 1987. 252 pp. (hc. 0-671-54771-2) $17.45;
(pbk. 0-671-66234-1) $6.95
Gr. 9-12. Miep Gies talks about how she and her husband spent more
than two years helping to hide the Frank family from the Nazis. An
incredibly powerful story of heroic people risking their lives for the
sake of others. An excellent companion to read with Anne's *Diary*.
Includes black-and-white photographs of the Frank family and artifacts
from the time, plus a layout of the annex.

053 Gissing, Vera. *Pearls of Childhood: The Poignant True Wartime
Story of a Young Girl Growing Up in an Adopted Land*. New York:
St. Martin's, 1988. 176 pp. (hc. 0-312-02963-2) $16.95
Gr. 5-12. Through letters and diary accounts of her wartime years, the

author tells of her experience as a ten-year-old escaping in 1939 from Nazi-occupied Czechoslovakia. Illustrated with black-and-white photographs.

054 Gold, Alison Leslie. *Memories of Anne Frank: Reflections of a Childhood Friend*. New York: Scholastic, 1997. 135 pp. (hc. 0-590-90722-0) $16.95
Gr. 5-9. This is a biography of Hannah Goslar, a close friend of Anne Frank and one of the last people to see her alive. There are some very good moments in this biography. One of the most moving is when Hannah and Anne are reunited in Bergen-Belsen after not seeing each other for several years. Overall, however, the narrative is not terribly engaging. Hannah's own important Holocaust story would have more impact if she had told it herself. As it stands, this is not one of the better Holocaust biographies, although it does offer another interesting dimension to Anne Frank's story.

055 Greene, Carol. *Elie Wiesel: Messenger from the Holocaust*. Chicago: Children's Press, 1987. 32 pp. (hc. 0-516-03490-1) $15.27
Gr. 2-5. A brief biography for younger readers of the Holocaust survivor and 1986 Nobel Peace Prize recipient. Generously illustrated with black-and-white photographs. Includes the text of Wiesel's acceptance speech for the Nobel Peace Prize and a timeline of the author's life.

056 Hart, Kitty. *Return to Auschwitz: The Remarkable Story of a Girl Who Survived the Holocaust*. New York: Atheneum, 1982. 178 pp. (hc. 0-689-11266-1) $12.95
Gr. 9-12. Kitty, a young girl at the time the Nazis invaded Poland, remembers her hometown of Bielsko, her life in Lublin's Jewish ghetto, and the nearly two years she spent in Auschwitz. Years after her liberation, Kitty returns to Auschwitz with her grown son. Includes black-and-white photographs and a subject index.

057 Heller, Fanya Gottesfeld. *Strange and Unexpected Love: A Teenage Girl's Holocaust Memoirs*. Hoboken, NJ: KTAV, 1993. 281 pp. (hc. 0-88125-467-3) $23.00; (pbk. 0-88125-531-9) $14.95
Gr. 9-12. Fanya Heller lived in a middle-class, traditional Jewish family in Eastern Poland when the Nazis invaded. Thanks to the courage of two Christian rescuers, Fanya and her family managed to survive the war. One of the rescuers, a Ukrainian shoemaker, turned out to be the man with whom Fanya would fall in love. This is a vividly detailed

personal narrative told with great drama and intensity.

058 Hoffman, Judy. *Joseph and Me: In the Days of the Holocaust.*
Hoboken, NJ: KTAV, 1979. 80 pp.
Gr. 4-8. The author, a German Jew, describes her experiences living
with a Christian family in Amsterdam.

059 Hurwitz, Johanna. *Anne Frank: Life in Hiding.* Illus. Vera
Rosenberry. New York: Beech Tree, 1993. 52 pp.
(pbk. 0-688-12405-4) $3.95
Gr. 3-6. A biography of Anne Frank for younger readers, focusing on
her years in hiding in the Secret Annex. Illustrated with black-and-
white drawings. Includes a chronology of important dates and a subject
index.

060 Hyams, Joseph. *A Field of Buttercups.* Englewood Cliffs, NJ:
Prentice-Hall, 1968. 273 pp.
Gr. 9-12. The story of Janusz Korczak, the Polish Jewish pediatrician
and educator who cared for the orphans transferred to the Warsaw
Ghetto and followed them to their deaths in Treblinka. The "field of
buttercups" refers to the author's observation of the pile of yellow stars
at the deportation point.

061 Ippisch, Hanneke. *Sky: A True Story of Resistance During World
War II.* New York: Simon & Schuster, 1996. 146 pp.
(hc. 0-689-80508-X) $16.00
Gr. 6-12. An episodic memoir of courage and heroism in Nazi-
occupied Holland. Ippisch, the daughter of a minister, took part in her
country's resistance movement helping Jews and other political
enemies of Nazi Germany move from one hiding place to another and
evade deportation to the concentration camps. Although the book's
short chapters will appeal to less motivated readers, there are
occasional lapses in coherence that could prove frustrating.

062 Isaacman, Clara with Joan Adess Grossmen. *Clara's Story.*
Philadelphia: Jewish Publication Society of America, 1984. 180 pp.
(pbk. 0-827-60243-X) $9.95
Gr. 3-7. The author describes her own and her family's experiences
during the two and one-half years they spent hiding in Antwerp,
Belgium during the war.

063 Isaacson, Judith Magyar. *Seed of Sarah: Memoirs of a Survivor.*

2nd. ed. Urbana, IL: University of Illinois Press, 1991. 278 pp. (hc. 0-252-06219-1) $12.95
Gr. 10-12. An exceptionally well-written narrative in which the author describes her joyful childhood in Hungary, her horrific adolescence as a prisoner in Auschwitz, and her life after liberation. Most remarkable about this narrative is Isaacson's utter lack of bitterness when remembering the horrors to which she was subjected. Includes black-and-white photographs and a subject index.

064 Joffo, Joseph. *A Bag of Marbles.* New York: Bantam, 1986. (pbk. 0-553-06407-X) $1.75
Gr. 9-12. The Joffo brothers, French Jews, manage to elude the Nazis and survive the Holocaust by hiding out in the Alps.

065 Karlin, Wayne. *Rumors and Stones: A Journey.* Willimantic, CT: Curbstone, 1996. 214 pp. (hc. 1-880684-42-X) $19.95
Gr. 9-12. This is a powerful narrative of Karlin's journey to Poland to the small town of Kolno to learn about his family's past. Karlin, a Vietnam veteran, learns that the 2,000 Jewish inhabitants of Kolno were machine-gunned in ditches in 1941. This experience compels Karlin to contemplate moral questions. This is a complex but profoundly moving book that explores some very important issues.

066 Klein, Cecilie. *Sentenced to Live: A Survivor's Memoir.* New York: Holocaust Library, 1989. 146 pp. (hc. 0-89604-097-6) $16.95; (pbk. 0-89604-128-X) $10.95
Gr. 7-12. Cecilie Klein describes the experiences of her and her family in the Jewish ghetto of Chust in Hungary and their deportation to Auschwitz. Includes black-and-white photographs and several poems by the author.

067 Klein, Rivkah Leah. *The Scent of the Snowflowers.* New York: Feldheim, 1989. 511 pp. (hc. 0-87306-498-4) (pbk. 0-87306-499-2)
Gr. 9-12. The author relates her experiences in Budapest during the Nazi occupation. Klein does a remarkable job conveying what daily life was like in that time and place.

068 Koehn, Ilse. *Mischling, Second Degree.* New York: Greenwillow, 1977. 240 pp. (hc. 0-688-80110-2) $13.00; (pbk. 0-140-34290-7) $5.99
Gr. 5-10. As a child of a Jewish father and a non-Jewish mother with one Jewish grandparent, the author was considered by the Nazis to be a

Mischling, second degree. She recounts her experiences in Hitler Youth camp in a vivid, straightforward narrative.

069 Kohn, Nahum and Howard Roiter. *A Voice from the Forest: Memoirs of a Jewish Partisan.* New York: Holocaust Library, 1980. 255 pp. $12.95
Gr. 9-12. When the life of a small-town watchmaker from a religious family in western Poland is torn apart by the war, he joins the Soviet partisan Medvedev. Includes black-and-white photographs.

070 Krall, Hanna. *Shielding the Flame: An Intimate Conversation with Dr. Marek Edelman, the Last Surviving Leader of the Warsaw Ghetto Uprising.* Trans. Joanna Stasinska and Lawrence Weschler. New York: Holt, 1986. (hc. 0-03-006002-8) $13.95
Gr. 9-12. An interview with Marek Edelman, one of the few Jews who survived the heroic but inevitably doomed Warsaw Ghetto uprising. He later went on to become a leading cardiologist and activist in Poland's Solidarity movement.

071 Kuper, Jack. *Child of the Holocaust: A True Story.* New York: Berkley, 1993. 272 pp. (pbk. 0-425-13582-9) $5.99
Gr. 9-12. Jakob Kuperblum, an eight-year-old Polish Jew comes home to find his family and friends were rounded up by the Germans only hours earlier. After this discovery, Jakob embarks on a desperate journey to find safety and shelter. A powerful and moving survival story.

072 Larsen, Anita. *Raoul Wallenberg: Missing Diplomat.* Illus. James Watling. New York: Crestwood House, 1992. 48 pp. (hc. 0-89686-616-5) $11.95
Gr. 3-7. Provides younger readers with an introduction to the Swedish diplomat who helped rescue thousands of Hungarian Jews from extermination and explores the circumstances surrounding his mysterious disappearance at the end of the war. Factual, well-organized, and easy to understand. Illustrated with black-and-white drawings. Includes a chronology, suggestions for further reading, and a subject index. From the *History's Mysteries* series.

073 Leitner, Isabella. *Fragments of Isabella: A Memoir of Auschwitz.* Ed.. Irving A. Leitner. New York: Dell, 1983. 128 pp. (pbk. 0-440-32453-X) $3.95
Gr. 7-12. Isabella tells of her deportation to and life in the Auschwitz

concentration camp. Includes an epilogue by Irving A. Leitner.

074 Leitner, Isabella with Irving A. Leitner. *The Big Lie: A True Story*. New York: Scholastic, 1992. 79 pp. (hc. 0-590-45569-9) $13.95 Gr. 5-12. The author offers in the leanest prose only the facts of her experiences as a prisoner in Auschwitz.

075 Leitner, Isabella and Irving A. Leitner. *Isabella: From Auschwitz to Freedom*. New York: Anchor, 1994. 233 pp. (pbk. 0-385-4731-4) $12.95 Gr. 5-10. Merges and re-works the author's two previously published works: *Fragments of Isabella* and *Saving the Fragments*.

076 Leitner, Isabella with Irving A. Leitner. *Saving the Fragments: From Auschwitz to New York*. New York: New American Library, 1985. 131 pp. (0-453-00502-0) $12.95 Gr. 6-12. Isabella Leitner describes her life as a Holocaust survivor since her liberation from Auschwitz. A powerful and poignant memoir. Includes an introduction by Howard Fast.

077 Lengyel, Olga. *Five Chimneys*. Chicago: Academy Chicago Publishers, 1992. 221 pp. (pbk. 0-897-3376-4) $12.00 Gr. 9-12. An Auschwitz survivor offers vivid eyewitness account of the everyday incidences of brutalities in the camp.

078 Lester, Elenore. *Wallenberg: The Man in the Iron Web*. Englewood Cliffs. NJ: Prentice-Hall, 1982. 183 pp. (hc. 0-13-944322-3) $12.95; (pbk. 0-13-944240-5) $6.95 Gr. 9-12. A biography of the Swedish diplomat whose daring, one-man rescue mission helped save thousands of Hungarian Jews. Told in a gripping, thriller-style narrative. Includes a foreword by Simon Wiesenthal, source notes, and a subject index.

079 Levi, Primo. *The Drowned and the Saved*. Trans. Raymond Rosenthal. New York: Vintage, 1988. (pbk. 0-679-72168-X) $11.00 Gr. 9-12. The Italian chemist recounts in vivid detail the utter hell of living in Auschwitz.

080 —. *Survival in Auschwitz*. New York: Simon & Schuster, 1995. (pbk. 0-684-82680-1) $11.00 Gr. 9-12. Levi offers another account of his experiences in Auschwitz.

Originally published by Macmillan in1987.

081 Linnea, Sharon. *Raoul Wallenberg: The Man Who Stopped for
     Death*. Philadelphia: Jewish Publication Society of America, 1993.
     151 pp. (hc. 0-8276-0440-8) $17.95; (pbk. 0-8276-0448-3) $9.95
Gr. 7-12. Traces the life of the heroic Swedish diplomat who saved
more than 100,000 Hungarian Jews from extermination and then
mysteriously disappeared after the Russians occupied Budapest.
Includes a map of wartime Budapest, black-and-white photographs, and
a subject index.

082 Marrin, Albert. *Hitler*. New York: Puffin, 1986. 249 pp.
     (pbk. 0-14-036526-5) $5.99
Gr. 7-12. An excellent biography for young adults, tracing Hitler's life
as a struggling artist in Austria to his rise from obscurity to dictator of
Germany. Includes black-and-white photographs, a bibliography, and a
subject index.

083 Muchman, Beatrice. *Never to Be Forgotten: A Young Girl's
     Holocaust Memoir*. Hoboken, NJ: KATV, 1997. 124pp.
     (hc. 0-88125-598-X) $23.00
Gr. 7-12. Beatrice Muchman and her family fled from Germany to
Belgium when Hitler came to power but, before they were able to
escape to the United States, Belgium was invaded and the family was
trapped. Beatrice was sent to live with a Catholic woman while her
parents moved from one place to another. Her parents were eventually
caught and killed by the Nazis. Muchman constructed this memoir from
her   fragmented   childhood   recollections,   documents,   and
correspondence from her parents she discovered after the war.

084 Mueller, Filip. *Eyewitness Auschwitz*. New York: Madison Books,
     1981. 192 pp. (pbk. 0-812-86084-5) $7.95
Gr. 9-12. A member of the Jewish commando ordered to assist with the
gassing of other prisoners offers vivid, first-hand accounts of the evil of
Auschwitz.

085 Neimark, Anne E. *One Man's Valor: Leo Baeck and the
     Holocaust*. New York: Lodestar, 1986. 113 pp. (hc. 0-525-67175-7)
     $14.95
Gr. 5-9. The story of Leo Baeck, a German Jew and a world-renowned
rabbi and scholar, who courageously fought against Nazi persecution.
Includes black-and-white photographs, suggestions for further reading,

and a subject index. From the *Jewish Biography Series.*

086 Noble, Iris. *Nazi Hunter: Simon Wiesenthal.* New York: Julian
Messner, 1979. 158 pp. (hc. 0-671-32964-2) $7.29
Gr. 5-12. Presents an account of Nazi hunter Simon Wiesenthal who
has successfully brought to justice hundreds of Nazis, many of whom
disappeared into hiding at the end of World War II.

087 Novac, Ana. *The Beautiful Days of My Youth: My Six Months in
Auschwitz and Plaszow.* Trans. George L. Newman. New York:
Holt, 1997. 314 pp. (hc. 0-8050-5018-3) $15.95
Gr. 9-12. In 1940 at the age of eleven in Transylvania, Ana Novac
began to faithfully keep a diary. Four years later when she was taken to
Auschwitz and Plaszow, Ana used scraps of paper and whatever else
she could find to write on to record what she felt and saw and thought.
This book is that diary as Ana wrote it during the six months she spent
in the death camps. Another extraordinary personal narrative full of
horrific detail and profound insight. Includes a glossary, notes, and a
subject index. Translated from the French.

088 Nyiszli, Miklos. *Auschwitz.* New York: Fawcett, 1981.
(pbk. 0-449-23848-2) $2.50
Gr. 9-12. A Jewish doctor is forced to participate in Josef Mengele's
horrible medical experiments on Auschwitz camp inmates. Originally
published by Seaver Books in 1960.

089 Oberski, Jona. *Childhood: A Remembrance.* Trans. Ralph
Manheim. New York: Doubleday, 1983. 119 pp.
(hc. 0-385-17768-2) $11.95
Gr. 7-12. Jona, a very young child, struggles to make sense of his new
life in the Bergen-Belsen concentration camp. Translated from the
Dutch.

090 Orenstein, Henry. *I Shall Live.* New York: Beaufort, 1997.
(pbk. 0-825-30500-4) $14.95
Gr. 9-12. Henry becomes a member of a special group that saves him
from immediate execution by the Nazis. Originally published by
Touchstone in 1989.

091 Perel, Solomon. *Europa, Europa: A Memoir of World War II.*
Trans. Margot Bettauer Dembo. New York: Wiley, 1997. 217 pp.
(hc. 0-471-17218-9)

Gr. 7-12. Fourteen-year-old Solomon Perel sets out from Nazi-occupied Poland for the Soviet frontier in the hope of finding safety. In an extraordinary twist of fate, however, he finds refuge in the most improbable place—in an elite Hitler Youth school where he passes himself as a student. A riveting first person account. Published in association with the United States Holocaust Memorial Museum. Translated from the German.

092 Perl, Lila and Marian Blumenthal Lazan. *Four Perfect Pebbles: A Holocaust Story*. New York: Greenwillow, 1996. 130 pp. (hc. 0-688-14294-X) $15.00
Gr. 5-10. Marian Blumenthal recounts her family's struggle to survive the Holocaust. The story opens in Bergen-Belsen, then flashes back to events leading to Blumenthal's imprisonment there. A harrowing and often moving account, a significant flaw is that the story is only partly told from Blumenthal's point of view. When told by an omniscient narrator, the story lacks emotional impact. Nonetheless, this is a book that will reach readers who appreciate the personal narrative form.

093 Poltawska, Wanda. *And I Am Afraid of My Dreams*. New York: Hippocrene, 1989. (hc. 0-87052-2745-2) $16.95
Gr. 7-12. Wanda is arrested by the Gestapo for helping "enemies of the state" and sent to the Ravensbruck concentration camp where death from execution, medical experiments, and starvation are daily possibilities. Originally published by Hippocrene in 1964.

094 Rabinovici, Schoschana. *Thanks to My Mother*. Trans. James Skofield. New York: Dial, 1998. 246 pp. (hc. 0-8037-2235-4) $17.99.
Gr. 7-12. An incredible story of how Susie Weksler (Rabinovici's name then) and her mother miraculously survived many horrors during the Holocaust. Weksler was eight years old when the Nazis occupied her native Vilnius, Lithuania, in 1941. Her mother went to extraordinary lengths to keep them together, from hiding her in a backpack to dressing her up in clothes and makeup that made her look like an adult. Weksler and her mother managed to survive the Kaiserwald, Stutthof, and Tauentzein concentration camps, and an eleven-day winter death march before being liberated by the Russian army. Includes black-and-white photographs and useful footnotes explaining concentration camp jargon.

095 Ramati, Alexander. *The Assisi Underground: The Priests Who*

Rescued Jews. New York: Stein and Day, 1978. 181 pp.
(hc. 0-8128-2315-X) $8.95
Gr. 7-12. The story of Father Rufino Niccacci who, with the help of
other fellow priests, sheltered and protected 300 Jews in the Italian
town of Assisi during the Nazi occupation.

096 Reichel, Sabine. *What Did You Do in the War Daddy?: Growing
Up German.* New York: Hill & Wang, 1989. (hc. 0-8090-9685-4)
$17.95
Gr. 9-12. German-born Reichel, now living in the United States, tries
desperately to come to terms with the shame and guilt of the Nazi past
of herself, her parents, and their generation. An extremely powerful and
interesting perspective on the Holocaust and World War II one does not
often see, particularly in books for young people.

097 Reiss, Johanna. *The Journey Back.* New York: Crowell, 1976. 212
pp. (pbk. 0-05-447042-3) $3.95
Gr. 5-10. In spring 1945, a Dutch Jewish girl is reunited with her
family after years of hiding and returns with them to post-war
Netherlands, where they try to rebuild their country and family. Sequel
to *The Upstairs Room.*

098 ——. *The Upstairs Room.* New York: Crowell, 1972. 196 pp.
(hc. 0-690-85127-8) $15.00; (pbk. 0-06-440370-X) $3.95
Gr. 5-10. A Dutch Jewish girl describes the two-and-one-half years she
spent hiding from the Nazis in the upstairs bedroom of a farmer's house
during World War II. A Newbery Honor winner.

099 Reisman, Arnold and Ellen. *Welcome Tomorrow.* Cleveland:
North Coast Publishing, 1983. 176 pp. (pbk. 0-68639-632-4) $6.95
Gr. 9-12. The memoirs of Arnold Reisman recall his early boyhood in
Lodz, Poland, and his many incredible adventures, including how his
family escaped to Russia and how they had to flee from one area to
another as the Germans conquered more and more territory.

100 Rigenblum, Emmanuel. *Notes from the Warsaw Ghetto: The
Journal of Emmanuel Rigenblum.* Ed. and Trans. Jacob Sloan. New
York: Schocken, 1974. 389 pp. (hc. 0-80520-460-1) $16.00
Gr. 9-12. Rigenblum, the archivist for the Warsaw Ghetto and a social
historian, wrote these day-by-day eyewitness accounts of what he
witnessed there and buried them before the Nazis executed him in
1944. The notes were discovered in 1946 and 1950. Translated from the

Polish. Includes a chronology and a subject index.

101 Roberts, Jack L. *The Importance of Oskar Schindler.* San Diego:
     Lucent, 1996. 111 pp. (hc. 0-56006-079-4) $17.95
Gr. 5-12. A biography of the heroic German businessman responsible
for saving the lives of hundred of Jews. After the war, Israel declared
Schindler a "Righteous Gentile." The author covers Schindler's early
life, his actions during the war, and life after. Includes black-and-white
photographs, chapter notes, suggestions for further reading, and a
subject index. From *The Importance Of Biography* series.

102 Roubickova, Eva. *We're Alive and Life Goes On: A
     Theresienstadt Diary.* Trans. Zaia Alexander. New York: Holt,
     1998. 189 pp. (hc. 0-8050-5352-2) $16.95
Gr. 7-12. Theresienstadt (also known as Terezin) was a "model"
concentration camp in Czechoslovakia designed by the Nazis for the
International Red Cross and other humanitarian organizations to
deceive them into believing Jews were being treated fairly.
Superficially, it appeared as though the Jews were treated well in the
camp. The reality, however, was far more grim. Eva Mandlova arrived
in Theresienstadt in December 1941 at the age of twenty-one. From
that day until she was freed three-and-one-half years later, she kept a
diary, which offers a fascinating, personal insight into what life was
like in this concentration camp. Includes a foreword by Virginia Euwer
Wolff, black-and-white photographs of Eva and her family, and a
detailed map of the Theresienstadt camp.

103 Schloss, Eva with Evelyn Julia Kent. *Eva's Story: A Survivor's
     Tale by the Step-Sister of Anne Frank.* New York: St. Martin's,
     1988. 224 pp. (hc. 0-312-02913-6) $16.95
Gr. 9-12. Like her stepsister, Anne, Eva and her family were deported
to Auschwitz, but Eva miraculously survived to offer this account of
her experiences. Eva's mother married Otto Frank, Anne's father, in
1953. Includes black-and-white photographs.

104 Schnabel, Ernst. *Anne Frank: A Portrait in Courage.* New York:
     Harcourt Brace, 1958. 181 pp.
Gr. 7-12. The author recounts the life of Anne Frank, based upon the
testimony of forty-two witnesses and upon personal and official
documents. Another important complement to Anne's own diary.

105 Schur, Maxine Rose. *Hannah Szenes: A Song of Light.* Illus.
Donna Ruff. Philadelphia: Jewish Publication Society of America,
1986. 106 pp. (hc. 0-8276-0251-0) $10.95
Gr. 5-10. A biography of Hannah Szenes (also spelled Senesh), the
young heroine who sacrificed her own life to help rescue Hungarian
Jews. Illustrated with black-and-white drawings.

106 Schweifert, Peter. *The Bird Has Wings: Letters of Peter
Schweifert.* Ed. Claude Lanzman. Trans. Barbara Lucas. New York:
St. Martin's, 1976. 188 pp. (hc. 0-15107-527-1) $7.50
Gr. 7-12. Peter Schweifert left Germany when he was twenty-one and
was killed when he was twenty-seven. In this collection of letters to his
mother, who denies she is Jewish, he tries to persuade her to declare
herself a Jew and take pride in her identity. Translated from the French.

107 Sender, Ruth Minsky. *The Cage.* New York: Simon & Schuster,
1986. 245 pp. (pbk.0-68981-321-X) $4.50
Gr. 9-12. Sender recounts her life as a teenager in Nazi-occupied
Poland, from the Lodz Ghetto to deportation to Auschwitz. Originally
published by Macmillan (0-02-781830-6, 1986).

108 —. *To Life.* New York: Simon & Schuster, 1997. 229 pp.
(hc. 0-02-781831-4) $14.95; (pbk. 0-14-034367-9) $4.99
Gr. 7-12. Sender continues the story of her life where she left off in *The
Cage.* She recounts her liberation from Auschwitz, her search for
surviving family members, and her long and difficult ordeal trying to
immigrate to the United States with her husband and two children.

109 Senesh, Hannah. *Hannah Senesh: Her Life and Diary.* Trans.
Marta Cohn. New York: Schocken Books, 1976. 257 pp.
(hc. 0-8052-0410-5) $16.00
Gr. 9-12. Hannah Senesh is one of Israel's most revered heroines. A
native of Hungary, she moved to Palestine on the eve of World War II
and joined the elite Jewish parachute unit organized by the British.
Hannah's mission was to parachute into Nazi-occupied Yugoslavia,
join the partisans, and then make her way across the border into
Hungary to warn the Jewish populations of their impending fate. After
successfully joining up with the partisans, Senesh was captured
immediately upon entering Hungary. She was brutally tortured and
finally executed in 1944 at the age of twenty-three. This book is taken
from the diaries Senesh kept since the age of thirteen. Includes an
introduction by Abba Eban.

110   Singer, Isaac Bashevis. *A Day of Pleasure: Stories of a Boy
      Growing Up in Warsaw.* New York: Galahad, 1992. 100 pp.
      (hc. 0-88365-798-8) $11.95; (pbk. 0-37441-696-6) $5.95
Gr. 7-12. The Nobel Laureate recounts his childhood in Warsaw in the
first decades of the twentieth century. Beautifully written. Includes
black-and-white photographs by Roman Vishniac. Winner of the 1970
National Book Award. Originally published by Farrar, Straus & Giroux
in 1969.

111   —. *In My Father's Court.* New York: Farrar, Straus & Giroux,
      1966. 317 pp. (hc. 0-37417-560-8) $10.95
Gr. 9-12. The author reminisces about growing up in Warsaw. He gives
special attention to his father, an impoverished rabbi often called upon
by his congregates to decide upon civil, personal, and ritual issues.

112   Stance, Alaine. *So Much to Forget.* Trans. Susan Altschul.
      Vanguard, 1977. 164 pp. (pbk. 0-77159-365-1) $6.95
Gr. 9-12. The author relates his experiences as a young child living in
Lithuania, first under Russian, and then Nazi, occupation. Translated
from the French. Originally published by Gage (0-77159-365-1).

113   Stern, Ella Norman. *Elie Wiesel: Witness for Life.* Hoboken, NJ:
      KTAV, 1982. 199 pp. (hc. 0-87068-766-2) $12.95;
      (pbk. 0-87068-767-0) $7.95
Gr. 9-12. A biography of the Nobel Peace Prize winner, from his
childhood in Sight, Hungary, through the Holocaust and after. Includes
black-and-white photographs and a bibliography.

114   Tames, Richard. *Anne Frank.* New York: Watts, 1990. 32 pp.
      (hc. 0-531-10763-9) $12.40; (pbk. 0-531-24608-6) $5.95
Gr. 3-6. A brief biography of Anne Frank for younger readers. Includes
many black-and-white photographs, a diagram of the Secret Annex, a
glossary, and a subject index. From the *Life & Times* series.

115   Tec, Nechama. *Dry Tears: The Story of a Lost Childhood.*
      Westport, CT: Wildcat, 1982. 216 pp. (hc. 0-941968-00-6) $12.95
Gr. 7-12. The author, who was eight years old when Lublin, Poland,
was occupied, talks about how her parents were able to pass off the
family as Christians and survive the war.

116   ten Boom, Corrie with John and Elizabeth Cheryl. *The Hiding
      Place.* New York: Bantam, 1984. 256 pp. (pbk. 0-553-25669-6)

$10.99
Gr. 7-12. The story of how Corrie ten Boom and her devout Christian family hid Jews in their home in Holland. Eventually captured, Corrie watches her older sister die in a concentration camp, but still forgives her persecutors. An inspiring story of compassion and courage.

117 Toll, Nelly S. *Behind the Secret Window: A Memoir of a Hidden Childhood During World War II*. New York: Dial, 1993. 161 pp. (hc. 0-8037-1362-2) $17.00
Gr. 5-12. The author recalls her experiences when she and her mother were hidden from the Nazis by a Gentile couple in L'vov, Poland, during World War II. Includes color prints of twenty-three watercolor paintings painted during this period of the author's life.

118 Tyler, Laura. *Anne Frank*. Illus. Gain Renee. Englewood Cliffs, NJ: Silver Burdette Press, 1990. 104 pp. (hc. 0-382-09975-3) $12.95; (pbk. 0-382-24002-2) $5.95
Gr. 4-8. An informative biography tracing Anne Frank's life, suitable for readers not ready for Anne's own *Diary*. Illustrated with unremarkable watercolors. This book is from the *What Made Them Great* series. It is adapted from *Anne Frank* by Linda Trident, originally published in the *Why They Became Famous* series.

119 Vinke, Hermann. *The Short Life of Sofia Scholl*. Trans. Hedwig Patter. New York: Harper & Row, 1984. 216 pp. (hc. 0-06-0263302-4) $10.95
Gr. 7-12. A biography of Sophie Scholl, a twenty-one-year-old German student executed by the Nazis for her activities with an underground resistance group called the White Rose. The author creates this account by putting together selections of Sofia's own letters and diary, and the recollections of family and friends. Includes black-and-white drawings and photographs. Translated from the German.

120 Vogel, Ilse-Margaret. *Bad Times, Good Friends: A Personal Memoir*. San Diego: HBO, 1992. 256 pp. (hc. 0-15-205528-2) $16.95
Gr. 9-12. In Berlin, between 1943 and 1945, Ilse-Margaret Vogel and her friends struggle to survive and work against the Nazis. A wonderful story of courage and friendship. Includes a chronology and glossary.

121 Von der Grun, Max. *Howl Like the Wolves: Growing Up in Nazi Germany*. Trans. Jan Van Heart. New York: Morrow, 1980.

228 pp. (hc. 0-688-22252-8) $13.50

Gr. 7-12. Interweaving memoirs with history and documents, the author talks about how he was brought up in an anti-Nazi family but taught by his mother to "howl like the wolves so as not to be eaten by them." Translated from the German.

122 Von der Rol, Ruud and Iran Verhoeven. *Anne Frank, Beyond the Diary: A Photographic Remembrance.* Trans. Tony Lanham and Ply Peters. New York: Viking, 1993. 113 pp.
(hc. 0-670-84932-4) $17.00; (pbk. 0-140-36926-0) $7.99

Gr. 5-12. Over one hundred photographs, illustrations, and maps accompany historical essays, diary excerpts, and interviews to provide additional insight into Anne's and her family's life. This revealing photobiography is a superb complement to Anne's *Diary of a Young Girl.* Includes a chronology and an index of people and places. Created for the Anne Frank House in Amsterdam. Translated from the Dutch.

123 Vos, Ida. *Hide & Seek.* Trans. Terries Edelstein and Ines Smite. New York: Houghton Mifflin, 1991. 144 pp. (hc. 0-395-556470-0) $15.00; (pbk. 0-140-36908-2) $3.99

Gr. 3-8. A young Jewish girl living in Holland tells of her experiences during the Nazi occupation, her years in hiding, and the aftershock that comes when the war finally ends. Translated from the Dutch.

124 Vrba, Rudolf and Alan Bestir. *Escape from Auschwitz.* New York: Grove Press, 1964.

Gr. 9-12. Rudolf Vrba was imprisoned in Auschwitz but managed to escape and vowed to tell the world of the horrors he witnessed.

125 Weinstein, Frida Scheps. *A Hidden Childhood: A Jewish Girl's Sanctuary in a French Convent, 1942-1945.* Trans. Barbara Lobe Kennedy. New York: Hill and Wang, 1985. 151 pp.
(pbk. 8-090-1529-3) $7.95

Gr. 5-12. The author talks about her life as one of the thousands of "hidden children," who survived the Holocaust by disguising their Jewish identities and going to live with Gentile families or in convents. Translated from the French.

126 Weitz, Sonny Schreiber. *I Promised I Would Tell.* Ed. Susan Belt Cagily. Brookline, MA: Facing History and Ourselves, 1993. 103 pp. (pbk. 0-9615841-3-0)

Gr. 10-12. Through poetry and testimony, the author recounts her experiences living in the Krakow, Poland, ghetto and in five Nazi concentration camps.

127 Wiesel, Elie. *Night*. New York: Bantam, 1982. 128 pp.
(pbk. 0-553-27253-5) $4.99
Gr. 9-12. The author's terrifying account of his and his family's experiences in the Auschwitz and Buchenwald concentration camps. An absolutely horrific, profoundly disturbing book that will stay permanently etched into the reader's memory.

128 Wilkomirski, Binjamin. *Fragments: Memories of a Wartime Childhood, 1939-1948*. New York: Schocken, 1996. 160 pp.
(hc. 0-8052-4139-6) $20.00; (pbk. 0-8052-1089-X) $11.00
Gr. 9-12. Found wandering on the outskirts of Auschwitz-Birkenau at the end of the war, Wilkomirski had been in several death camps since the age of four. His parents dead, he was adopted by a Swiss family who brought him up to forget everything about his experiences. With the help of an analyst, Wilkomirski recalls his memories of his time in the camps and records them in this book.

129 Willenberg, Samuel. *Surviving Treblinka*. Ed. Wladyslaw T. Bartoszewski. London: Blackwell, 1989. 210 pp.
(hc. 0-631-16261-5) $19.95
Gr. 9-12. A personal narrative by one of only seventy survivors of the 900,000 Jews sent to the Treblinka death camp. An intensely personal, vivid memoir. Includes chapter notes, a glossary, and a subject index.

130 Woolf, Jacqueline. *"Take Care of Jostle:" A Memoir in Defense of Occupied France*. New York: Watts, 1981. (hc. 0-531-09861-3) $9.95
Gr. 9-12. When their parents are arrested by the Gestapo, fourteen-year-old Jacqueline and four-year-old Jostle Glicenstein, who always thought of themselves as more French than Jewish, must try to live out the rest of the war on their own in Occupied France. With the help of their heroic Gentile friends, neighbors, and fellow citizens, the two girls manage to survive. This memoir is a tribute to those ordinary people who heroically helped the Jews.

131 Wolf, Marion Fryer. *The Shrinking Circle: Memories of Nazi Berlin, 1933-1939*. New York: UH Press, 1989. 133 pp.
(pbk. 0-8074-0419-5) $7.95
Gr. 6-12. A highly readable personal narrative. Includes black-and-

white photographs, a chronology, bibliography, glossary, and subject index.

132 Zar, Rose. *In the Mouth of the Wolf.* Philadelphia: Jewish Publication Society of America, 1983. 225 pp. (hc. 0-8276-0225-1) $10.95; (pbk. 0-8276-0382-7) $9.95
Gr. 6-12. The author describes her experiences in wartime Poland and how she survived the Holocaust by passing herself off as an Aryan.

133 Zassenhaus, Hiltgunt. *Walls: Resisting the Third Reich—One Woman's Story.* Boston: Beacon Press, 1993. 256 pp. (pbk. 0-8070-6345-2) $10.00
Gr. 9-12. The author tells the story of how she first worked with the Nazis, censoring the mail of political prisoners, but gradually turned against them and became part of the resistance movement. Originally published in 1974 (0-8070-6388-6).

134 Zucker-Bujanowska, Liliana. *Liliana's Journal: Warsaw, 1939-1945.* New York: Dial, 1980. 162 pp. (hc. 0-8037-4997-X) $9.95
Gr. 7-12. The author relates her experiences living as a Jew in Poland before and during the war. Written in 1946, the memoir was translated from the Polish by the author. Includes black-and white photographs.

135 Zuckerman, Abraham. *A Voice in the Chorus: Life as a Teenager in the Holocaust.* Union, NJ: AM, 1990. 161 pp. (hc. 0-96274-130-2) $19.95
Gr. 9-12. Born and raised in Krakow, Poland, Zuckerman spent his teenage years in Nazi concentration camps and, at the end of the war, came to the United States to become a successful businessman. Zuckerman's survival is owed in part to Oskar Schindler to whose factory he was assigned. Since the war, Zuckerman has devoted himself to memorializing Schindler. Includes black-and-white photographs. Previously published by KTAV (0-88125-369-3).

136 Zyskind, Sara. *Stolen Years.* New York: Learner, 1981. 288 pp. (hc. 0-8225-0766-8) $11.95; (pbk. 0-451-14339-6) $3.95
Gr. 6-12. Sara tells her own story of how, when she was eleven years old, the Nazis came and sent her and her family to first the ghettoes and then the death camps.

137 —. *Struggle.* Minneapolis: Learner, 1989. 284 pp. (hc. 0-8225-0772-2) $16.95

Gr. 7-12. The true story of Lure, a teenage boy from Bzezin, Poland, who has to endure homelessness, ghettos, and, finally, Auschwitz. An intense, moving story.

Drama

One will find listed in this section collections of plays by single and multiple authors, and individual works. Another resource of interest about Holocaust drama is Janet Rubin's *Voices: Plays for Studying the Holocaust* published by Scarecrow Press.

138 Brecht, Bertolt. *The Jewish Wife and Other Short Plays*. Trans. Eric Bentley. New York: Grove, 1965. 174 pp. (pbk. 0-802150-98-5) $9.95
Gr. 11-12. Six plays depicting life for Jews in Nazi Germany before Hitler implemented his Final Solution. Includes: *The Jewish Wife, In Search of Justice, The Informer, The Elephant Calf, The Measures Taken,* and *The Exception and the Rule*. Translated from the German.

139 Fuchs, Elinor, ed. *Plays of the Holocaust: An International Anthology*. New York: Theatre Communications Group, 1987. 310 pp. (hc. 0-930452-67-4) $24.95; (pbk. 0-930452-63-1) $12.95
Gr. 9-12. As of 1997, this is the only anthology of Holocaust drama available. The anthology represents works from the following countries: France, Germany, Great Britain, Israel, Poland, Sweden, and the United States. All non-English plays are translated. In her introduction, Fuchs offers background information on each of the plays. Includes an excellent annotated, selected bibliography of Holocaust drama from around the world.

140 Goodrich, Francis and Albert Hackett. *The Diary of Anne Frank*. New York: Random House, 1956. (hc. 0-394-40564-1) $16.00; (pbk. 0-822-20307-3) $5.25
Gr. 9-12. A drama adapted from Anne's *Diary*. Not as effective as its source, but a strong, important work nonetheless. An excellent dramatization of the experiences of Anne and her family in the attic.

141 Hochhuth, Rolf. *The Deputy*. Trans. Richard and Clara Winston. Baltimore: Johns Hopkins UP, 1997. 391 pp. (pbk. 0-801856-53-1) $15.95
Gr. 9-12. As a young German Protestant, Hochhuth became convinced of the complicity of Pope Pius XII and the Roman Catholic Church in

the Holocaust. This drama explores the author's view of how the Roman Catholic Church failed to respond to the Holocaust. Translated from the German. Originally published by Grove Press in 1964.

142 Miller, Arthur. *Arthur Miller's Playing for Time: A Full-Length Stage Play*. Chicago: Dramatic Publishing Co., 1985. 91 pp. (pbk. 0-871-29267-X) $5.95
Gr. 9-12. A dramatization of the novel of the same title by Fania Fenelon. See the annotation for the work in the "Fiction" section. Miller adapted this play from the television film he wrote.

143 —. *Broken Glass*. New York: Penguin, 1995. 162 pp. (pbk. 0-140-24938-9) $7.95
Gr. 10-12. Set in New York in the late 1930s, the drama centers on Phillip Gellburg and his wife Sylvia. An executive, he is the only Jew among the WASPs at a Wall Street bank. Sylvia, obsessed with the news of Nazi Germany, becomes paralyzed in the legs when she sees a photograph of old Jewish men being forced to scrub a sidewalk with toothbrushes. Miller's story serves as a metaphor for the denial and inaction of the United States government while Jews were being persecuted in Nazi Germany. An intriguing, provocative play.

144 —. *Incident at Vichy*. New York: Penguin, 1985. 80 pp. (pbk. 0-140-48193-1) $8.95
Gr. 9-12. Set in 1942, in a place of detention in Vichy, France, a group of people have been rounded up for interrogation. Miller confronts directly issues of anti-Semitism and the Holocaust.

145 Rembrandt, Elaine. *So Young to Die: The Story of Hannah Senesh*. *Heroes, Heroines & Holidays: Plays for Jewish Youth*. Denver: Alternatives in Religious Education, 1981. pp. 89-104. (pbk. 0-86705-002-0) $6.50
Gr. 7-12. A one-act play about the young Jewish heroine. For eight characters. Includes production notes.

146 Rosenfeld, Ruth H. *Imagining Hitler*. Bloomington, IN: Indiana University Press, 1985. 121 pp. (hc. 0-25313-960-0) $15.00
Gr. 11-12. This drama explores the idea that everyone has the capacity to do the evil done by Hitler.

147 Shaw, Robert. *The Man in the Glass Booth*. New York: Grove, 1969. (pbk. 0-394-17314-7) $2.95

Gr. 9-12. Modeled after the trial of Adolf Eichmann in Jerusalem, Shaw universalizes Nazi identity by making the main character a Jew who poses as a Nazi posing as a Jew.

148 Skloot, Robert, ed. *The Theatre of the Holocaust: Four Plays.* Madison: University of Wisconsin Press, 1982. 333 pp. (pbk. 0-187-3274-2)
Gr. 9-12. Includes *Resort 76* by Shimon Wincelberg, *Throne of Straw* by Harold and Edith Lieberman, *The Cannibals* by George Tabori, and *Who Will Carry the Word?* by Charlotte Delbo.

149 Steinhorn, Harriet and Edith Pick Lowy. *Shadows of the Holocaust: Plays, Readings, and Program Resources.* Rockville, MD: KAR-BEN Copies, 1983. 80 pp. (pbk. 0-930494-25-3) $6.95
Gr. 4-10. A collection of seven plays and five songs appropriate for older elementary, middle, or high school students to perform. The plays are brief and include stage directions and production notes. Includes a glossary, suggestions for holding a meaningful Holocaust assembly, a suggested format for a Holocaust memorial program, and a brief bibliography.

150 Sylvannus, Erwin. *Doctor Korczak and the Children.*
Gr. 9-12. This drama depicts the life of Janusz Korczak, the legendary educator, physician, and humanitarian who cared for orphans in the Warsaw Ghetto. On August 5, 1942, he and 200 orphans were rounded up and sent to Treblinka where they were all exterminated.

151 Weiss, Peter. *The Investigation: An Oratorio in 11 Cantos.* New York: Marion Boyars, 1996. 208 pp. (pbk. 0-714-50301-0) $14.95
Gr. 9-12. A fascinating play based upon war crimes trials of Nazi perpetrators in Frankfurt, Germany. Much of the dialogue is taken from actual court testimony.

152 Whitman, Ruth. *The Testing of Hanna Senesh.* Detroit: Wayne State University Press, 1986. 115 pp. (hc. 0-814-31853-3) $17.95; (pbk. 0-814-31854-1) $11.95
Gr. 9-12. A play based upon the life of the legendary heroine, one of a group of Palestinian Jews who parachuted into Nazi-occupied Europe in order to help fellow Jews. Senesh parachuted into Yugoslavia in 1944, spent three months with Tito's partisans, and then crossed the border into Hungary with the intention of helping Jews there, but she was captured immediately. She was imprisoned and tortured for

information about other members of her group, but she never talked. Senesh was executed by a firing squad for treason. Includes historical background by Livia Rothkirchen.

Fiction

One will find listed in this section novels, novellas, short story collections written by a single author, and chapter books for younger children.

153 Aaron, Chester. *Gideon: A Novel.* New York: Lippincott, 1982.
181 pp. (hc. 0-397-31992-4)
Gr. 7-12. When Gideon, a Jewish boy, loses all his family and friends, he buries his religion and identity in order to survive the Warsaw Ghetto and Treblinka concentration camp.

154 Ackerman, Karen. *The Night Crossing.* Illus. Elizabeth Sayles.
New York: Knopf, 1994. 56 pp. (hc. 0-679-87040-7) $14.00;
(pbk. 0-679-87040-7) $4.50
Gr. 2-5. In 1938, when the Nazis take over Austria and begin to persecute the Jews, Clara and her family flee to Switzerland. An excellent fictional introduction to the Holocaust for younger readers.

155 Almagor, Gila. *Under the Domim Tree.* Trans. Hillel Schenker.
New York: Simon & Schuster, 1995. 164 pp. (hc. 0-671-89020-4)
$15.00
Gr. 7-12. Chronicles the joys and troubles experienced by a group of teenage girls, many of whom are Holocaust survivors, living at a settlement in 1953 Israel. Translated from the Hebrew.

156 Ambrose, Kenneth. *The Story of Peter Cronheim.* Illus. Elisabeth
Grant. New York: Duell, Sloan and Pearce, 1962. 159 pp.
Gr. 4-8. In 1932, in a small town in northern Germany, Peter celebrates his bar mitzvah, but soon after things change for the worst for Jews. By the end of the story, Peter has fled to England for safety. Illustrated with black-and-white drawings.

157 Appelfeld, Aharon. *For Every Sin: A Novel.* Trans. Jeffrey M. G.
Green. New York: Weidenfeld & Nicolson, 1989. 168 pp.
(hc. 1-55584-318-2) $15.95
Gr. 7-12. Theo, a young Holocaust survivor, struggles to understand his recent experiences. Translated from the Hebrew.

158 —. *Tzili: The Story of a Life*. Trans. Dalya Bilu. New York:
      Dutton, 1983. 185 pp. (hc. 0-525-24187-6) $12.95;
      (pbk. 0-802-13455-6) $11.00
Gr. 7-12. Told as a parable, this is the story of Tzili, a poor, simple-
minded Jewish girl in Poland left behind by her parents when they flee,
but still able to survive the Holocaust with the help of local peasants.
An often anguished story, but not totally bleak. *Tzili* completes a
trilogy begun with *Badenheim 1939* and *The Age of Wonders*.
Translated from the Hebrew.

159 Arnold, Elliott. *A Kind of Secret Weapon*. New York: Charles
      Scribner's Sons, 1969. 191 pp.
Gr. 5-9. When Denmark is occupied by the Nazis in 1940, Peter
Andersen's parents become involved with an underground newspaper.
Soon, Peter also joins the resistance movement. An exciting story with
a lot of dialogue and short chapters, making for a quick read.

160 Arrick, Fran. *Chernowitz!* Scarsdale, NY: Bradbury Press, 1981.
      165 pp. (hc. 0-87888-190-5) $8.95
Gr. 9-12. In post-World War II America, Bobby Cherno, a ninth grader,
is tormented by Emmett Sundlock, an anti-Semitic peer. When the
bully recruits a group of followers, the harassment extends to Bobby's
family. In response to these incidents, the school stages an assembly at
which films of concentration camps and their victims are shown. The
education changes the attitudes of many of the students, but not
Emmett.

161 Baer, Edith. *A Frost in the Night*. New York: Schocken, 1980. 224
      pp. (pbk. 0-8052-0857-7) $7.95
Gr. 7-12. The experiences of Eva, a young Jewish girl, living in
Germany during Hitler's rise to power. A very well-written novel that
looks at what life was like for German Jews in-between Hitler's rise to
power and the implementation of the Final Solution.

162 Baylis-White, Mary. *Sheltering Rebecca*. New York: Lodestar,
      1989. 99 pp. (hc. 0-525-67349-0) $14.95
Gr. 4-8. In England in the days before World War II, Sally is asked to
look after Rebecca Muller, the new girl at school. As Sally and
Rebecca grow closer as friends, Sally learns what it meant for Rebecca
to be a Jew in Nazi Germany.

163 Benchley, Nathaniel. *Bright Candles: A Novel of the Danish Resistance*. New York: Harper Collins, 1974. 256 pp. (hc. 06-020461-3) $13.95

Gr. 7-12. Jens, a sixteen-year-old Danish boy in Copenhagen defies his parents who believe cooperation is the safest course and joins the resistance, helping many of his fellow Jewish citizens escape. An interesting book to compare to Lois Lowry's *Number the Stars* or Carol Matas's *Lisa's War*.

164 Benjamin, Ruth. *Stranger to Her People*. New York: CIS, 1993. 207 pp. (hc. 1-56062-210-5) (pbk. 1-56062-231-8)

Gr. 9-12. Jenny, a twenty-six-year-old South African teacher and convert to Judaism goes to Europe to participate in a "March of the Living" event. Although written as a young adult novel, the protagonist is too old, the tone of the story is too didactic, and the writing is simply not good.

165 Bergman, Tamar. *Along the Tracks*. Trans. Michael Siversky. Boston: Houghton Mifflin, 1991. 245 pp. (hc. 0-395-55328-8) $14.95; (pbk. 0-395-74513-6) $5.95

Gr. 5-10. The adventures of a young Jewish boy who is driven from his home in Poland during the German invasion, becomes a refugee in the Soviet Union, where he is separated from his family, and undergoes many hardships before enjoying a normal home again. Based upon the author's real life experiences. Translated from the Hebrew.

166 —. *The Boy from Over There*. Trans. Hillel Halkin. Boston: Houghton Mifflin, 1988. 181 pp. (hc. 0-395-43077-1) $13.95; (pbk. 0-395-64370-8) $4.95

Gr. 5-10. The story of life in a children's house on a kibbutz in the Jordan valley during Israel's War of Independence is told through the eyes of Avramik, an orphaned Holocaust survivor and Rina, whose father was killed in Europe fighting with the Jewish Brigade.

167 Bezdekov, Zdenka. *They Called Me Leni*. Illus. Eva Bednarova. Trans. Stuart R. Amor. Indianapolis: Bobbs-Merrill, 1973. 84 pp. (hc. 0-74041-665-2) $4.50

Gr. 3-6. A haunting and touching story of Leni, a young girl abducted from Czechoslovakia by the Germans and brought to Germany to be raised as an Aryan. The text is complemented with striking black-and-white illustrations. Translated from the Czech.

48   Fiction

168 Bishop, Claire Huchet. *Twenty and Ten*. Illus. William Pene
     DuBois. New York: Peter Smith, 1984. 76 pp. (hc. 0-84-466168-2)
     $18.00; (pbk. 0-14-031076-2) $3.99
Gr. 2-5. Twenty French children help hide and protect ten refugee
children during the German occupation. Based upon a true story.
Illustrated with black-and-white drawings.

169 Bloch, Marie Halum. *Displaced Persons*. New York: Lothrop, Lee
     and Shepard, 1978. 191 pp. (hc. 0-688-41860-0)
Gr. 9-12. Fourteen-year-old Stefan, a Ukrainian refugee, struggles to
survive in a displaced persons camp in Germany.

170 Blume, Judy. *Starring Sally J. Freedman as Herself*. New York:
     Simon & Schuster, 1982. 251 pp. (pbk. 0-440-48253-4) $4.50
Gr. 4-8. In 1947, Sally J. Freedman leaves New Jersey to spend a
school year in Miami with her mother and convalescing brother. There,
she imagines the next door neighbor is Hitler.

171 Borkas-Nemetz, Lillian. *The Old Brown Suitcase: A Teenager's
     Story of War and Peace*. Port Angeles, WA: Ben-Simon, 1994. 148
     pp. (hc. 0-027-11070-20 $17.00; (pbk. 0-91453-10-8) $9.50
Gr. 5-10. Slava, a fourteen-year-old Polish Jewish girl, escapes from
the Warsaw Ghetto and hides out the rest of the war. After the war,
Slava immigrates to Canada where she struggles to learn a new
language and customs, while being haunted by memories of Nazi
persecution.

172 Bush, Lawrence. *Rooftop Secrets and Other Stories of Anti-
     Semitism*. Illus. Martin Lemelman. New York: Union of American
     Hebrew Congregations, 1986. 157 pp. (pbk. 0-8074-0314-8) $7.95
Gr. 5-10. A collection of eight short stories spanning five hundred years
of Jewish history. Written from the perspective of a child experiencing
anti-Semitic or racial prejudice, the settings include Spain during the
Inquisition, Colonial America, and Nazi Germany. A fascinating
collection revealing anti-Semitism as a persistent and continuing
problem. Each story is prefaced with a commentary placing it in
historical context. This book lends itself especially well to classroom
use.

173 Charney, Ann. *Dobryd*. Sag Harbor, NY: Permanent Press, 1996.
     170 pp. (hc. 1-877946-66-4) $22.00
Gr. 5-10. An extraordinary tale of a young girl living in Nazi-occupied

Poland who manages to have a "happy" childhood despite the devastations and horrors that consume her life. A memorable and moving story depicting the resiliency of a child living in utterly horrific circumstances.

174 Cohen, Barbara. *Benny.* New York: Lothrop, Lee & Shepard, 1977. 154 pp. (hc. 0-688-41804-X)
Gr. 5-8. In 1939, when his aunt and uncle take in Arnulf, a German refugee, Benny Rifkind is given a chance to prove he really is concerned with more than baseball and the World's Fair.

175 Cormier, Robert. *Tunes for Bears to Dance To.* New York: Delacorte, 1992. 101 pp. (hc. 0-385-30818-3) $15.00; (pbk. 0-440-21903-5) $3.99
Gr. 7-12. Eleven-year-old Henry escapes his family's problems when he befriends Mr. Levine, an elderly Holocaust survivor, but the bigoted Mr. Hariston manipulates Henry to turn on his friend. A fascinating, compelling story that examines evil and how easily power can be abused.

176 Dank, Milton. *The Dangerous Game.* New York: Lippincott, 1977. 157 pp. (hc. 0-397-31753-0) $6.95
Gr. 4-9. Fifteen-year-old Charles Marceau, the son of a French father and an American mother, joins the resistance in Paris after the Nazis occupy France.

177 Degens, T. *The Visit.* New York: Viking, 1982. 150 pp. (hc. 0-670-74712-2) $10.95
Gr. 9-12. At a family gathering in Berlin years after World War II, Kate Hofmann relives some of the events described in the diary of her dead Aunt Sylvia, who was once a Hitler Youth member.

178 Demetz, Hannah. *The House on Prague Street.* New York: St. Martin's, 1970. 186 pp. (hc. 0-312-39322-9) $8.95
Gr. 9-12. Helene Richter's idyllic life in pre-war Czechoslovakia gradually deteriorates as the situation for Jews grows more desperate. Translated from the German by the author.

179 Dillon, Eilis. *Children of Bach.* 164 pp. New York: Scribner, 1992. 176 pp. (hc. 0-684-19440-6) $14.95
Gr. 5-8. When their parents are arrested by the Nazis, a group of Jewish Hungarian children from a family of talented musicians escape a

similar fate.

180 Douglas, Kirk. *The Broken Mirror: A Novella*. New York: Simon
    & Schuster, 1997. 88 pp. (hc. 0-689-81493-3) $13.00
Gr. 4-8. After the Nazis destroy his family in Munich, twelve-year-old
Moishe gives up his Jewish faith, calls himself Danny, and is taken to
New York where he tries to make the best of his life in a Roman
Catholic orphanage. This is a touching story of the loss of faith and its
recovery told with honesty and simplicity.

181 Drucker, Malka and Michael Halperin. *Jacob's Rescue: A
    Holocaust Story*. New York: Bantam, 1993. 119 pp.
    (hc. 0-553-08976-5) $15.00
Gr. 4-8. In answer to her questions, a father tells his daughter of his
terrifying childhood during the Holocaust when he and other Jewish
children were hidden from the Nazis by Alex and Mela Roslan, a brave
Polish couple. Based on a true story.

182 Evenhuis, Gertie. *What About Me?* Trans. Lance Salway. Illus.
    Ron Stenberg. New York: Lodestar, 1976. 96 pp.
    (hc. 0-5256-6524-2) $6.95
Gr. 4-8. In 1943 German-occupied Amsterdam, eleven-year-old Dirk
Waterman joins the resistance movement and helps fight against the
occupation. Illustrated with black-and-white drawings. Translated from
the Dutch.

183 Field, Hermann H. *Angry Harvest*. New York: Crowell, 1958.
Gr. 9-12. The story of a Jewish girl who hides from the Nazis on a farm
with a Polish family.

184 Fink, Ida. *The Journey*. New York: Farrar, Straus & Giroux, 1993.
    Trans. Joanna Weschler and Francine Prose. 224 pp.
    (hc. 0-374-28541-1) $20.00; (pbk. 0-452-27015-4) $10.00
Gr. 9-12. In autumn 1942, as the Nazis begin the deportation of Jews
imprisoned in the ghettos, two sisters escape from theirs. With forged
identity papers, they pose as Polish peasant girls volunteering for work
in Germany. A harrowing, suspenseful story.

185 —. *A Scrap of Time and Other Stories*. Trans. Francine Prose and
    Madeline Levine. New York: Pantheon, 1987. 192 pp.
    (hc. 0-3945-5806-5) $15.95; (pbk. 0-8101-1259-0) $12.95
Gr. 9-12. Told in spare, powerful prose, this is a collection of short

stories, many of which feature young people who survived to tell of the Nazi terrors they suffered. Translated from the Polish.

186 —. *Traces: Stories.* Trans. Philip Boehm and Francine Prose. New York: Metropolitan, 1997. 210 pp. (hc. 0-8050-4557-0) $23.00 Gr. 9-12. In this collection of short stories, the author depicts everyday life in occupied Poland. Fink's prose is vivid and lean. Based upon the author's own wartime experiences. Translated from the Polish.

187 Firer, Benzion. *The Twins.* Trans. Braca Sloe. New York: Feldheim, 1983. 229 pp. (hc. 0-87306-279-5) $10.95; (pbk. 0-87306-343-0) $7.95 Gr. 9-12. A novel about boy and girl twins separated in Poland during the Holocaust. He goes to Israel and she to a Polish convent, but they are eventually reunited. Translated from the Hebrew.

188 Forman, James. *Ceremony of Innocence.* New York: Dutton, 1970. 249 pp. (hc. 0-80151-140-2) $7.95 Gr. 9-12. Brother and sister Hans and Sophie School, students at Munich University, join in the German resistance movement. The story is based upon real people and events.

189 —. *Horses of Anger.* New York: Farrar, Straus & Giroux, 1967. 224 pp. (hc. 0-37433-333-5) $3.95 Gr. 7-12. In 1944 Germany, fifteen-year-old Hans Amann, sickened by the war, begins to act against the Nazi philosophy instilled in him over the years.

190 —. *My Brother, My Enemy.* New York: Scholastic, 1972. 250 pp. (pbk. 0-59004-477-X) $2.25 Gr. 5-10. Danny, a Polish Jew and concentration camp survivor, joins three young people on a dangerous trek across Europe and on to Israel.

191 —. *The Survivor.* New York: Farrar, Straus & Giroux, 1976. 288 pp. (hc. 0-374-37312-4) $11.95 Gr. 7-12. A grim and affecting story of the disintegration of a Jewish family during the Nazi occupation of Holland.

192 —. *The Traitors.* New York: Farrar, Straus & Giroux, 1968. 256 pp. (hc. 0-37437-722-7) $3.95 Gr. 7-12. The story of two half-brothers, one who becomes a Nazi, the other who helps his pastor father save a Jewish friend.

193 —. *The White Crow*. New York: Farrar, Straus & Giroux, 1976.
227 pp. (hc. 0-374-38386-3) $7.95
Gr. 9-12. A fictionalized account of Adolf Hitler's youth, from 1907 at age eighteen to his unsuccessful attempt to gain power with the *Beer Hall Putsch* in 1923. This is an interesting speculative portrait of a fanatic, showing the roots of hate, prejudice, and rage that would later be set loose upon the world.

194 Friedman, Carl. *Nightfather*. Trans. Arnold J. Pomerans and Erica Pomerans. New York: Persea, 1994. 144 pp. (hc. 0-89255-193-3) $18.50; (pbk. 0-89255-210-7) $7.95
Gr. 9-12. An autobiographical novel by a Dutch poet and translator whose father is a Holocaust survivor. The story is made up of a series of intense, vivid episodes about a young girl in The Netherlands in the 1950s and 1960s who tells how her father's stories of his life in the concentration camps are part of family life. Translated from the Dutch.

195 Gehrts, Barbara. *Don't Say a Word*. Trans. Elizabeth D. Crawford. New York: McElderry, 1986. 192 pp. (hc. 0-68950-412-8) $13.95
Gr. 7-12. In the early days of World War II Berlin, Anna and her family grow more and more aware of the terrible direction their country is taking under Hitler. Among the many grim realities Anna confronts is the death of her Jewish schoolmate and her family. Translated from the German.

196 Gille, Elisabeth. *Shadows of a Childhood: A Novel of War and Friendship*. Trans. Linda Coverdale. New York: New Press, 1998. 138 pp. (hc. 1-56584-388-6) $23.00
Gr. 7-12. Gille was five years old when her mother, a Russian writer, was deported to Auschwitz and never seen again. Hidden in the French countryside with her sister until the war was over, Gille uses her experiences to tell this story of two sisters hidden in a Bordeaux convent for the duration of the war. A poignant, memorable novel. Translated from the French.

197 Ginsburg, Marvell. *The Tattooed Torah*. Illus. Jo Gershman. New York: Union of American Hebrew Congregations, 1983. 32 pp. (hc. 0-8074-0252-4) $10.95
Gr. 2-4. A small Torah in a synagogue in Brno, Czechoslovakia, is stolen and desecrated by Nazi soldiers, but it is eventually rescued, restored, and returned.

198 Goldreich, Gloria. *Season of Discovery*. New York: Lodestar,
     1977. 156 pp. (hc. 0-5256-6523-4) $4.50
Gr. 5-10. Lisa, a young Jewish girl in the year of her bat mitzvah,
learns about the Holocaust from Mrs. Rothenberg, a woman Lisa reads
to at the Jewish Community Center.

199 Goldstein, Lisa. *The Red Magician*. New York: TOR, 1993. 192
     pp. (hc. 0-312-85462-5) $18.95; (pbk. 0-312-89007-9) $10.95
Gr. 7-12. A fantasy that takes place in a small backwoods village in
Nazi-occupied eastern Europe. A highly original, beautifully told tale.
An American Book Award winner.

200 Gotfryd, Bernard. *Anton the Dove Fancier and Other Tales of the
     Holocaust*. New York: Washington Square Press, 1990. 175 pp.
     (pbk. 0-671-69137-6) $7.95
Gr. 10-12. Short stories relate the experiences of a young Polish boy
before World War II, during the war, and immediately after. The stories
are based upon the author's own wartime experiences, spending time in
six concentration camps. The stories make for poignant and memorable
reading.

201 Greene, Bette. *Morning is a Long Time Coming*. New York: Dial,
     1978. 261 pp. (hc. 0-8037-5496-5) $10.95; (pbk. 0-4402-1893-4)
     $4.50
Gr. 5-12. In this sequel to *Summer of My German Soldier*, Patty Bergen
is now eighteen years old and graduating from Jenkinsville High
School. Although Anton is dead, he remains the most compelling
person in Patty's life. She travels to Germany, hoping to find something
to fill the void she feels exists in her life. While in Paris, Patty meets
Roger and has her first love affair, which makes her finally begin to
appreciate the value of her own life.

202 —. *Summer of My German Soldier*. New York: Dell, 1993. 199
     pp. (pbk. 0-440-21892-6) $4.99
Gr. 5-10. Patty Bergen, a Jewish girl living in a small Arkansas town
falls in love with Anton, a German soldier who escaped from a nearby
prisoner-of-war camp. A wonderful, exceptionally written story of
relationships.

203 Haugaard, Erik Christian. *Chase Me, Catch Nobody!* Boston:
     Houghton Mifflin, 1980. 209 pp. (hc. 0-395-29208-5) $8.95
Gr. 5-10. On a school trip to Germany in 1937, fourteen-year-old Erik

from Denmark meets a stranger and finds himself involved with the
anti-Nazi underground.

204 Herman, Erwin and Agnes. *The Yanov Torah*. Illus. Katherine
     Janus Kohn. Rockville, MD: Kar-Ben Copies, 1985. 48 pp.
     (hc. 0-930494-45-8) $10.95; (pbk. 0-930494-46-6) $5.95
Gr. 2-4. Despite enormous personal risk, Jews in a work camp in
Yanov, in the Nazi-occupied city of L'vov, Poland, smuggle in a Torah
piece by piece. Illustrated with black-and-white drawings.

205 Hersey, John. *The Wall*. New York: Bantam, 1981.
     (pbk. 0-553-20053-4) $3.25
Gr. 9-12. A fictional account of the Warsaw Ghetto Uprising in 1943.

206 Holm, Anne. *North to Freedom*. Trans. L.W. Kingsland. San
     Diego: HBJ, 1963. 190 pp. (pbk. 0-15-666100-4) $5.95
Gr. 5-10. Twelve-year-old David escapes from an eastern European
concentration camp and tries to make it back to his home in Denmark.
A riveting adventure. Translated from the Danish.

207 Isherwood, Christopher. *The Berlin Stories*. Cambridge, England:
     Robert Bentley, 1979. (hc. 0-837-60449-4) $18.00
Gr. 11-12. A collection of short stories showing the decline of German
cultural and social life of Germany in the 1920s, leading up to the rise
of Nazism in the early 1930s. The musical *Cabaret* is based upon these
stories.

208 Jules, Jacqueline. *The Grey-Striped Suit: How Grandma and
     Grandpa Survived the Holocaust*. Los Angeles: Alef Design Group,
     1993. 64 pp. (hc. 1-881283-06-2) $13.95
Gr. 2-4. When Frannie, visiting her grandparents, discovers a grey-
striped shirt in a closet, she starts asking questions, which prompts
them to tell her of their experiences in the Holocaust. An excellent
introduction to the Holocaust for younger readers. Illustrated with
black-and-white drawings.

209 Kanfer, Stefan. *The Eighth Sin*. New York: Random House, 1978.
     288 pp. (hc. 0-394-41476-4) $8.95
Gr. 9-12. A novel about Benoit, a Gypsy boy, who survives the
concentration camps and is adopted by a Jewish couple in New York
City after the war.

Fiction   55

210 Kay, Mara. *In the Face of Danger.* New York: Crown, 1977. 210
    pp. (hc. 0-517-53119-4) $6.95
Gr. 5-9. Caught in Nazi Germany when her uncle is injured in an auto
accident, Ann Lindsay hides two Jewish girls in her house. An exciting,
suspenseful story.

211 Keneally, Thomas. *Schindler's List.* New York: Penguin, 1983.
    (pbk. 0-671-88031-4) $12.00
Gr. 11-12. A fictional account of Oskar Schindler and his heroic efforts
to save Jews in Poland.

212 Kerr, Judith. *The Other Way Round.* New York: Putnam, 1977.
    191 pp. (hc. 0-6892-0335-6) $8.95
Gr. 4-8. In this sequel to *When Hitler Stole Pink Rabbit,* Anna lives in
London for the duration of the war coping with the pains of growing
up, her fears during the Blitz, and her responsibilities toward her
parents. Originally published by Coward, McCann & Geoghegan
(1975, 0-020-1231-4).

213 ——.*When Hitler Stole Pink Rabbit.* New York: Putnam, 1997.
    191 pp. (pbk. 0-6898-11589-9) $4.95
Gr. 3-8. In 1933, Anna, her brother, and mother escape to Switzerland
where they unite with Anna's father and begin their journey as refugees
from the Nazis. Illustrated with black-and-white drawings by the
author. Originally published by Coward, McCann & Geoghegan (1972,
0-689-20182-5).

214 Kerr, M. E. *Gentlehands.* New York: HarperCollins, 1978. 183 pp.
    (hc. 0-06-023177-7) $16.89; (pbk. 0-06-447067-9) $3.95
Gr. 7-12. Buddy Boyle and Skye Pennington fall in love one summer in
Long Island, but the bliss of their romance is shattered when Buddy
learns his eccentric grandfather might be "Gentlehands," a Nazi war
criminal. A beautifully written young adult novel, as good as it gets.

215 Kranzler, Gershon. *Seder in Helrin and Other Stories for Girls.*
    Illus. Joyce Klavan. Brooklyn, NY: Merkos L'inyonei Chinuch,
    1975. 108 pp.
Gr. 5-9. Short stories based upon religious commandments, several of
which are about the Holocaust. Illustrated with black-and-white
drawings.

216 Laird, Christina. *But Can the Phoenix Sing?* New York:

Greenwillow, 1993. 230 pp. (hc. 0-688-13612-5) $15.00
Gr. 7-12. Seventeen-year-old Richard learns of his stepfather's hidden past as a Warsaw Ghetto survivor and partisan fighter in an autobiographical letter.

217 —. *Shadow of the Wall*. New York: Greenwillow, 1990. 144 pp. (hc. 0-688-09336-1) $12.95
Gr. 7-12. Living in the Warsaw Ghetto with his mother and two sisters, Misha is befriended by Dr. Korczak and joins the resistance organization. Includes a postscript on Janusz Korczak, a real person who serves as a central character in the novel.

218 Lasky, Kathryn. *Prank*. New York: Macmillan, 1984. 171 pp. (hc. 0-02-751690-3) $12.95
Gr. 7-12. Sixteen-year-old Birdie Flynn, an Irish-Catholic teenager living in East Boston, is prompted to study the events of the Holocaust when her brother Timmy takes part in vandalizing a synagogue.

219 Levin, Jane Whitebread. *Star of Danger*. New York: Harcourt, Brace & World, 1966. 160 pp.
Gr. 9-12. Eighteen-year-old Peter and his friend Karl escape first from Germany in 1939 to Denmark and later to Sweden with the help of the Danish Resistance.

220 Levitin, Sonia. *Journey to America*. New York: Aladdin, 1987. 150 pp. (pbk. 0-689-71130-1) $3.95
Gr. 5-8. The Platts, a Jewish family in Germany on the eve of World War II, flee the Nazis to start a new life in America. Illustrated with black-and-white drawings. Originally published by Atheneum in 1970.

221 —. *Silver Days*. New York: Aladdin, 1989. 186 pp. (pbk. 0-689-71570-6) $3.95
Gr. 5-8. In this sequel to *Journey to America*, the Platt family safely escapes the horrors of Nazi Germany and reunites in America. For thirteen-year-old Lisa, being a Jewish refugee from Germany during World War II is not easy, even in America. There is still poverty and prejudice of a different kind with which she must cope.

222 Levoy, Myron. *Alan and Naomi*. New York: Harper Trophy 1987. 192 pp. (pbk. 0-06-440209-6) $3.95
Gr. 5-8. In 1944 New York, Alan tries to befriend Naomi, a victim of Nazi brutality in France.

223 Lowry, Lois. *Number the Stars*. Boston: Houghton Mifflin, 1989.
137 pp. (hc. 0-395-51060-0) $12.95; (pbk. 0-440-40327-8) $3.50
Gr. 4-7. In 1943 in German occupied Denmark, ten-year-old
Annemarie learns the meaning of courage when she helps her Jewish
friend hide from the Nazis. Winner of the 1990 Newbery Medal.

224 Lustig, Arnost. *Darkness Casts No Shadow*. Trans. Jeanne
Nemcova. Washington, D.C.: Inscape, 1976. 144 pp.
(hc. 0-87953-406-0)
Gr. 7-12. Two teenage boys escape from the transport taking them to a
concentration camp and try to make their way through Germany to their
native Prague. This is a terrifying story told with stunning subtlety.
Based upon the author's own experiences.

225 Mace, Elisabeth. *Brother Enemy*. New York: Beaufort, 1979. 175
pp. (hc. 0-8253-0031-2) $10.95
Gr. 9-12. In 1937 Germany, nine-year-old Andreas, a *Mischling*, finds
out what it means to be part Jewish in a Nazi country.

226 Madison, Winifred. *Becky's Horse*. New York: Scholastic, 1975.
152 pp. (hc. 0-590-07361-3) $6.95
Gr. 4-8. In order for her family to bring her refugee cousin from Austria
to live with them in 1938, Becky gives up her dream of owning a horse.

227 Matas, Carol. *After the War*. New York: Simon & Schuster, 1996.
120 pp. (hc. 0-689-80350-8) $16.00; (pbk. 0-689-80722-8) $3.95
Gr. 5-10. Recently liberated from the Buchenwald concentration camp,
fifteen-year-old Ruth returns to Poland to search for family and friends.
She finds herself the sole survivor of over eighty relatives. With
nowhere to go, Ruth joins up with an underground organization
smuggling displaced Jews to Palestine. She and several other young
adult survivors lead a group of orphans on a harrowing journey to the
new homeland. Matas shows in this novel that the persecution of
European Jews did not end with the Holocaust. The story is unique in
that it is one of the few that looks at what happens to Holocaust
survivors immediately following liberation. Beautifully written,
touching, and memorable.

228 —. *Code Name Kris*. New York: Charles Scribner's Sons, 1990.
152 pp. (hc. 0-684-19208-X) $12.95
Gr. 5-10. In this sequel to *Lisa's War*, seventeen-year-old Jesper
continues his work in the underground Danish resistance movement

helping Jews escape from the Nazis. Also published in paperback by
Scholastic as *Kris's War* (0-590-45034-4, $3.25).

229 —. *Daniel's Story*. New York: Scholastic, 1993. 136 pp.
   (hc. 0-590-46920-7) $13.95; (pbk. 0-590-46588-0) $3.99
Gr. 5-10. Daniel describes his imprisonment in a concentration camp
and his eventual liberation. A powerful study of courage and survival.
This novel was published in conjunction with an exhibit called
"Daniel's Story: Remember the Children" at the United States
Holocaust Memorial Museum in Washington, D.C.

230 —. *The Garden*. New York: Simon & Schuster, 1997. 102 pp.
   (hc. 0-689-80349-4) $15.00
Gr. 7-12. In this sequel to *After the War*, concentration camp survivor
Ruth Mendelson lives in British-controlled Palestine on Kibbutz David
as the United Nations prepares to vote on partitioning the country
between Arabs and Jews. An engrossing, provocative story depicting a
time and place seldom explored in fiction for young people. Includes a
glossary.

231 —. *Lisa's War*. New York: Scholastic, 1989. 111 pp.
   (hc. 0-684-19010-9) $15.00; (pbk. 0-590-43517-5) $2.99
Gr. 5-10. In Denmark, Lisa and her family join in the resistance against
the Nazi occupation of their homeland. They join their countrymen and
women in helping Danish Jews escape deportation to the concentration
camps. This is an engrossing, exciting story that should be compared
with Lois Lowry's *Number the Stars*.

232 —. *Greater Than Angels*. New York: Simon & Schuster, 1998.
   133 pp. (hc. 0-689-81353-8) $16.00
Gr. 6-10. Anna, a teenaged German refugee, tells how she and other
Jewish children were saved from deportation to concentration camps by
the "Righteous Gentile" citizens of Le Chambon-sur-Lignon in France
during the German occupation. Like Matas's other Holocaust novels
this one is excellent. She successfully blends history with an engrossing
and compelling story of human drama. Anna is a wonderful character, a
strong and feisty young woman readers will appreciate and remember.
Matas concludes the novel with some notes on how she went about
researching the facts for this story.

233 Mazer, Harry. *The Last Mission*. New York: Dell, 1979. 188 pp.
   (pbk. 0-440-94797-9) $3.99

Fiction   59

Gr. 6-10. Fifteen-year-old Jack Raab, determined to save the Jews in
Eastern Europe, uses a false I.D. to lie his way into the Air Force in
1944. While flying a bombing mission over Europe, Jack's plane is
shot down and Jack, a Jew, is captured and sent off to a German POW
camp. An exciting, moving story that offers an interesting twist on
other Holocaust stories.

234 Moran, Thomas. *The Man in the Box*. New York: Riverhead,
     1997. 260 pp. (hc. 1-57322-060-4) $21.95
Gr. 9-12. A strange but engrossing and elegantly written story told
through the eyes of Niki Lukasser, an adolescent. Niki's father has
walled Jewish Dr. Weiss in his barn loft. At first, Niki sees hiding Dr.
Weiss as an exciting adventure but, as the tension of having this secret
weighs more heavily upon the family, his father in particular, Niki is
forced to assume the burden of caring for Dr. Weiss.

235 Morpurgo, Michael. *Waiting for Anya*. New York: Viking, 1991.
     172 pp. (hc. 0-670-83735-0) $13.99
Gr. 5-8. In Vichy France, a young man, a reclusive widow, and an
entire town work together to hide escaping Jews.

236 Moskin, Marietta. *I Am Rosemarie*. New York: John Day, 1972.
     190 pp. $5.95
Gr. 7-12. Rosemarie's happy childhood in Amsterdam is shattered
when the Nazis invade and occupy Holland. Like other Dutch Jews,
Rosemarie and her family are forced out of their homes and sent first to
the Westerbork transit camp and later Bergen-Belsen, where she
miraculously manages to stay alive to be liberated.

237 Murray, Michele. *Crystal Nights*. New York: Houghton Mifflin,
     1979. 310 pp.
Gr. 7-12. Elly feels the effects of war when relatives come to stay on
her family's Connecticut farm after fleeing Nazi Germany. Originally
published by Seabury Press (1973, 0-8164-3098-5).

238 Napoli, Donna Jo. *Stones in Water*. New York: Dutton, 1997. 209
     pp. (hc. 0-525-45842-5) $15.99
Gr. 5-12. Two Italian boys, Roberto and Samuele, living in Venice are
taken by the Nazis to Germany to work as slave labor. Samuele, who is
Jewish, dies but Roberto manages to escape when taken to the Russian
front and desperately tries to make his way back home. A gripping,
superbly written Holocaust story told from a little-known perspective.

239 Neshamit, Sarah. *The Children of Mapu Street*. Trans. David S.
     Segal. Philadelphia: Jewish Publication Society of America, 1970.
     324 pp.
Gr. 9-12. The story of Jewish children in Kovno, Lithuania, who endure
the German invasion, Nazi terror, and the hatred of their non-Jewish
neighbors. Translated from the Hebrew.

240 Nolan, Han. *If I Should Die Before I Wake*. San Diego: Harcourt
     Brace, 1994. 293 pp. (hc. 0-15-238040-X) $12.00;
     (pbk. 0-15-238041-8) $6.00
Gr. 7-12. As sixteen-year-old Hillary Burke, an anti-Semite and neo-
Nazi initiate, lies in a coma, she is transported through time to Poland
at the beginning of World War II and into the life of a Jewish teenager.
A compelling, deep, and memorable story that ties the Holocaust with
the present. A must for middle and high school library collections.

241 Orgel, Doris. *A Certain Magic*. New York: Dial, 1976. 176 pp.
     (hc. 0-8037-5405-1) $7.95
Gr. 5-9. Two lives, thirty-six years apart, come together when eleven-
year-old Jenny discovers her Aunt Trudl's old diary and learns of her
experiences in Vienna before and after the Nazis took power.

242 ———. *The Devil in Vienna*. New York: Puffin, 1988. 264 pp.
     (pbk. 0-14-032500-X) $4.99
Gr. 5-10. Thirteen-year-olds Inge Dorenwald and Lieselotte Vessely
are the best of friends until the Nazis rise to power in 1937 Vienna.
Inge, a Jew, and Lieselotte, the daughter of a Nazi official, struggle to
keep their friendship alive.

243 Orlev, Uri. *The Island on Bird Street*. Trans. Hillel Halkin.
     Boston: Houghton Mifflin, 1984. 162 pp. (hc. 0-395-3387-5) $14.95
Gr. 5-9. Alex is left on his own for months in a ruined house in the
Warsaw Ghetto, where he must learn all the tricks of survival under
constantly life-threatening conditions. Translated from the Hebrew.

244 ———. *The Lead Soldiers*. Trans. Hillel Halkin. New York: Taplinger,
     1980. 234 pp. (hc. 0-8008-4576-5) $9.95
Gr. 7-12. A semi-autobiographical novel of young Yurik"s and his kid
brother Kazik's journey from a suburb in Warsaw to the ghetto and
finally to Bergen-Belsen. Translated from the Hebrew.

245 ———. *The Man from the Other Side*. Trans. Hillel Halkin. Boston:

Houghton Mifflin, 1991. 186 pp. (hc. 0-395-53808-4) $13.95;
(pbk. 0-14-037088-9) $3.99
Gr. 5-10. Fourteen-year-old Marek and his grandparents shelter a
Jewish man on the outskirts of the Warsaw Ghetto days before the
uprising. A very engrossing thriller.

246 Ossowski, Leonie. *Star Without a Sky*. Minneapolis: Lerner, 1985.
214 pp. (hc. 0-8225-0771-4) $19.95
Gr. 5-10. In the final chaotic days of World War II, five young
Germans discover a Jewish boy hiding in a cellar and are torn over
whether or not to turn him over to the Nazi authorities. A powerful,
thoughtful story of young people struggling over moral responsibilities.

247 Ozick, Cynthia. *The Shawl*. New York: Knopf, 1990.
(hc. 0-394-57976-3) $12.95; (pbk. 0-679-72926) $7.95
Gr. 9-12. Rosa Lublin is the character who connects this short story and
novella together. In the title story, she cradles her baby in the death
camp until a guard rips it away from her and hurls the infant at an
electrified fence. In "Rosa," she is a survivor in America struggling to
cope with her anger and grief. A powerful, memorable work.

248 Pausewang, Gudrun. *The Final Journey*. Trans. Patricia Compton.
New York: Viking, 1996. 155 pp. (hc. 0-670-86456-0) $14.99
Gr. 7-10. Alice, a young Jewish girl, reflects on the past and present as
she travels to her death aboard a crowded cattle car. A relentlessly
bleak, profoundly moving story. Translated from the German.

249 Provost, Gary and Gail Levine. *David and Max*. Philadelphia:
Jewish Publication Society, 1988. 180 pp. (0-8276-0315-0) $12.95
Gr. 3-8. While spending the summer with his grandfather Max, twelve-
year-old David searches for a friend believed to have died in the
Holocaust. In his search, David learns about the terrible years of Nazi
persecution.

250 Ramati, Alexander. *And the Violins Stopped Playing: A Story of
the Gypsy Holocaust*. New York: Watts, 1986. 237pp.
(hc.0-531-15028-3) $15.95
Gr. 9-12. Like the Jews, the Gypsies in Europe were also targeted by
the Nazis for extermination in the Final Solution. In this novel, Ramati
tells of how Polish Gypsies were persecuted during the Holocaust.

251 Ray, Karen. *To Cross a Line*. New York: Orchard, 1994. 154 pp.

(hc. 0-531-06831-5) $15.95; (pbk. 0-140-37587-2) $3.99
Gr. 5-9. Seventeen-year-old Egon Katz isn't allowed to have a driver's license because, in 1938 Germany, Jews aren't allowed to drive. Despite that, Egon drives anyway and ends up in an accident, which puts him in a situation that makes him realize how desperate life is becoming for Jews.

252 Richter, Hans Peter. *Friedrich*. Trans. Edite Kroll. New York: Dell, 1973. 157 pp. (pbk. 0-14-032205-1) $4.99
Gr. 4-8. The friendship between two boys, one of whom is Jewish, in Nazi Germany. Includes a chronology.

253 ——. *I Was There*. Trans. Edite Kroll. New York: Puffin, 1987. 224 pp. (pbk. 0-140-32206-X)
Gr. 5-8. Two members of the Hitler Youth movement become disillusioned with Nazism. Originally published by Holt in 1972.

254 Romm, J. Leonard. *The Swastika on the Synagogue Door*. Illus. Spark. Los Angeles: Alef Design Group, 1993. 167 pp. (pbk. 1-881283-05-4) $5.95
Gr. 5-10. With the help of a rabbi and a Holocaust survivor, a teenage brother and sister try to solve the mystery of who desecrated a Long Island synagogue with a swastika and anti-Semitic slogan. Short chapters with a lot of action and dialogue make this book a good choice for reluctant readers.

255 Rose, Anne. *Refugee*. New York: Dial, 1977. 118 pp. (hc. 0-8037-7285-8) $6.95.
Gr. 5-10. Traces the life of Elke, a Belgian Jewish girl, during World War II, from the time she flees the German invasion of Belgium at age twelve to her life in New York at eighteen.

256 Roseman, Kenneth. *Escape from the Holocaust*. New York: Union of American Hebrew Congregations, 1985. 179 pp. (pbk. 0-8074-0307-5) $7.95
Gr. 7-12. An interesting Holocaust novel that follows a "plot-your-own-story" format. At the bottom of the page, the reader chooses which direction he or she would like to take in the story. The choice the reader makes can mean the difference between freedom and slavery and life and death. The main character of the story is a medical student and the setting is 1930s Berlin. Includes a glossary and a map of World War II Europe.

257 Roth-Hano, Renee. *Touch Wood: A Girlhood in Occupied France.*
New York: Four Winds Press, 1988. 234 pp. (hc. 0-02-777340-X)
$12.95
Gr. 7-12. In this autobiographical novel set in Nazi-occupied France,
Renee, a young Jewish girl, and her family leave their home in Alsace
for Paris where they live a dangerous, uncertain existence until Renee
and her sister find shelter in a Catholic women's residence.

258 Samuels, Gertrude. *Mottele: A Partisan Odyssey.* New York:
Harper and Row, 1976. 181 pp. (hc. 0-06-013759-2) $8.85
Gr. 5-9. When twelve-year-old Mottele returns home from his music
lesson to find his home destroyed and family murdered by the
Germans, he joins up with Uncle Misha's partisans to take revenge.
Based upon true episodes from Jewish partisan experiences.

259 Schleimer, Sarah M. *Far from the Place We Called Home.* New
York: Feldheim, 1994. 238 pp. (hc. 0-87306-667-7)
Gr. 5-12. Evacuated to England from Germany when the Nazis take
over, several Jewish boys try to stay faithful to their Judaism, rebuild
their lives, and search for their parents after the war.

260 Schnur, Steven. *The Shadow Children.* Illus. Herbert Tauss. New
York: Morrow, 1994. 87 pp. (hc. 0-688-13281-2) $14.00
Gr. 3-6. While spending the summer on his grandfather's farm in the
French countryside, eleven-year-old Etienne discovers a secret from
World War II and encounters ghosts of Jewish children who were
murdered by the Nazis. Illustrated with black-and-white drawings.

261 Schur, Maxine Rose. *Sacred Shadows.* New York: Dial, 1997.
(hc. 0-803-72295-8) $14.99
Gr. 5-10. When her German hometown becomes a part of Poland at the
end of World War I, Lena Katz and her family, German Jews, become
victims of anti-Semitism and anti-German hatred. An exceptional
coming-of-age novel that explores the prejudices of a time and place
seldom depicted in literature. Based upon the author's own family
history.

262 Schwartz-Bart, Andre. *The Last of the Just.* New York:
Atheneum, 1973.
Gr. 9-12. A fascinating historical novel that begins with the persecution
of Jews in Europe and ends with the Holocaust.

263 Segal, Lore. *Other People's Houses*. New York: New Press, 1990.
312 pp. (pbk. 1-56584-143-3) $11.95
Gr. 9-12. Nine months after the Nazis take over, a ten-year-old Austrian girl leaves Vienna on a train with several hundred other refugee children and spends the next seven years living in the houses of people willing to give her refuge. Originally published in 1963 by Harcourt Brace Jovanovich.

264 Serrailier, Ian. *The Silver Sword*. Illus. C. Walter Hodges. New York: S. G. Phillips, 1959. (hc. 0-875-99104-1) $30.95
Gr. 5-8. Three young Poles struggle to find their parents after the family becomes separated following the 1939 Nazi invasion. Based upon a true story. Illustrated with black-and-white drawings.

265 Shemin, Margaretha. *The Empty Moat*. New York: Coward-McCann, 1969. 159 pp.
Gr. 5-8. In Holland, Elizabeth van Swaenenburgh first cooperates with the Nazis who promise to spare her beautiful castle, but later defies them by hiding a British soldier and a Jewish girl.

266 —. *The Little Riders*. Illus. Peter Spier. New York: Putnam, 1988.
76 pp. (hc. 0-399-21462-3) $12.95; (pbk. 0-688-12499-2) $4.95
Gr. 3-6. Eleven-year-old Johanna is visiting her grandparents when the Germans invade Holland. Separated from her parents in America, she takes comfort in watching the clock tower from her bedroom window, particularly the twelve metal horseback riders the clock sends out when it strikes the hour. When the Germans threaten to melt down the riders to make ammunition, she plots to steal and hide them away in her grandparents' house. Illustrated with black-and-white drawings.

267 Siegal, Aranka. *Grace in the Wilderness: After the Liberation, 1945-1948*. New York: Farrar, Straus & Giroux, 1985.
(hc. 0-374-32760-2) $15.00; (pbk. 0-14-036967-8) $4.99
Gr. 5-12. Liberated from the Bergen-Belsen concentration camp at the end of the war but haunted by her experiences, fifteen-year-old Piri Davidowitz starts a strange new life as a Jew in Sweden. A sequel to *Upon the Head of a Goat: A Childhood in Hungary, 1939-1945*.

268 —. *Upon the Head of a Goat: A Childhood in Hungary, 1939-1945*. New York: Farrar, Straus & Giroux, 1981. 214 pp.
(hc. 0-374-380597) $16.00; (pbk. 0-14-036966-X) $4.99
Gr. 5-12. The ordeal of thirteen-year-old Piri Davidowitz living as a

Jew in World War II Hungary in the Beregszasz Ghetto. A 1982 Newbery Honor Book and winner of the Janusz Korczak Literary Award.

269 Sommerfelt, Aimee. *Miriam*. Trans. Pat Shaw Iverson. New York: Criterion, 1963. 160 pp.
Gr. 4-8. In Nazi-occupied Oslo, Jewish Miriam and her family are hidden away by kind neighbors and helped by the Norwegian Underground to escape to Sweden. Translated from the Norwegian.

270 Stiles, Martha Bennett. *Darkness Over the Land*. New York: Dial, 1966. 260 pp.
Gr. 9-12. The story of Mark Elend who, in 1938 as a young impressionable man, is mesmerized by the Nazis and becomes a loyal follower. As the war rages on, however, Mark begins to question the choices he made.

271 Suhl, Yuri. *On the Other Side of the Gate*. New York: Watts, 1975. 149 pp. (hc. 0-531-02792-9) $5.90
Gr. 7-12. With the help of the Polish underground, Herschel and Lena are able to smuggle David, their infant son, out of the ghetto to live with a sympathetic Polish family.

272 —. *Uncle Misha's Partisans*. New York: Scholastic, 1973. 211 pp. (hc. 0-590-07295-1) $6.95
Gr. 5-8. Twelve-year-old Mottele escapes to the woods to join a famous group of Jewish partisans known as Uncle Misha's Partisans. Based upon the real-life experiences of a Jewish partisan group that fought in the Ukraine. A fast-paced, suspenseful story. See also Gertrude Samuels's *Mottele: A Partisan Odyssey*.

273 Szambelan-Strevinsky, Christine. *Dark Hour of Noon*. New York: Lippincott, 1982. 215 pp. (hc. 0-397-32013-2) $10.50
Gr. 5-10. Trina organizes a small group of resistance fighters in Poland during World War II. The group calls itself the Gray Knights and none of its members are older than fourteen. Includes a glossary of Polish terms.

274 Taylor, Kressman. *Address Unknown*. Cincinnati: Story Press, 1995. (hc. 1-884910-17-3) $12.99
Gr. 7-12. Written in 1938 on the eve of the Holocaust, as a series of letters between an American living in San Francisco and his former

business partner who returned to Germany, the story revealed the poison of Nazism. Originally published in the September-October issue of *Story*, the story was reissued in 1995 to commemorate the 50th anniversary of the liberation of the concentration camps. An immensely powerful work.

275   Tene, Benjamin. *In the Shade of the Chestnut Tree.* Trans. Reuben
       Ben-Joseph. Illus. Richard Sigberman. Philadelphia: Jewish
       Publication Society of America, 1981. 136 pp. (hc. 0-8276-0186-7)
       $8.95
Gr. 4-8. Twelve autobiographical stories describe the dreams, frustrations, and problems of young Jewish boys and girls growing up in Warsaw between the two world wars. Illustrated with black-and-white drawings. Translated from the Hebrew.

276   Tresder, Terry Walton. *Hear O Israel: A Story of the Warsaw
       Ghetto.* Illus. Lloyd Bloom. New York: Atheneum, 1990. 48 pp.
       (hc. 0-689-31456-6) $13.95
Gr. 3-6. Isaac and his family live in the Warsaw Ghetto until they are deported to Treblinka for extermination, where they courageously meet their fate. Illustrated with powerful black-and-white reproductions of oil paintings. The impact of these illustrations would be all the more powerful in color.

277   Uhlman, Fred. *Reunion.* New York: Farrar, Straus & Giroux,
       1977. 112 pp. (pbk. 0-374-52515-3) $10.00
Gr. 7-12. A novella about two schoolboys in Germany in the early 1930s. One is the son of a Jewish doctor, the other of a Jewish aristocrat.

278   Uris, Leon. *Exodus.* New York: Bantam, 1983. 608 pp.
       (pbk. 0-553-25847-8) $7.99
Gr. 9-12. The epic story of Jews fighting for an independent Israel following World War II. A long, involved story with a huge cast characters, but also quite dramatic and engrossing. Motivated high school readers will appreciate this work.

279   —. *Mila 18.* New York: Bantam, 1983. 576 pp.
       (pbk. 0-553-324160-5) $7.99
Gr. 9-12. A fictionalized account of some of the Jews in the Warsaw Ghetto who decided to fight back. See also John Hersey's *The Wall.*

280 Van Dijk, Lutz. *Damned Strong Love: The True Story of Willi G.
and Stephan K.* Trans. Elizabeth D. Crawford. New York: Holt,
1995. (hc. 0-8050-3770-5) $15.95
Gr. 9-12. When Poland falls to the Germans in 1939, Stephan K.'s
father is taken away to a labor camp and the fifteen-year-old is left to
help care for his family. On his sixteenth birthday, Stefan discovers he
is gay and falls in love with Willi, an Austrian and member of the
German air force. Everything about their relationship is damned, but
they pursue it, blind to all the dangers. When the Gestapo discover their
relationship, they find their love and their lives in grave danger. This is
an amazing story of two young men who fall in love with each other at
the worst of all possible places and times. The story is based upon the
real life experiences of Stefan K., who writes a letter to readers at the
end of the book. This autobiographical novel is one of the first to
dramatize the Nazi persecution of homosexuals. Translated from the
German. See also Richard Plant's *The Pink Triangle: The Nazi War on
Homosexuals.*

281 van Stockum, Hilda. *The Borrowed House.* New York: Farrar,
Straus & Giroux, 1975. 215 pp. (hc. 0-374-30888-8) $6.95
Gr. 5-8. In occupied Holland, twelve-year-old Janna, a German girl,
moves into a "borrowed" house in Amsterdam with her parents and
discovers the possessions of the previous Jewish owners, including a
closet full of clothes for a girl her own age. Janna later learns a great
deal from neighbors and servants about this Jewish family and she finds
her new knowledge disturbingly at odds with what she learned in the
Hitler Youth.

282 Vivier, Colette. *The House of Four Winds.* Trans. and Ed. Miriam
Morton. Garden City, NY: Doubleday, 1969. 190 pp.
Gr. 5-10. In 1943 Nazi-occupied Paris, Michel and his family hide a
Jewish family threatened with deportation in their apartment house.

283 Voigt, Cynthia. *David and Jonathan.* New York: Scholastic, 1992.
249 pp. (hc. 0-590-45165-0) $14.95; (pbk. 0-590-45166-9) $3.95.
Gr. 7-12. Henry and Jonathan are the best of friends until David,
Jonathan's cousin and a Holocaust survivor, comes to live with him. A
wonderful, sensitive novel about friendship and relationships in general
with the Holocaust serving as an important element in the story.

284 Vos, Ida. *Anna Is Still Here.* Trans. Terese Edelstein and Inez
Smidt. New York: Puffin, 1995. 139 pp. (pbk. 0-14-036909-0)

68 Fiction

$3.99
Gr. 5-10. Thirteen-year-old Anna, a "hidden child" in Nazi-occupied Holland during the war, gradually learns to deal with the realities of being a survivor. A thoughtful, moving story.

285 —. *Dancing on the Bridge of Avignon.* Trans. Terese Edelstein and Inez Smidt. Boston: Houghton Mifflin, 1995. 183 pp. $14.95
Gr. 5-8. Ten-year-old Rosa de Jong tries to forget the everyday life of Nazi-occupied Holland through dreams and her violin music. An engrossing, dramatic story. Translated from the Dutch.

286 Werstein, Irving. *The Long Escape.* New York: Charles Scribner's Sons, 1964. 190 pp.
Gr. 5-10. Justine Raymond, director of a convalescent home on Belgium's seacoast, leads fifty of her youngest charges to safety when they make a harrowing escape from the invading Germans. Based upon a true story.

287 Wiesel, Elie. *Dawn.* New York: Bantam, 1961. 102 pp. (pbk. 0-553-22536-7) $4.99
Gr. 9-12. In British-controlled Palestine, Elisha, a young Israeli freedom fighter and Holocaust survivor, holds an English officer prisoner. His assignment is to kill the officer in retaliation for the execution of a Jewish prisoner by the British but, haunted by his past, he cannot bring himself to commit cold-blooded murder. An eloquent, emotional story of moral conflict.

288 —. *The Gates of the Forest: A Novel.* Trans. Frances Frenaye. New York: Schocken, 1995. 240 pp. (pbk. 0-8052-1044-X) $13.00
Gr. 9-12. Wiesel explores the spiritual impact wartime experiences have upon teenage Gregor, the lone survivor of his family, who is hiding from the Nazis. After a mysterious stranger saves his life, he finds himself involved with a group of Jewish partisans. A haunting, memorable story. Translated from the French. Originally published in 1982.

289 Wiesenthal, Simon. *The Sunflower.* New York: Schocken, 1977.
Gr. 9-12. A philosophical tale depicting a dying Nazi asking the forgiveness of a Jew for his role in the Holocaust.

290 Williams, Laura E. *Behind the Bedroom Wall.* Illus. A. Nancy Goldstein. Minneapolis, MN: Milkweed, 1996. 169 pp.

(pbk. 1-57131-606-X) $6.95
Gr. 4-8. In 1942 Germany, thirteen-year-old Korinna Rehme is an active member of her local Jungmadel, a Nazi youth group, along with many of her friends. When Korinna discovers her parents are hiding Jews in a secret space behind her bedroom wall, she must decide whether to report them to the Gestapo. An excellent portrait of how the Nazis manipulated Germany's youth. Illustrated with black-and-white drawings.

291 Wuorio, Eva-Lis. *Code: Polonaise.* New York: Holt, Rinehart & Winston, 1971. 198 pp.
Gr. 5-8. The story of a small group of young Polish partisans and their work against the Nazis.

292 —. *To Fight in Silence.* New York: Holt, Rinehart & Winston, 1973. 216 pp. (hc. 0-03-080241-5)
Gr. 4-8. Karen and Kristian take part in the Danish Resistance's daring plan to rescue their country's Jews.

293 Yolen, Jane. *Briar Rose.* New York: TOR, 1992. 185 pp. (hc. 0-312-85135-9) $17.95; (pbk. 0-8125-5862-6) $4.99
Gr. 7-12. The fairy tale "Sleeping Beauty" is retold in the setting of the European Holocaust. An intriguing, surprisingly successful blend of a bright fantasy tale and one of the darkest moments in human history. Includes an author's note and recommendations for further reading. From *The Fairy Tale Series* created by Terri Windling.

294 —. *The Devil's Arithmetic.* New York: Viking Kestrel, 1988. 170 pp. (hc. 0-670-81027-4) $15.99; (pbk. 0-14-034535-3)
Gr. 5-10. Hannah resents the traditions of her Jewish heritage but, when she opens the door to symbolically welcome the prophet Elijah at her family's Passover Seder, she is transported back in time to a small village in Nazi-occupied Poland. Despite the intrusive time travelling device, Yolen crafts a disturbing, realistic portrait of the Holocaust.

295 Zei, Alki. *Petros's War.* New York: Dutton, 1972. Trans. Edward Fenton. 236 pp. (hc. 0-525-36962-7) $8.95
Gr. 5-8. Based upon the author's own experiences in German-occupied Greece, this is the story of Petros, his sister Antigone, and Rita, a Jewish girl, who are all involved in the resistance movement. Translated from the Greek.

Nonfiction

Not all nonfiction books cited in this book are listed in this bibliography. Excluded are anthologies, drama, poetry and songs, and reference works.

296 Abells, Chanya Byers. *The Children We Remember*. New York: Greenwillow, 1986. 48pp. (hc. 0-688-06371-3) $16.00
Gr. 1-3. The fate of Jewish children at the hands of the Nazis is told in brief text and with powerful black-and-white photographs from the archives of Yad Vashem at The Matryrs and Heroes Remembrance Authority in Jerusalem. An extraordinarily moving work. An excellent book to read aloud. Originally published in 1983 by Kar-Ben Copies.

297 Adelson, Alan and Robert Lapides, comp. and ed. *Lodz Ghetto: Inside a Community Under Siege*. New York: Penguin, 1989. 525 pp. (hc. 0-670-82983-8); (pbk. 0-14-013228-7), $17.95
Gr. 9-12. A collection of excerpts from diaries, journals, letters, poems, and illustrations of some of the 200,000 Polish Jews who struggled to survive in the Lodz Ghetto. This is an amazing collection of what the editors call the "collected consciousness" of the Lodz Ghetto. Includes illustrations in black-and-white and color, maps, black-and-white photographs, textual notes, a glossary, and an author index.

298 Adler, David A. *Hiding from the Nazis*. Illus. Karen Ritz. New York: Holiday House, 1997. 32pp. (hc. 0-8234-1288-1) $15.95
Gr. 2-6. This is the true story of Lore Baer who, at the age of four, was placed by her parents with a Christian family in the Dutch countryside to protect her from Nazi persecution. A moving story told in simple text and effectively complemented with bold watercolor illustrations. Lore's story is brought up-to-date with her reunion with her parents and their emigration to the United States. An author's note explains the historical context of the story. This story introduces very young children to the subject of "hidden children" and the Holocaust. See also Howard Greenfield's *The Hidden Children*.

299 ——. *The Number on My Grandfather's Arm*. Illus. Rose
Eichenbaum. New York: UAHC Press, 1987. 32 pp.
(hc. 0-8074-0328-8) $9.95
Gr. 1-3. A grandfather explains to his seven-year-old granddaughter
how he came to have a number tattooed on his arm: as a prisoner in the
Auschwitz concentration camp. Illustrated with black-and-white
photographs. An excellent book to introduce very young readers to the
Holocaust.

300 ——. *We Remember the Holocaust*. New York: Holt, 1989. 147 pp.
(hc. 0-8050-0434-3); (pbk. 0-8050-3715-2) $10.95
Gr. 5-10. The events of the Holocaust are chronicled through personal
narratives of people who experienced it. Vivid remembrances make for
a profoundly moving reading experience. Abundantly illustrated with
black-and-white photographs. Includes a chronology, glossary, and
suggestions for further reading. Indexed by subject.

301 Altshuler, David A. *Hitler's War Against the Jews*. New York:
Berhman House, 1978. 190 pp. (hc. 0-87441-222-6) $9.95
Gr. 4-8. An adaptation of *The War Against the Jews, 1933-1945* and *A
Holocaust Reader* by Lucy S. Dawidowicz for younger readers. This is
an excellent historical overview of the Holocaust. Altshuler divides the
contents into two parts: "The Final Solution," which looks at the
Holocaust from the Nazi perspective; and "The Holocaust," which
offers the perspective of the victims. Includes black-and-white
illustrations, reproductions of documents, maps, a list of important
dates, and a subject index. An essential resource with a wealth of
information.

302 Ayer, Eleanor H. *The United States Holocaust Memorial Museum:
America Keeps the Memory Alive*. New York: Dillon, 1994. 79 pp.
(hc. 0-87518-649-1) $14.95; (pbk. 0-382-24728-0) $7.95
Gr. 4-12. A floor-by-floor description of the museum's exhibits and
holdings, accompanied by color and black-and-white photographs of its
many artifacts. Includes a timeline of the Holocaust, suggestions for
further reading, and a subject index.

303 Ayer, Eleanor with Helen Waterford and Alfons Heck. *Parallel
Journeys*. New York: Atheneum, 1995. 244 pp. (hc. 0-689-31830-8)
$15.00
Gr. 7-12. A fascinating look at two completely different perspectives of
the Holocaust in one book. Alfons Heck was a proud, obedient follower

of Adolf Hitler and member of the Hitler Youth movement. Helen Waterford was a young Jewish girl in Germany when Hitler came to power. They escaped to Holland but, when the Nazis took over there, she and her family were shipped off to Auschwitz. A unique account offering two entirely different perspectives on the same events. Includes black-and-white photographs, chapter notes, a bibliography, and a subject index.

304 Bachrach, Deborah. *The Resistance.* New York: Lucent, 1997. 112 pp. (hc. 1-56006-092-1) $17.96
Gr. 5-10. A fine overview of some the most well-known organized resistance movements that occurred in different parts of Nazi-occupied Europe. Among the movements attention is devoted to are: the Warsaw Ghetto Uprising; the partisan groups formed by Polish and Soviet Jews; the villagers of Le Cambon-sur-Lignon, France, who collectively hid hundreds of Jews; and the heroic efforts of the Danish people to save their Jews. The text is complemented throughout with informative boxes and sidebars. Illustrated throughout with archival black-and-white photographs. A thoroughly researched, well-organized, and concisely written work. Includes maps, chapter notes, a chronology, suggestions for further reading, a bibliography, and a subject index. From the *Holocaust Library* series.

305 Bachrach, Susan D. *Tell Them We Remember: The Story of the Holocaust.* New York: Little, Brown, 1994. (hc. 0-316-69264-6) $21.95; (pbk. 0-316-07484-5) $12.95
Gr. 4-10. Produced by the United States Holocaust Memorial Museum, this is a very good overview of the Holocaust that briefly discusses broad issues like "Jewish Life in Europe Before the Holocaust" and "Anti-Semitism" to specific events and incidents like "The Night of Broken Glass" and "The Voyage of the *St. Louis.*" The book is richly illustrated with black-and-white and color photographs. A wonderful feature are pictures of individuals who experienced the Holocaust accompanied by their brief personal stories. The individuals appear throughout the book as their stories unfold at different points between 1933-1945. Includes a glossary, suggestions for further reading, and a subject index.

306 Bauer, Yehuda and Nili Keren. *A History of the Holocaust.* New York: Watts, 1982. 416 pp. (hc. 0-531-09862-1); (pbk. 0-531-05641-4) $14.95
Gr. 9-12. Set against a background of Jewish-Gentile relationships, a

summary of Jewish history, and the roots of anti-Semitism, the author reviews the Holocaust years in great detail, country by country. Includes maps, charts, tables, chapter notes, a bibliography, glossary, and subject index. An outstanding resource, particularly for the high school level.

307 Bauminger, Arieh L. *The Righteous Among the Nations.* Jerusalem: Ahva Press, 1990. 203 pp
Gr. 7-12. A tribute to "Righteous Gentiles" who went to extraordinary measures to aid Jews during the Holocaust. Nearly every country in Europe is represented here. Includes black-and white photographs of the people profiled and a subject index.

308 Beller, Ilex. *Life in the Shtetl: Scenes and Recollections.* Trans. Alastair Douglas Pannell. New York: Holmes & Meier, 1986. 140 pp. (hc. 0-8419-1095-2) $49.50
Gr. 7-12. A series of paintings depicting the way Jews lived in the Shtetls of Poland. Shtetl life was utterly destroyed by the Holocaust. Beller created the paintings as a means of preserving a record of shtetl life. The artist describes his return to Poland in recent years and expresses his views on the need to remember and study the lessons learned from the tragedy of the Holocaust. The color plates are of excellent quality. Titles of the works are printed in English and Hebrew. Translated from the French.

309 Berenbaum, Michael. *The World Must Know: The History of the Holocaust as Told in the United States Holocaust Memorial Museum.* Boston: Little, Brown, 1993. 240 pp. (hc. 0-316-09135-9) $40.00; (pbk. 0-316-09134-0) $21.95
Gr. 7-12. Artifacts and photographs from the United States Holocaust Memorial Museum complement an informative text to offer an excellent general overview of the Holocaust. A handsome, organized book. Includes an afterword about the museum and a subject index.

310 Bernbaum, Israel. *My Brother's Keeper: The Holocaust through the Eyes of an Artist.* New York: Putnam, 1985. 64 pp. (hc. 0-399-21242-6) $16.95
Gr. 4-12. Israel Bernbaum escaped to the Soviet Union from Nazi-occupied Warsaw just before the ghetto walls were erected. Bernbaum describes the Holocaust and explains how he tries to tell the story of it through his art. The paintings are vivid and disturbing. Bernbaum's horrific images convey the utter brutality and inhumanity of the

Holocaust.

311 Berwick, Michael. *The Third Reich*. New York: Putnam, 1972.
   128 pp.
Gr. 7-10. A historical survey of Nazi Germany, beginning with the rise
of Hitler and concluding with the Nuremberg Trials, and giving
Holocaust information from 1933 to 1945. Includes many black-and-
white photographs and maps. There are suggestions for further reading,
source notes, and a very useful chronology of major events in the
history of the Third Reich. Indexed by subject.

312 Bierman, John. *Odyssey*. New York: Simon & Schuster, 1984. 255
   pp. (hc. 0-671-50156-9) $16.45
Gr. 9-12. The story of the *Pentcho*, a ship carrying five hundred Jews
from Bratislava to Palestine. Many complications turned the anticipated
one-month voyage into a harrowing four-year struggle for survival.
Includes black-and-white photographs, and an author's note on the
sources.

313 Blatter, Janet and Sybil Milton. *Art of the Holocaust*. New York:
   Rutledge, 1990. 272 pp. (hc. 0-8317-0418-7) $29.95
Gr. 7-12. An extraordinary collection of over 350 artworks created in
ghettos, concentration camps, and in hiding. The color and black-and-
white plates are captioned and contain the following information: the
artist's name; title of the work; place and date the work was completed;
the medium and size of the work; and the museum or individual
holding the work. Henry Friedlander offers an informative historical
introduction and the book concludes with brief biographical sketches of
each of the artists. Includes a preface by Irving Howe, a directory of
Holocaust museums and memorials, and a bibliography.

314 Block, Gay and Malka Drucker. *Rescuers: Portraits of Moral
   Courage in the Holocaust*. New York: Holmes & Meier, 1992. 256
   pp. (hc. 0-8419-1322-6) $49.95; (pbk. 0-8419-1323-4), $29.95
Gr. 9-12. A collection of interviews with forty-nine people from ten
countries who risked their lives to help Jews in their homelands.
Countries represented include: Belgium, Bulgaria, Czechoslovakia,
France, Germany, Hungary, The Netherlands, Poland, the Soviet Union
and Ukraine, and Yugoslavia. Includes black-and-white and color
photographs of the rescuers and a selected bibliography.

315 Blum, Howard. *Wanted! The Search for Nazis in America.* New York: Touchstone, 1977. 269 pp. (pbk. 0-671-67607-5) $8.95
Gr. 9-12. The story of Anthony DeVito, an Immigration and Naturalization Service agent, who led a crusade to find and expose four Nazis living as respected members of American society since World War II. An engaging and engrossing story.

316 Boas, Jacob. *We Are Witnesses: Five Diaries of Teenagers Who Died in the Holocaust.* New York: Henry Holt, 1995. 196 pp. (hc. 0-8050-3702 -0) $15.95
Gr. 7-12. Heartbreaking personal narratives of teenagers from Belgium, Hungary, Lithuania, and Poland who perished in the Holocaust. Young adult readers will find this book especially moving because these are the experiences of people their own age. Includes chapter notes and a subject index.

317 Brecher, Elinor J. *Schindler's Legacy: True Stories of the List Survivors.* New York: Plume, 1994. 442 pp. (pbk. 0-452-27353-6) $14.95
Gr. 9-12. A collection of testimonies from some of the Jews, or from their children, saved by Oskar Schindler. These honest, poignant narratives offer a revealing look at the experiences of the *Schindlerjuden* and of Schindler himself. An excellent companion to the novel *Schindler's List.* Includes black-and-white photographs of the contributors and a foreword by Thomas Keneally.

318 Chaikin, Miriam. *A Nightmare in History: The Holocaust, 1933-1945.* New York: Clarion, 1987. 150 pp. (hc. 0-89919-461-3) $14.95
Gr. 5-12. A history of the Holocaust that opens with a discussion of anti-Semitism, tracing its history from Biblical times through its manifestation in Nazi Germany. In her discussion of Hitler's plans to exterminate European Jews, the author focuses upon the Warsaw Ghetto and Auschwitz-Birkenau concentration camp. Includes black-and-white photographs, an excellent bibliography, suggestions for further reading, and a thorough subject index.

319 Chicago, Judy. *Holocaust Project: From Darkness Into Light.* New York: Penguin, 1993. 205 pp. (pbk. 0-14-01-5991-6) $22.50
Gr. 7-12. A book chronicling the creation of a series of Holocaust-related artworks by Judy Chicago. The artist shows the research involved with creating the works, and their evolution. The

reproductions of the works, represented in color plates, are of excellent quality.

320 Conot, Robert E. *Justice at Nuremberg*. New York: Carroll & Graff, 1984. (hc. 0-881-84032-7) $13.95
Gr. 9-12. An account of how the perpetrators of the Holocaust were brought to justice by the International War Crimes Tribunal conducted following the war.

321 Costanza, Mary S. *The Living Witness: Art in the Concentration Camps and Ghettos*. New York: Free Press, 1982. 196 pp. (hc. 0-02-9666-3) $19.95
Gr. 9-12. This is a more scholarly in-depth study of Holocaust art than one finds in *Art of the Holocaust*. Presenting 100 works of art from camps and ghettos, from small fragments of drawings to watercolors, paintings, and sculptures, Costanza describes the history of each work. Reproductions are offered only in black-and-white. Includes chapter notes and a subject index.

322 Cowan, Lore. *Children of the Resistance*. New York: Pocket, 1969. 179 pp. (pbk. 0-671-2934-8) $1.25
Gr. 10-12. True stories of boys and girls who played active, dangerous roles in underground resistance movements against the Nazis during World War II. Many of the children profiled helped Jews escape deportation. Countries represented include: Czechoslovakia, Denmark, France, Germany, Holland, Italy, Norway, and Yugoslavia.

323 Czarnecki, Joseph P. *Last Traces: The Lost Art of Auschwitz*. New York: Atheneum, 1989. 175 pp. (hc. 0-689-12022-2) $29.95
Gr. 7-12. An incredible collection of photographs of drawings, paintings, and graffiti by prisoners of Auschwitz. The photographs, all black-and-white, are of excellent quality. Each photograph is captioned with a description of the work, its location and artist if known. Descriptive text accompanies each of the photographs. This book offers wonderful examples of the astonishing resilience of the human spirit. Includes endnotes and an introduction by Chaim Potok.

324 David, Kati. *A Child's War: World War II through the Eyes of Children*. New York: Avon, 1989. 210 pp. (hc. 0-941423-24-7) $17.95; (pbk. 0-380-71109-5) $7.95
Gr. 7-12. An extraordinary collection of personal narratives of fifteen European children who experienced the horrors of World War II. The

countries represented are: Austria, Belgium, Czechoslovakia, Denmark, England, Estonia, France, Germany, Holland, Hungary, Italy, Poland, Romania, the Soviet Union, and Switzerland. Not all of the stories have to do with the Holocaust, but many do. These are touching, memorable narratives.

325　Dawidowicz, Lucy S., ed. *A Holocaust Reader*. New York: Behrman House, 1976. 397pp. (hc. 0-87441-219-6); (pbk. 0-87441-236-6)
Gr. 9-12. A remarkable collection of documents pertaining to Nazi Germany's plan to destroy Europe's Jews. Divided into two parts, Part One is called "The Final Solution," tracing the rise of the anti-Semitic sentiment and legislation in Germany in the 1920s and 30s, and Hitler's preparations for mass deportation and extermination of Jews. Part Two, titled "The Holocaust," looks at the Jewish perspective taken from communal records, diaries, folk literature and other sources. Includes suggestions for further reading, source notes, and a subject index.

326 ——. *The War Against the Jews, 1933-1945*. New York: Holt, 1976. 640 pp. (hc. 0-030-13661-X) $15.00
Gr. 9-12. A scrupulously researched, detailed account of the Holocaust viewed as the completion of the Nazi vision and its effect upon the Jews of eastern Europe.

327　Del Calzo, Nick. *The Triumphant Spirit: Portraits and Stories of Holocaust Survivors . . . Their Messages of Hope and Compassion*. Denver: Triumphant Spirit Foundation, 1997. 172 pp. (hc. 0-9655260-0-3); (pbk. 0-9655260-1-1) $29.95
Gr. 7-12. This is a handsome collection of photographs of and brief interviews with Holocaust survivors. Del Calzo's black-and-white photography is striking. Includes an introduction by Thomas Keneally, a bibliography, and a subject index.

328　De Silva, Cara, ed. *In Memory's Kitchen: A Legacy from the Women of Terezin*. Trans. Bianca Steiner Brown. Northvale, NJ: Jason Aronson, 1996. 112 pp. (hc. 1-56821-902-4) $25.00; (pbk. 0-38531-922-3) $12.95
Gr. 9-12. *In Memory's Kitchen* is likely to be one of the oddest Holocaust books one will find. What makes the book so unique is that it is a collection of recipes written by women who were imprisoned in the Terezin (also known as Theresienstadt) concentration camp in Czechoslovakia. Suffering from disease, hunger, and everyday Nazi

brutalities, these women somehow managed to write their family recipes to leave as their legacy. Collected by Mina Pachter, a primary author of the cookbook, she entrusted the collection to a friend just before she died of hunger sickness on Yom Kippur in 1944. The original recipes were written on whatever scraps of paper the women were able to find. *In Memory's Kitchen* is much more than a cookbook. It is, as Michael Berenbaum says in his Foreword to the book, "a manifestation of defiance." The recipes are presented in the original Czech or German with the English translation. Also included are poems and letters Mina Pachter composed while imprisoned in Terezin.

329 Dobroszycki, Lucjan and Barbara Kirshenblatt-Gimblett. *Image Before My Eyes: A Photographic History of Jewish Life in Poland Before the Holocaust.* New York: Schocken, 1977. 269 pp. (pbk. 0-8052-1026-1) $25.00
Gr. 7-12. Before the Holocaust, Poland had the largest Jewish population in Europe. It was a world center of Jewish cultural creativity. This collection of 300 photographs selected from over ten thousand housed at the YIVO Institute for Jewish Research offers a pictorial account of all aspects of Polish-Jewish life. An incredible, revealing book. Includes demographic statistics of the Jewish population in pre-Holocaust Poland, and indexes of names and places.

330 Dolan, Jr., Edward F. *Anti-Semitism.* New York: Watts, 1985. 135 pp. (hc. 0-531-10068-5) $12.90
Gr. 7-12. Chronicles the history of anti-Semitism, from its earliest beginnings, through the Holocaust, to contemporary times. An excellent study examining the roots of anti-Semitism, its many manifestations, and why it persists. An excellent background resource to use in Holocaust studies. Includes black-and-white photographs, suggestions for further reading, and a subject index.

331 —. *Victory in Europe: The Fall of Hitler's Germany.* New York: Watts, 1988. 179 pp. (hc. 0-531-10522-9) $13.90
Gr. 5-12. Surveys the final months of World War II in Europe, including the liberation of the Nazi death camps. Includes black-and-white photographs, maps, suggestions for further reading, and a subject index.

332 Eckman, Lester and Chaim Lazar. *The Jewish Resistance: The History of the Jewish Partisans in Lithuania and White Russia During the Nazi Occupation, 1940-1945.* New York: Shengold,

1977. 282 pp. (hc. 0-88400-050-8) $10.00
Gr. 9-12. A history of the Jewish men, women, and children who fought valiantly as partisans against the Germans during World War II. Hundreds of interviews with partisans are collected here to create an extraordinary factual account of a little known, but important part of history. Includes a bibliography, black-and-white photographs, and a subject index.

333 Eisenberg, Azriel. *Witness to the Holocaust.* New York: Pilgrim Press, 1981. 649 pp. (hc. 0-8298-0432-3) $17.95
Gr. 9-12. A collection of over 600 readings, mostly eyewitness accounts, covering all aspects of the Holocaust. The readings are divided into twenty-five topics, each section including an introduction and bibliography. This would be an excellent reference book for a high school media center.

334 Eliach, Yaffa. *Hasidic Tales of the Holocaust: The First Original Hasidic Tales in a Century.* New York: Oxford University Press, 1982. 266 pp. (hc. 0-19-503199-7) $15.95
Gr. 9-12. A collection of eighty-nine stories based on interviews and oral histories. This is the first anthology of Hasidic stories about the Holocaust, and the first ever in which women play a significant role.

335 Eliach, Yaffa, ed. *We Were Children Just Like You.* New York: Center for Holocaust Documentation and Research, 1990. 124 pp. (pbk. 0-9609-9970-8) $15.00
Gr. 7-12. A photographic study of children during the Holocaust, produced as part of the Oral History Project of the Center for Holocaust Studies in Brooklyn, New York. All photographs are captioned.

336 Eliav, Arie L. *The Voyage of the Ulua.* Trans. Israel I. Taslitt. New York: Sabra, 1969. 191 pp.
Gr. 9-12. The author, the captain of the *Ulua*, tells the story of how his ship carried 800 Holocaust survivors, "illegal" immigrants in the eyes of the British authorities, to Israel before its independence. The ship successfully ran a British blockade and safely entered Israel. An exciting story. Includes a glossary and a map of the *Ulua's* route. Translated from the Hebrew.

337 Epstein, Helen. *Children of the Holocaust: Conversations with Sons and Daughters of Survivors.* New York: Putnam, 1979. 308 pp. (hc. 0-79105-143-3); (pbk. 0-553-2250-0) $3.95

Gr. 9-12. Epstein, the daughter of survivors of Auschwitz and Terezin, relates her own struggle to come to terms with her parents' past, as well as the struggles of hundreds of other children of survivors she interviewed. An outstanding, important work.

338 Feinstein, Stephen C. *Witness and Legacy: Contemporary Art about the Holocaust.* Minneapolis: Lerner, 1995. 64 pp. (pbk. 0-8225-3148-8) $17.00
Gr. 7-12. Published in conjunction with an exhibition, this book looks at works of contemporary American artists who have chosen the Holocaust as the subject of one or more of their works. Artworks represented include drawings, paintings, and sculptures. Color plates of the works are captioned with the date, medium, size, and title of the works.

339 Fest, Joachim C. *The Face of the Third Reich: Portraits of the Nazi Leadership.* Trans. Michael Bullock. New York: Pantheon, 1977. 402 pp. (hc. 0-394-73407-6) $13.56
Gr. 11-12. Eighteen sketches of Hitler and his henchmen who helped devise and maintain totalitarian rule in Nazi Germany. This is a scholarly work including extensive notes, bibliography, and subject index. Translated from the German.

340 Finkelstein, Norman H. *Remember Not to Forget: A Memory of the Holocaust.* Illus. Lois and Lars Hokanson. New York: Watts, 1985. 31 pp. (hc. 0-531-04892-6); (pbk. 0-688-11802-X) $4.95
Gr. 2-4. A brief introduction to the Holocaust for younger readers, accompanied with black-and-white illustrations.

341 Flender, Harold. *Rescue in Denmark.* New York: Holocaust Library, 1963. 281 pp. (pbk. 0-89604-018-6) $5.95
Gr. 9-12. Another well-researched account of the Danish resistance movement and how they saved nearly all of their Jewish countrymen. Recommended for older young adult readers. Includes black-and-white illustrations, chapter notes, and a subject index.

342 Forman, James D. *Nazism.* New York: Watts, 1978. 122pp. (hc. 0-531-01473-8) $5.90
Gr. 5-12. Describes the influences of nineteenth-century philosophers and World War I on the origins and growth of Nazism and Hitler's rise to power. This is an informative text in its discussion of Nazi Germany, but it fails to offer any discussion of post-World War II Nazism in

Europe or the rest of the world. Includes a bibliography and subject index.

343 Frank, Anne. *Anne Frank's Tales from the Secret Annex*. Trans. Ralph Manheim and Michel Mok. Garden City, NY: Doubleday, 1984. 136 pp. (hc. 0-385-18715-7) $14.95
Gr. 5-12. A collection of short stories, essays, and recollections Anne wrote while in hiding in a separate journal. The pieces reveal Anne's gift for writing. Reading the selections makes one wonder what impact she might have made upon the literary world had she lived. Recommend using this book as a companion to Anne's *Diary*. Translated from the Dutch.

344 Friedman, Ina R. *Escape or Die: True Stories of Young People Who Survived the Holocaust*. Reading, MA: Addison-Wesley, 1982. 146 pp. (hc. 0-201-10477-6) $9.95
Gr. 5-12. True stories of twelve young men and women, Jews and non-Jews, who survived the Holocaust. The survivors range in age from eleven to eighteen and represent the following countries: Austria, Belgium, Czechoslovakia, France, Germany, Holland, Hungary, Palestine, Poland, and the Ukraine. Includes a glossary and subject index.

345 —. *The Other Victims: First Person Stories of Non-Jews Persecuted by the Nazis*. Boston: Houghton Mifflin, 1990. 214 pp. (hc. 0-395-50212-8) $14.95; (pbk. 0-395-74515-2) $4.95
Gr. 7-12. Personal narratives of Christians, Gypsies, homosexuals, deaf people, and other non-Jews persecuted by the Nazis. Countries represented include: Czechoslovakia, Germany, Poland, and Yugoslavia.

346 Friedman, Philip. *Their Brothers' Keepers: The Christian Heroes and Heroines who Helped the Oppressed Escape the Nazi Terror*. New York: Holocaust Library, 1978. 232 pp. (pbk. 0-89604-002-X) $4.95
Gr. 7-12. Profiles of Christians who heroically helped people persecuted by the Nazis. Countries represented include: Belgium, Belorussia, Bulgaria, Czechoslovakia, Estonia, France, Greece, Holland, Hungary, Italy, Latvia, Lithuania, the Ukraine, and Yugoslavia. Includes a bibliography, notes and references, and a subject index.

347 Gilbert, Martin. *The Boys: The Untold Story of 732 Young Concentration Camp Survivors.* New York: Holt, 1996. 511 pp. (hc. 0-8050-4402-7) $30.00

Gr. 9-12. In 1945, Great Britain offered to take in 1,000 young survivors of concentration camps but only 732 could be found. Although women were among them, this group of young adults became collectively known as "the boys." They became a close-knit group of friends and remained friends despite many migrating to Canada and the United States. Gilbert chronicles the experiences of many of the survivors, some of whom had never before spoken of them. This is an amazing collection of personal Holocaust experiences. Includes black-and-white photographs, maps, a glossary, and subject index.

348 —. *Final Journey: The Fate of the Jews in Nazi Europe.* New York: Mayflower, 1979. 224 pp. (hc. 0-8317-3325-X) $12.95

Gr. 9-12. Short chapters of information combining eyewitness accounts with contemporary evidence to offer a good, historical overview of the Holocaust. Generously illustrated with black-and-white photographs and maps. Includes a thorough subject index.

349 —.*The Macmillan Atlas of the Holocaust.* New York: Macmillan, 1982. (hc. 0-02-54338-0) $25.00

Gr. 5-12. An outstanding resource containing dozens of maps and some black-and-white photographs. Includes a thorough bibliography and index. The information is very well organized and easily accessible. An essential tool for both educators and students.

350 —. *Maps and Photographs: A Record of the Destruction of Jewish Life in Europe During the Dark Years of Nazi Rule.* New York: Braun Center for Holocaust Studies, 1992. (pbk. 0-88464-141-4) $8.45

Gr. 5-12. An account of the Holocaust through black-and-white photographs and maps. A stunning look at history through visual images. Includes a list of sources and suggested readings.

351 Gray, Ronald. *Hitler and the Germans.* New York: Cambridge University Press, 1983. 32 pp. (pbk. 0-521-27702-X) $4.95

Gr. 5-10. A historical study of Hitler's Third Reich, tracing the roots of its beginnings to its collapse with the end of World War II. The format of the book lends itself particularly well to homework assignments and classroom use. Includes black-and-white photographs, a chronology of key dates, and brief biographical sketches of major Nazi leaders.

352 Greenfeld, Howard. *The Hidden Children*. New York: Ticknor & Fields, 1993. 118 pp. (hc. 0-395-66074-2) $15.95
Gr. 3-10. Describes the experiences of those Jewish children who were forced into hiding during the Holocaust and survived to tell about it. Includes black-and-white photographs of the survivors, suggestions for further reading, and a subject index.

353 Gruber, Ruth. *Haven: The Unknown Story of 1,000 World War II Refugees*. New York: Coward-McCann, 1983. 335 pp. (hc. 0-689-11182-6)
Gr. 9-12. This is a little-known story of the one thousand refugees brought to the United States as "guests" of the government by order of President Roosevelt. After a harrowing journey from Europe, hunted by German planes and U-boats, the refugees arrived only to find themselves forced to live in an internment camp behind fences and barbed wire in Oswego, New York. The majority of refugees were Jews, but there were others who had fled their countries conquered by Hitler. Includes black-and white photographs and a subject index.

354 Grunfeld, Frederic V. *The Hitler File: A Social History of Germany and the Nazis, 1918-1945*. New York: Random House, 1974. 374 pp.
Gr. 4-12. An essentially pictorial book illustrated with over 750 black-and-white and forty-eight pages of color illustrations. Includes art, cartoons, photos, and posters produced in Germany before and during the Nazi regime. This book will have particular appeal for reluctant readers.

355 Haas, Gerda S. *Tracking the Holocaust*. New York: Lerner, 1995. 176 pp. (hc. 0-822-53157-7) $22.95
Gr. 5-10. The author interweaves the stories of eight individuals, including her own, with factual events of the Holocaust making for an unusual and fascinating chronological account. Haas brings an important and powerful personal dimension to history in this well-researched and skillfully written book. Includes black-and-white photographs, maps, and a subject index.

356 Hallie, Philip. *Lest Innocent Blood Be Shed: The Story of Le Chambon and How Goodness Happened There*. New York: Harper Collins, 1980. 303 pp. (pbk. 0-06-092517-5) $13.00
Gr. 9-12. The story of how the villagers of Le Chambon, a small Protestant town in southwestern France, worked together to save

thousands of Jews from the Nazis. A remarkable, inspiring story. Includes black-and-white photographs, source notes, and a subject index.

357 Handler, Andrew and Susan V. Meschel, comp. and ed. *Young People Speak: Surviving the Holocaust in Hungary.* New York: Watts, 1993. 144 pp. (0-531-1044-3) $22.70
Gr. 6-12. Eleven survivors of the Holocaust in Hungary recollect their childhood experiences with Hitler's implementation of the Final Solution. Includes black-and-white photographs of the survivors profiled, suggestions for further reading, and a subject index.

358 Hartmann, Erich. *In the Camps.* New York: Norton, 1995. 111 pp. (hc. 0-393-03772-X) $35.00
Gr. 4-12. A collection of chilling photographs of some of the most infamous Nazi concentration and death camps in Europe. Hartmann has captured some incredibly moving images. Highly recommended for reluctant readers. Includes an afterword by Hartmann.

359 Heartfield, John. *Photomontages of the Nazi Period.* New York: Universe, 1977. 143 pp. (hc. 0-876-63281-9) $12.50; (pbk. 0-876-63954-6) $6.95
Gr. 5-12. Heartfield, a German Dadaist, Communist, and artist created scathingly satirical anti-Nazi works, which appeared in German periodicals throughout the 1930s and are collected in this volume. Includes more than ninety illustrations. This is another very good book for reluctant readers.

360 Hellman, Peter. *Avenue of the Righteous: Portraits in Uncommon Courage of Christians and the Jews They Saved from Hitler.* New York: Atheneum, 1980. 267 pp. (0-689-11109-6) $11.95
Gr. 9-12. On August 19, 1953, Yad Vashem, also known as the Martyrs and Heroes Remembrance Act, was established by Israeli law as a memorial to those Jews who were victims of what has come to be known as the Holocaust. The law also mandated that a "place and name" also be given to non-Jews who acted to save their fellow human beings. This place came to be known as the "Avenue of the Righteous." In this book, Hellman tells the stories of several of these non-Jews who are honored at this place at Yad Vashem. Includes black-and-white photographs.

361 Heydecker, Joe J. *The Warsaw Ghetto: A Photographic Record,*
     1941-1944. London: I. B. Tauris, 1990. 124 pp. (1-85043-155-8)
Gr. 7-12. Joseph Heydecker, a German soldier attached to a propaganda
unit as a photographer, secretly photographed everyday life in the
Warsaw Ghetto. This is a fascinating, candid look at what ghetto life
was like for Jews. The black-and-white photographs are striking and
poignant. It is particularly interesting to see how living conditions in
the ghetto progressively worsened until its total liquidation in 1944.
Includes a foreword by Heinrich Boll and an introduction by the author.

362 Heyes, Eileen. *Children of the Swastika: The Hitler Youth.*
     Brookfield, CT: Millbrook, 1993. 96 pp. (hc. 1-56294-237-9)
Gr. 6-10. A very good overview of the Hitler Youth movement in Nazi
Germany. The author offers very detailed information on how boys and
girls were indoctrinated into the organization and in what ways they
were asked to serve the state. Particularly interesting are excerpts from
interviews with former Hitler Youth members who offer interesting
insight into that time. Illustrated throughout with black-and-white
photographs. Includes chapter notes, suggestions for further reading, a
chronology, and a subject index.

363 Hillel, Mark and Clarissa Henry. *Of Pure Blood.* New York:
     McGraw-Hill, 1977. 256 pp. (hc. 0-070-28895-X) $10.00;
     (pbk. 0-685-86808-7) $2.50
Gr. 7-12. A shocking story of the *Lebensborn* (Fountain of Life)
organization which kidnapped children from all over Europe who were
considered "racially valuable," were "Germanized," and that were
raised to be used for breeding a "master race." Over 200,000 children
were taken from Poland alone.

364 Josephs, Jeremy. *Swastika Over Paris: The Fate of the Jews in*
     France. New York: Arcade, 1989. 192 pp. (hc. 1-55970-036-X)
     $19.95
Gr. 9-12. Focusing on the stories of two French Jewish families,
Josephs gives an account of how 80,000 French Jews were sent to the
gas chamber. Includes black-and-white photographs and a subject
index.

365 Judd, Denis. *Posters of World War II.* New York: Random House,
     1993. 160 pp. (hc. 0-517-09318-9) $14.99
Gr. 7-12. This extensive collection contains many outstanding
examples of anti-Semitic propaganda. Posters are indexed by country

and artist. Originally published by St. Martin's Press in 1973.

366 Justman, Stuart. *The Jewish Holocaust for Beginners.* Illus. Rebecca Shope. New York: Writers and Readers, 1995. 120 pp. (pbk. 0-86316-182-0) $11.00
Gr. 7-12. The story of the Holocaust is told in a comic book format that will appeal to young adult readers. The author offers a general but informative history. Black-and-white photographs are interspersed with striking, disturbing illustrations. Includes a timeline, bibliography of sources, and a subject index.

367 Katz, William Loren. *An Album of Nazism.* New York: Watts, 1979. 90 pp. (hc. 0-531-01500-9) $11.60
Gr. 4-8. The Nazi movement in 1930s and 1940s Germany and in the contemporary world is explored through photographs and text. Although this book is dated in discussing post-World War II Nazism, it is still useful in its description and discussion of Nazi Germany. The text is generously illustrated with many excellent black-and-white photographs. Includes a subject index and a bibliography.

368 Kluger, Ruth and Peggy Mann. *The Secret Ship.* New York: Doubleday, 1978. 136 pp. (hc. 0385-11328-5) $5.95
Gr. 5-8. Adapted from *The Last Escape: The Launching of the Largest Secret Rescue of All Time*, the author relates the Herculean effort to rescue European Jews by secretly and illegally transporting them to Palestine aboard the ship *Hilda*. Short chapters with large print makes this a good book to recommend to reluctant readers.

369 Kugelmass, Jack and Jonathan Boyarin, ed and trans. *From a Ruined Garden: The Memorial Books of Polish Jewry.* New York: Schocken, 1983. 275 pp. (hc. 0-8052-3867-0) $18.95
Gr. 9-12. A collection of excerpts from over 100 community memorial books written by Holocaust survivors. Most of the book deals with life before the Holocaust. The book provides a revealing look at the rich, vibrant life of the Jewish communities in Poland. Includes an exhaustive bibliography of Eastern European memorial books and a geographical index and gazetteer.

370 Kurzman, Dan. *The Bravest Battle: The Twenty-Eight Days of the Warsaw Ghetto Uprising.* New York: Putnam, 1976. 386 pp. (hc. 0-306-80533-2) $14.95
Gr. 11-12. A detailed, well-researched, step-by-step account of the

uprising. Includes notes and an extensive bibliography. No index.

371 Lace, William W. *The Nazis*. New York: Lucent, 1997. 111 pp.
(hc. 1-56006-0910-3) $17.96
Gr. 5-10. An excellent historical overview of Germany's National
Socialist German Workers' Party. Lace examines the origins of the
party, its ideology, and its growth under Hitler's leadership. The author
also gives considerable attention to Hitler's personality: his paranoia,
later inability to distinguish between fantasy and reality, and the
megalomania that would drive him to acts of mass destruction. Written
in concise, straightforward prose, the informative text is complemented
with black-and-white photographs that appear throughout. Includes a
chronology, suggestions for further reading, a bibliography, and a
subject index. From the *Holocaust Library* series.

372 Landau, Elaine. *Nazi War Criminals*. New York: Watts, 1990. 160
pp. (hc. 0-531-15181-6) $12.40
Gr. 7-12. Examines the cases of four prominent Nazi war criminals:
Josef Mengele, Adolf Eichmann, Klaus Barbie, and Kurt Waldheim,
and also looks at several lesser known perpetrators. Includes black-and-
white photographs, chapter notes, suggestions for further reading, and a
subject index.

373 —. *The Warsaw Ghetto Uprising*. New York: Macmillan, 1992.
143 pp. (hc. 0-02-751392-0) $14.95
Gr. 10-12. Chronicles the resistance organized by Jews in the Warsaw
Ghetto a few days prior to its liquidation. Includes black-and-white
photographs, source notes, suggestions for further reading, and a
subject index.

374 —. *We Survived the Holocaust*. New York: Watts, 1991. 144 pp.
(hc. 0-531-15229-4) $22.70
Gr. 6-12. A collection of memoirs of sixteen Jewish Holocaust
survivors from Austria, Czechoslovakia, Germany, Holland, Hungary,
Poland, and Transylvania. Includes black-and-white photographs of the
survivors, a glossary, suggestions for further reading, and a subject
index.

375 Lang, Daniel. *A Backward Look: Germans Remember*. New York:
McGraw-Hill, 1979. 112 pp. (hc. 0-07-036239-4) $8.95
Gr. 10-12. Interviews with Germans who lived through Hitler's Nazi
Germany as perpetrators and victims. People interviewed include

rescuers who helped smuggle Jews out of Germany and a guard from the Buchenwald concentration camp. The interviewees talk about what life was like in that time and how their experiences have affected them since.

376 Langbein, Hermann. *Against All Hope: Resistance in the Nazi Concentration Camps, 1938-1945.* Trans. Harry Zohn. New York: Paragon, 1994. 502 pp. (hc. 1-55578-363-2) $ 29.95
Gr. 9-12. In this comprehensive, in-depth study, Langbein shatters the myth that all concentration camp prisoners went passively to their deaths. Includes extensive chapter notes and a thorough subject index.

377 Langer, Lawrence L. *Holocaust Testimonies: The Ruins of Memory.* New Haven: Yale University Press, 1991. 216 pp. (hc. 0-300-04966-8) $25.00
Gr. 9-12. Quoting extensively from interviews in the Fortunoff Video Archives for Holocaust Testimonies, Langer analyzes how oral Holocaust studies enable us to confront the human dimensions of the tragedy. This is an in-depth, scholarly analysis recommended for advanced students. Includes chapter notes, but no index.

378 Lawliss, Charles. . . . *and God Cried: The Holocaust Remembered.* New York: JG Press, 1994. 175 pp. (hc. 1-57215-036-X)
Gr. 7-12. A good general overview of the Holocaust abundantly illustrated with captioned photographs from the archives of the Simon Wiesenthal Center and the United States Holocaust Memorial Museum. Provides an excellent introduction to the Holocaust. No index.

379 Lindwer, Willy. *The Last Seven Months of Anne Frank.* Trans. Alison Meersschaert. New York: Pantheon, 1991. 204 pp. (hc. 0-679-40145-8); (pbk. 0-385-42360-8) $12.95
Gr. 9-12. The last seven months of Anne Frank's life are traced through the testimonies of six Jewish women who survived the war. Detailed eyewitness accounts follow Anne and her family from the Westerbork transit camp to Auschwitz, and finally to Bergen-Belsen where she and her sister Margot perished. This is a fascinating and heartbreaking reconstruction of Anne's ordeal in the final months of her life. A necessary complement to Anne's own diary.

380 Linenthal, Edward T. *Preserving Memory: The Struggle to Create*

America's Holocaust Museum. New York: Viking, 1995. 336 pp. (hc. 0-670-86067-0) $27.95

Gr. 9-12. The remarkable story of the fifteen-year struggle to build the United States Holocaust Memorial Museum in Washington, D.C. Told in a straightforward, engaging style. Includes black-and-white photographs, extensive chapter notes, and a subject index.

381 Lyttle, Richard B. *Nazi Hunting.* New York: Watts, 1982. 101 pp. (hc. 0-531-04410-6) $8.90

Gr. 4-10. Brief reconstructions of the pursuit of some of the more notorious Nazi fugitives, including Josef Mengele, Martin Bormann, and Adolf Eichmann. The reconstructions are written in a dramatic style that will appeal to reluctant readers. Includes black-and-white photographs and a subject index.

382 Marks, Jane. *The Secret Survivors of the Holocaust.* New York: Fawcett Columbine, 1993. 307 pp. (pbk. 0-449-90686-8) $12.00

Gr. 10-12. An excellent account for older young adult readers of hidden Jewish children. Well-researched and well-written.

383 Mayer, Milton. *They Thought They Were Free: The Germans, 1933-1945.* 2nd Ed. Chicago: University of Chicago Press, 1966. 354 pp. (hc. 0-266-51192-8) $16.50

Gr. 9-12. The rise of Nazism as seen through the eyes of ten ordinary citizens in a small German city, which, for them, meant employment, a sense of pride, and security. An interesting look at differing perspectives on historical events.

384 Meltzer, Milton, ed. *The Jewish-Americans: A History in Their Own Words, 1650-1950.* New York: HarperCollins, 1982. 174 pp. (hc. 0-690-04227-2)

Gr. 5-12. Personal experiences of Jewish-Americans are collected here, taken from letters, journals, diaries, autobiographies, speeches, and other documents. Two segments pertain to the Holocaust. Howard Katzender, one of the American soldiers who liberated the Buchenwald concentration camp offers a vivid and horrific account of what he witnessed; Israel Green, a diamond cutter in Antwerp before the war, was sent to Auschwitz shortly after the Nazis occupied his country, but miraculously survived and settled in the United States. He too offers a vivid and terrifying remembrance.

385 Meltzer, Milton. *Never to Forget: The Jews of the Holocaust.* New York: HarperCollins, 1976. 217 pp. (hc. 0-06-024175-6) $15.89;

(pbk. 0-06-446118-1) $6.95

Gr. 6-12. An outstanding historical study of the European Holocaust divided into three sections: the anti-Semitic sentiments in Germany that led up to the Holocaust; the methods and means of Hitler's Final Solution; and how Jews resisted their persecution. A scrupulously researched historical study. Includes statistics, a chronology, an excellent bibliography for further study, and a very thorough index. A must for all children's and young adult collections.

386 ——. *Rescue: The Story of How Gentiles Saved Jews in the Holocaust.* New York: Harper Collins, 1988. 168 pp.
(hc.0-06-024210-8) $15.89; (pbk. 0-06-446117-3) $6.95

Gr. 6-12. A recounting of the numerous individual heroic acts of Gentiles to save Jews from extermination. A thoroughly researched historical study. Includes a bibliography for further reading and a subject index.

387 ——. *The World of Our Fathers: The Jews of Eastern Europe.* New York: Farrar, Straus & Giroux, 1974. 274 pp. (hc. 0-374-38530-0) $7.95

Gr. 10-12. The author chronicles Jewish life in eastern Europe from the Middle Ages through the Holocaust. Typical of Meltzer's work, this book is scrupulously researched, richly informative, and highly readable. Includes a glossary, bibliography, and a subject index.

388 Milton, Sybil. ed. and trans. *The Art of Jewish Children: Germany, 1936-1941.* New York: Philosophical Library, 1989. 159 pp. (hc. 0-8022-2558-6) $35.00

Gr. 7-12. From the Dusseldorf City Museum. A collection of 125 drawings, paintings, and other works of art produced by Jewish children in segregated schools they were forced to attend before Hitler implemented his Final Solution. The collection survives through the efforts of artist-teacher Juno Levin. In addition to the children's artwork are selected works by Levin and his circle, essays on the works, and historical background on the collection. The artworks are extraordinarily poignant. The quality of the plates is excellent. When available, the artist, title, and date of the work is given. Translated from the German.

389 Morin, Isobel V. *Days of Judgement: The World War II War Crimes Trials.* Brookfield, CT: Millbrook, 1995. 144 pp. (hc. 1-56294-442-8) $16.40

Gr. 7-12. A history of the international war crimes trials following World War II. Equal attention is given to trials of German and Japanese war criminals. The book examines the reasoning that led to the trials and their outcomes. Brief biographical profiles of the defendants are also offered. Includes black-and-white photographs, a bibliography, and subject index.

390 Mosse, George L., ed. *Nazi Culture: Intellectual, Cultural, and Social in the Third Reich.* New York: Schocken, 1981. 432 pp. (hc. 0-8052-0668-X) $15.16

Gr. 7-12. A fascinating anthology of intellectual and cultural products from Nazi Germany, including: a Nazi children's prayer; a section of a novel by Joseph Goebbels, the Nazi propaganda minister; a children's story portraying Hitler as a friend of young people; and a speech by Hitler against the equal status of women. Includes a lengthy general introduction by the editor, and introductions to each section and selection.

391 Nomberg-Przytyk, Sara. *Auschwitz: True Tales from a Grotesque Land.* Trans. Roslyn Hirsch. Ed. Eli Pfefferkorn and David H. Hirsch. Chapel Hill: University of North Carolina Press, 1985. 185 pp. (hc. 0-8078-1629-9); (pbk. 0-8078-4160-9) $13.95

Gr. 11-12. The author draws a series of raw, powerful portraits and vignettes from her experiences and observations as a prisoner in Auschwitz.

392 Noren, Catherine Hang. *The Camera of My Family.* New York: Knopf, 1976. 239 pp. (0-394-48838-5) $20.00

Gr. 4-12. A collection of photographs and memorabilia of five generations of a German-Jewish family, spanning from their lives in Germany at the end of the nineteenth century to the present in America. Several chapters deal with the Nazi period in Germany and the Holocaust. A poignant, visually striking book.

393 Patterson, Charles. *Anti-Semitism: The Road to the Holocaust and Beyond.* New York: Walker, 1982. 150 pp. (hc. 0-8027-6470-3) $11.95

Gr. 9-12. Tracing the roots of anti-Semitism in ancient history to an examination of it in contemporary times, Patterson explains how the Holocaust was not an isolated chapter in history, but rather a culmination of centuries of persecution of Jews. A well-researched, concise study of anti-Semitism. Includes suggestions for further reading and a subject index.

394 Pettit, Jayne. *A Place to Hide: True Stories of Holocaust Rescuers.*
New York: Scholastic, 1993. 114 pp. (pbk. 0-590-45353-X)
Gr. 5-10. Brief profiles of people who helped rescue Jews from the
Nazis during the Holocaust. Miep Gies and Oskar Schindler are among
the individuals profiled. Other topics covered include the efforts of the
Danish Resistance to save their country's Jews and the Assisi
Underground. Includes a few black-and-white, captioned photographs.
No index.

395 ——. *A Time to Fight Back: True Stories of Wartime
Resistance.* Boston: Houghton Mifflin, 1996. 163 pp.
(hc. 0-395-76504-8) $14.95
Gr. 5-8. The stories of eight young boys and girls in Asia and Europe
who accomplished heroic feats during World War II. Among these
stories is that of Elie Wiesel and Nachama Bawnik whose family
helped hide Jews from the Nazis in Poland. Included is a good
bibliography of Holocaust and other World War II literature for
children.

396 Plant, Richard. *The Pink Triangle: The Nazi War Against
Homosexuals.* New York: Holt, 1986. 257 pp.
(hc. 0-8050-0059-3) $19.95; (pbk. 0-8050-0600-1) $13.00
Gr. 11-12. Among the many cultural, ethnic, and religious groups
persecuted in Nazi Germany were homosexuals. Plant's book is the first
comprehensive study of this subject. Plant, himself a refugee from Nazi
Germany, offers a well-researched account of the systematic
persecution Hitler's Nazi regime employed against homosexuals. The
pink triangle refers to the marking homosexual prisoners wore in
concentration camps. Includes a chronology, chapter notes, a selected
bibliography, and a subject index.

397 Prager, Arthur and Emily. *World War II Resistance Stories.* Illus.
Steven Assel. New York: Watts, 1979. 90 pp. (hc. 0-531-02296-X)
$9.90; (pbk. 0-440-99800-X) $2.25
Gr. 4-7. The secret activities of six members of resistance movements
in Europe and Japan during World War II are described. Two of the
stories pertain to the Holocaust. Witold Pilecki organized a movement
to help save Polish Jews and other political prisoners from Auschwitz
by allowing himself to be arrested and sent to the camp. Pere Marie
Benoit and Fernande Leboucher helped French Jews escape deportation

from unoccupied France. Includes black-and-white drawings and a subject index.

398 Prager, Moshe. *Sparks of Glory.* Trans. Mordecai Schreiber. New York: Shengold, 1974. 154 pp. (0-88400-000-1) $5.95
Gr. 9-12. The stories of Jews who, despite all of their unspeakable sufferings during the Holocaust, still kept their faith alive. A very inspiring book.

399 Proktor, Richard. *Nazi Germany: The Origins and Collapse of the Third Reich.* New York: Holt, 1970. 153 pp. (hc. 0-03-089479-4)
Gr. 5-9. A vivid, thoughtful study of Hitler and Nazi Germany. Illustrated with black-and-white photographs. Includes suggestions for further reading and a subject index.

400 Rabinsky, Leatrice and Gertrude Mann. *Journey of Conscience: Young People Respond to the Holocaust.* Cleveland: William Collins, 1979. 112 pp. (pbk. 0-529-05679-8) $2.95
Gr. 7-12. Two dedicated teachers and their students, wanting to learn about the Holocaust, studied its literature and, from their studies, came up with the idea to retrace the path of the Holocaust in a "journey of conscience," taking them to the Terezin and Auschwitz concentration camps, the Warsaw Ghetto, Lidice, and the Anne Frank House. The book recalls the emotional impact this pilgrimage had on all who took part.

401 Rashke, Richard. *Escape from Sobibor.* New York: Avon, 1987. 416 pp. (pbk. 0-380-75394-4) $3.95
Gr. 9-12. The inmates of the Sobibor death camp revolt against the Nazis and some escape.

402 Read, Anthony and David Fisher. *Kristallnacht: The Nazi Night of Terror.* New York: Random House, 1989. 294 pp.
(hc. 0-8129-1723-5) $19.95; (pbk. 0-87226-237-5) $10.95
Gr. 9-12. Dramatic eyewitness testimony and information from secret German documents are used to create this vivid, thorough account of *Kristallnacht,* "The Night of Broken Glass," when Jews all over Germany were terrorized as an act of revenge for the assassination of a Nazi diplomat. Includes black-and-white photographs, source notes, a bibliography, and a subject index.

403 Rice, Earle J. *Nazi War Criminals.* New York: Lucent, 1997. 111

pp. (hc. 1-56006-097-2) $17.96
Gr. 5-10. In addition to a thoroughly researched discussion of the
Nuremberg War Trials, the author offers excellent profiles of the most
notorious Nazi villains, including: Adolf Eichmann, Reinhard
Heydrich, Heinrich Himmler, Rudolf Hoss, Josef Mengele, and Julius
Streicher. This is a thorough, informative, and highly readable book.
The text is complemented with black-and-white photographs that
appear throughout and informative sidebars. Includes chapter notes, a
chronology, glossary, and suggestions for further reading, an extensive
bibliography, and subject index. From the *Holocaust Library* series.
See also Rice's *The Nuremberg War Trials*.

404 Rittner, Carol and Sondra Myers. *The Courage to Care: Rescuers
    of Jews During the Holocaust*. New York: New York University
    Press, 1986. 157 pp. (pbk. 0-8147-7406-7) $19.50
Gr. 9-12. Profiles of fourteen "Righteous Gentiles," who risked their
lives trying to save Jews. Countries represented include: Bulgaria,
Denmark, France, Italy, The Netherlands, Norway, and Poland. The
story of the tiny village of Le Chambon-sur-Lignon in Vichy France is
also told. The entire village worked together to serve as a refuge for
Jews. Includes black-and-white photographs, a subject index, a
foreword by Elie Wiesel, and several brief essays by historians
discussing the courageous people profiled.

405 Rittner, Carol and John K. Roth. *Different Voices: Women and the
    Holocaust*. New York: Paragon, 1993. 435 pp. (hc. 1-5578-503-1)
    $26.95; (pbk. 1-55778-504-X) $18.95
Gr. 9-12. A thorough examination of women's experiences in the
Holocaust. Divided into three parts, the first section of the book
recounts experiences of survivors related through personal narratives.
The second section consists of contemporary insights from women
scholars of the Holocaust. The third section consists of women artists
and intellectuals who also offer reflections upon the Holocaust.
Includes a glossary and subject index. This is an in-depth, exhaustively
researched, scholarly study recommended for advanced students.

406 Rogasky, Barbara. *Smoke and Ashes: The Story of the Holocaust*.
    New York: Holiday House, 1988. 187 pp. (hc. 0-8234-0697-0)
    $19.95; (pbk. 0-8234-0878) $12.95
Gr. 6-12. Examines the causes, events, and legacies of the Holocaust.
Another fine general introduction to the Holocaust. The chapters are
brief and the text is supported with black-and-white photographs,

illustrations, and replications of some official documents. Includes a bibliography of sources and a thorough subject index.

407 Rosenberg, Maxine B. *Hiding to Survive: Stories of Jewish Children Rescued from the Holocaust.* New York: Clarion, 1994. 166 pp. (hc. 0-395-65014-3) $15.95; (pbk. 0-395-90020-4) $8.95
Gr. 4-8. First person accounts of fourteen Holocaust survivors who, as children, were hidden from the Nazis by non-Jews. A distinguished work on the subjects of hidden children and righteous Gentiles. Includes black-and-white photographs of the survivors, a brief glossary, and suggestions for further reading. No index.

408 Rossel, Seymour. *The Holocaust: The Fire that Raged.* New York: Watts, 1981. 148 pp. (hc. 0-531-04351-7) $11.90
Gr. 6-12. The author traces the European Holocaust from Hitler's rise to power in 1933 to the Nuremberg War Crimes Tribunal following World War II. This is a solid historical overview of the Holocaust. Includes black-and-white maps of Europe under Hitler's control and of concentration camp locations. Suggestions for further reading and a subject index are also included.

409 Rothchild, Sylvia, ed. *Voices from the Holocaust.* New York: NAL, 1981. 456 pp. (0-453-00396-6) $14.95
Gr. 9-12. A collection of testimonies from 250 Holocaust survivors from all over Europe. The testimonies are divided into "life before the Holocaust," "life during the Holocaust," and "life in America." This is an amazing, outstanding collection of oral history. An absolute must for collections. Includes a foreword by Elie Wiesel and a glossary.

410 Rubenstein, Eli, ed. *For You Who Died I Must Live On . . . : Reflections on the March of the Living: Contemporary Jewish Youth Confront the Holocaust.* New York: Mosaic Press, 1993. 121 pp. (hc. 0-88962-510-7) $17.95
Gr. 5-12. Jewish high school students, primarily from Canada, express through art, poetry, prose, and song their feelings after touring some of Europe's most infamous extermination camps. A powerful, moving collection of work by young people. Includes black-and-white and color photographs. See also *Liberating the Ghosts.*

411 Rubin, Arnold P. *Hitler and the Nazis: The Evil that Men Do.* New York: Bantam, 1979. 177 pp. (pbk. 0-533-12283-5)
Gr. 7-12. Presents many facets of the Holocaust: anti-Semitism,

Jewish-Christian relations, and the lack of rescue efforts on behalf of Jewish victims. Well-researched and well-written. Includes a bibliography and subject index. Originally published as *The Evil that Men Do: The Story of the Nazis* by Messner in 1977.

412 Rubinstein, Richard L. and John K. Roth. *Approaches to Auschwitz: The Holocaust and Its Legacy*. Atlanta: John Knox, 1987. 422 pp. (hc. 0-8042-0778-X); (pbk. 0-8042-0777-1) $23.00
Gr. 11-12. An analytical study of the Holocaust examining the Nazi attempt to exterminate all European Jews and the historical events that led up to the genocide. This is a difficult, heavily researched, academic text suitable only for older, motivated young adults. The book might best be used as a text for advanced Holocaust studies in the senior high school grades.

413 Sender, Ruth Minsky. *The Holocaust Lady*. New York: Macmillan, 1992. 192 pp. (hc. 0-02-781832-2) $14.95
Gr. 6-12. A powerful, inspiring story of a Holocaust survivor who has dedicated her life to teaching others about it so that it will never be forgotten. This is a wonderful survivor story that demonstrates the importance of passing on the memories of the Holocaust to younger generations.

414 Sherrow, Victoria. *Amsterdam*. New York: New Discovery Books, 1992. 96 pp. (hc. 0-02-782465-9) $14.95
Gr. 5-10. A brief account, including many firsthand observations, of the German occupation of Amsterdam from 1940-1945. Attention is given to the persecution of the city's Jewish population. Generously illustrated with black-and-white photographs. Includes chapter notes, suggestions for further reading, and a subject index. From the *Cities at War* series.

415 Shevelev, Raphael with Karen Schomer. *Liberating the Ghosts: Photographs and Texts from The March of the Living Including Excerpts from the Writings of Participants*. Portland, OR: Lens Works, 1996. 129 pp. (hc. 1-888803-01-0); (pbk. 1-888803-00-2) $19.95
Gr. 6-12. A powerfully moving book commemorating the Holocaust with The March of the Living, a modern annual pilgrimage of remembrance begun in 1988. The book documents the event with stunning black-and-white photographs and writings by some of the participants. Several thousand young adults from around the world,

along with educators and survivors, go to Poland and are confronted with the sites and the meaning of the Holocaust. The event culminates in a silent march from Auschwitz to the gas chambers of Birkenau. A profoundly moving work.

416 Shirer, William L. *The Rise and Fall of Adolf Hitler*. New York:
     Landmark, 1984. 180 pp. (pbk. 0-394-86270-8) $2.95
Gr. 5-9. A comprehensive documentary of Nazi Germany and its leaders from its beginning to end. An excellent historical overview for young readers. Includes black-and-white photographs, maps, and a subject index.

417 —. *The Rise and Fall of the Third Reich: A History of Nazi
     Germany*. New York: Simon & Schuster, 1960. 1,264 pp.
     (hc. 0-671-72869-5) $35.00; (pbk. 0-671-72868-7) $16.00
Gr. 9-12. A detailed, well-researched, and highly readable chronicle of the Third Reich, from Hitler's early life to his suicide in Berlin. See also Louis L. Snyder's *Hitler's Third Reich: A Documentary History*.

418 Sichrovsky, Peter. *Born Guilty: Children of Nazi Families*. Trans.
     Jean Steinberg. New York: Basic Books, 1988. 178 pp.
     (hc. 0-465-00742-2) $17.95
Gr. 11-12. A collection of interviews with children and grandchildren of Nazi war criminals. A fascinating psychological study that considers the legacies of the Holocaust. Translated from the German.

419 Silver, Eric. *The Book of the Just: The Unsung Heroes Who
     Rescued Jews from Hitler*. New York: Grove Press, 1992. 175 pp.
     (hc. 0-8021-1347-8) $19.95
Gr. 9-12. Using personal testimonies, Silver offers profiles of some of the more than 10,000 men and women who risked their lives to save Jews all over Europe from Nazi slaughter. Includes black-and-white photographs, source notes, and a subject index.

420 Snyder, Louis L. *Hitler and Nazism*. New York: Bantam, 1967.
     182 pp.
Gr. 7-12. A biography of Hitler and a brief history of the significant events during the Third Reich. Written in a simple, straightforward style, the text is divided into short, vivid and dramatic chapters that will be especially appealing to young adult readers.

421 —. *Hitler's Third Reich: A Documentary History*. Chicago:

Nelson-Hall, 1981. 637 pp. (hc. 0-882-29705-8) $43.95;
(pbk. 0-882-29793-7) $25.95
Gr. 9-12. An account of the Third Reich is presented through a variety
of original documents: official publications, reportage, speeches,
excerpts from diaries and letters, transcripts of radio talks, and court
records. The materials cover the periods between the post-World War I
Weimar Republic through the rise of Nazi Germany to immediately
following the war. Snyder provides connective material to place each
selection in its historical context. An excellent, invaluable resource. See
also William L. Shirer's *The Rise and Fall of the Third Reich*.

422 Spiegelman, Art. *Maus: A Survivor's Tale. Part I: My Father
Bleeds History*. New York: Pantheon, 1986. 159 pp.
(hc. 0-394-541-553) $22.00; (pbk. 0-394-74723-2) $14.00
Gr. 7-12. An autobiographical account of a Holocaust survivor told in a
graphic novel format. Spiegelman portrays Nazis as cats and Jews as
mice. The author depicts himself being told about the Holocaust by his
Polish father. The story explores a troubled relationship between father
and son, as well as the concentration camp experience. The story and
black-and-white illustrations are grim and powerful. Reluctant readers
will find the comic book format especially appealing.

423 —. *Maus: A Survivor's Tale: Part II: And Here My Troubles
Began*. New York: Pantheon, 1991. 136 pp. (hc. 0-679-40641-7)
$18.00; (pbk. 0-679-72977-1) $14.00
Gr. 7-12. Spiegelman continues the story of his father's Holocaust
experiences in the same graphic novel format. In this book, the father's
Auschwitz experiences are depicted in his life after liberation. A
powerful, horrific book and an outstanding sequel.

424 Stadtler, Bea. *The Holocaust: A History of Courage and
Resistance*. Ed. Morrison David Bial. Illus. David Stone Martin.
New York: Behrman House, 1973. 210 pp. (pbk. 0-87441-578-1)
$7.95
Gr. 3-6. An outstanding history of the Holocaust written specifically as
a textbook for elementary school age children. Each chapter ends with
three questions that can be used for classroom discussion or an in-class
or homework writing assignment. Illustrated with black-and-white
drawings. Includes a preface by Yehuda Bauer, a bibliography, and
source notes.

425 Stein, Andre. *Hidden Children: Forgotten Survivors of the*

Holocaust. New York: Penguin, 1994. 273 pp.
   (pbk. 0-14-017051-0) $12.95
Gr. 10-12. Another well-researched account of hidden Jewish children
in Europe suitable for older, young adult readers. Here, the stories of
ten of those children are recounted.

426 Stein, R. Conrad. *Hitler Youth.* Chicago: Children's Press, 1985.
     48 pp. (0-516-04736-9) $15.00
Gr. 3-6. From the *World at War* series. Describes for younger readers
the origin and growth of the Hitler Youth movement and what roles it
played in Nazi Germany before and during the war. Illustrated with
many black-and-white photographs. Includes a subject index.

427 ——. *The Holocaust.* Chicago: Children's Press, 1986. 48 pp.
     (hc. 0-516-04767-1) $15.00; (pbk. 0-516-44767-X) $2.95
Gr. 2-6. From the *World at War* series. A good, general history of the
Holocaust written specifically for younger readers. Generously
illustrated with captioned black-and-white photographs, some quite
graphic. Indexed by subject. An excellent piece of nonfiction to use to
introduce young people to the Holocaust.

428 ——.*Warsaw Ghetto.* Chicago: Children's Press, 1985. 47 pp.
     (hc. 0-516-04779-5)
Gr. 3-6. From the *World at War* series. Recounts for younger readers
what life was like for Jews in the Warsaw Ghetto, from its erection to
its destruction. Illustrated with many black-and-white photographs.
Includes a subject index.

429 Steiner, Jean-Francois. *Treblinka.* Trans. Helen Weaver. New
     York: Meridian, 1994. 415 pp. (hc. 0-452-01124-8) $13.95
Gr. 9-12. Six hundred prisoners revolt and close down the death camps
at Treblinka. Includes a preface by Simone de Beauvoir. Translated
from the French. Originally published by Simon & Schuster in 1967.

430 Strahinich, Helen. *The Holocaust: Understanding and
     Remembering.* Springfield, NJ: Enslow, 1996. 112 pp.
     (0-89490-725-5)
Gr. 7-12. From the *Issues in Focus* series. A brief, general discussion of
what the Holocaust was and circumstances that allowed it to happen.
This is a good basic introduction to the Holocaust for young adults.
Occasional black-and-white photographs support the text. Included are
chapter notes, a glossary, subject index, suggestions for further reading,

and a directory of Holocaust museums in the United States and Canada.

431 Suhl, Yuri, ed. *They Fought Back: The Story of the Jewish Resistance in Nazi Europe*. New York: Schocken, 1975. 327 pp. (0-8052-0479-2) $9.95
Gr. 9-12. Thirty-three dramatic, true tales of revolts and escapes led by heroes of the Jewish underground in the camps, the ghettos, and with the partisans. Countries represented include: Belgium, Czechoslovakia, France, Italy, Poland, and Russia. Includes notes and a subject index.

432 Switzer, Ellen. *How Democracy Failed*. New York: Atheneum, 1975. 169 pp. (hc. 0-689-30459-5) $7.95
Gr. 9-12. A German-born writer goes back to interview people her own age, evoking memories of living their teenage years under Nazism and discussing the effects it had upon themselves and their families. An interesting, personalized account of the history of the period. Includes black-and-white photographs and a subject index.

433 Tatelbaum, Itzhak B. *Through Our Eyes: Children Witness the Holocaust*. Jerusalem: I.B.T., 1985. 187 pp.
Gr. 4-8. Another excellent textbook for Holocaust studies in upper elementary or middle school grades. The history of the Holocaust is covered in chronological order through eighteen study units. Each unit is comprised of children's diary entries and survivor's testimony representing various countries, times, and events. Each unit ends with questions that could be used for class discussion or written assignments. The book is generously illustrated with black-and-white photographs and other illustrations. Includes a bibliography.

434 Thalmann, Rita and Emmanuel Feinermann. *Crystal Night: 9-10 November 1938*. Trans. Gilles Cremonesi. New York: Holocaust Library, 1980. 192 pp.
Gr. 7-12. An account of the events surrounding the rioting that led to the *Kristallnacht*, when all of the synagogues in Germany were destroyed, Jewish businesses looted, and thousands of Jews terrorized and imprisoned. Based upon authenticated documents and testimonies. Translated from the French.

435 Vegh, Claudine. *I Didn't Say Goodbye: Interviews with Children of the Holocaust*. Trans. Ros Schwartz. New York: Dutton, 1984. 179 pp. (hc. 0-525-24308-9) $14.95
Gr. 7-12. Interviews with twenty-eight French men and women who, as

children, lost some or all of their families to the Holocaust. An outstanding collection of powerful, very moving testimonials. Includes a black-and-white map of World War II France, a Holocaust chronology, and an afterword by Bruno Bettelheim. Translated from the French.

436 Vishniac, Roman. *Polish Jews: A Pictorial Record.* New York:
      Schocken, 1975. 31 pp. (pbk. 0-8052-0910-7) $11.95
Gr. 5-12. Black-and-white photographs with captions depict the cultural, social, and spiritual life of Polish Jews before the Holocaust. Includes an introductory essay by Abraham Joshua Heschel.

437 von der Rol, Ruud and Rian Verhoeven. *Anne Frank: Beyond the
      Diary.* New York: Viking, 1993. (hc. 0-670-84932-4) $17.00
Gr. 5-12. Photographs, illustrations, and maps from the Anne Frank House archives accompany historical essays, diary excerpts, and interviews providing insight into Anne Frank's life and the world around her. An excellent companion to Anne's diary. Includes an introduction by Anna Quindlen, a chronology, and a subject index.

438 Werstein, Irving. *That Denmark Might Live: The Saga of the
      Danish Resistance in World War II.* Philadelphia: Macrae Smith,
      1967. 143 pp. $4.25
Gr. 7-12. The story of the Danish resistance movement organized against the German occupation. One of their most incredible accomplishments is the rescue of nearly all Danish Jews. Includes black-and-white photographs and a subject index.

439 —. *The Uprising of the Warsaw Ghetto, November 1940-May
      1943.* New York: Norton, 1968. 157 pp.
Gr. 5-10. Drawn from interviews with survivors, journals from those who did not survive, and trial records, the author tells the story of the Warsaw Ghetto. Includes a map of the Ghetto, black-and-white photographs, and a subject index.

440 Wiesenthal, Simon. *The Murderers Among Us.* New York:
      McGraw-Hill, 1973.
Gr. 9-12. The legendary Nazi hunter who brought over 1,000 criminals to trial discusses his work. An inspiring and compelling book. Includes black-and white photographs and a glossary.

441 Williamson, David. *The Third Reich*. New York: Watts, 1989. 63
   pp. (hc. 0-531-18261-4) $13.40
   Gr. 4-8. Presents a clear understanding of the political, economic, and
   social circumstances that led to the rise of Nazism in Germany. The
   Holocaust is given only superficial coverage. Includes biographical
   sketches of twelve Nazi leaders, a chronology of important dates, a
   glossary, suggestions for further reading, and a subject index.
   Generously illustrated with maps and photographs. From the *Witness
   History Series*.

442 Zeinert, Karen. *The Warsaw Ghetto Uprising*. Brookfield, CT:
   Millbrook Press, 1993. 112 pp. (hc. 1-56294-282-4) $16.40
   Gr. 6-12. Describes life in the Warsaw Ghetto and focuses upon the
   valiant but ultimately hopeless resistance Jews organized prior to the
   ghetto's liquidation. Illustrated with black-and-white photographs.
   Includes a timeline, bibliography, chapter notes, suggestions for further
   reading, and a subject index.

443 Ziemian, Joseph. *The Cigarette Sellers of Three Crosses Square*.
   Trans. Janina David. Minneapolis: Lerner, 1975. 166 pp.
   (hc. 0-8225-0757-9) $6.95
   Gr. 5-12. An incredible true story of a group of children who managed
   in 1942 to escape from the Warsaw Ghetto to the Aryan section of the
   city. Some of the children were later caught and killed, but most
   survived. Three Crosses Square refers to the place the children went to
   peddle cigarettes, an enterprise that helped keep them alive. Includes
   black-and-white photographs. Translated from the Polish.

Picture Books

Not all picture books are cited in this section. Two books, *Hiding from the Nazis* and *The Number on My Grandfather's Arm*, both by David A. Adler, are included in "Nonfiction." Two other books by Adler, *A Child of the Warsaw Ghetto* and *A Picture Book of Anne Frank*, are cited in "Autobiography and Biography." I chose to restrict this section to fictional works because librarians typically shelve them separately while interfiling nonfiction and biographical picture books.

444 Adler, David A. *One Yellow Daffodil: A Hanukkah Story*.
    Illus. Lloyd Bloom. San Diego: Harcourt Brace, 1995. 32 pp.
    (hc. 0-1520-0537-4) $16.00
Gr. 2-5. Morris Kaplan, a survivor of Auschwitz, is a kind but lonely flower shop owner who looks forward to weekly visits from a young brother and sister. When they come to buy flowers for Hanukkah, memories are stirred up of Morris's family celebrating Hanukkah in Poland before the war, and he is prompted to unpack an old menorah his family used before they were sent to Auschwitz. Invited to celebrate the holiday, Morris brings the menorah to the children's home and shares the story of Holocaust experiences of the single yellow daffodil, which gave him hope for survival. A gentle, hopeful story illustrated with deep-toned acrylic paintings. The bright flowers shine out of surrounding darkness, emphasizing the poignancy of the story and its hopeful tone.

445 Bunting, Eve. *Terrible Things*. Illus. Stephen Gansmell. New
    York: Harper & Row, 1980. 26 pp. (hc. 0-06-020903-8) $7.95
Gr. 1-4. A picture book story based upon Pastor Martin Niemoller's famous statement: "In Germany, they came first for the communists, and I didn't speak up because I wasn't a communist. Then they came for the Jews, and I didn't speak up because I wasn't a Jew. Then they came for the trade unionists, and I didn't speak up because I wasn't a trade unionist. Then they came for the Catholics and I didn't speak up because I wasn't a Catholic. Then they cam for me—and by that time there was nobody left to speak up." Bunting creates a fascinating story about animals in the forest who are taken away by the Terrible Things. Big Rabbit finds reasons for each of these "round-ups" until the rabbits

are all that are left in the forest and the Terrible Things come for them too. Illustrated with haunting black-and-white drawings.

446 Feder, Paula Kurzband. *The Feather-Bed Journey*. Illus. Stacey
     Schuett. Morton Grove, IL: Albert Whitman, 1995. 30 pp.
     (hc. 0-8075-2330-5) $15.95
Gr. 2-5. When Rachel and Lewis tear their grandmother's feather pillow while playing, their grandmother tells them the story of how she came to have the pillow and the special meaning behind it. In the story, she talks about her childhood in Poland and how she and her family were persecuted by the Nazis for being Jews. A warm, simply told story that connects the Holocaust between generations. Schuett's acrylic and pastel illustrations are colorful and expressive. Includes an author's note, which places the story in historical context.

447 Hoestlandt, Jo. *Star of Fear, Star of Hope*. Illus. Johanna Kang.
     Trans. Mark Polizzotti. New York: Walker, 1995. 32 pp.
     (hc. 0-8027-8373-2) $15.95
Gr. 2-4. In German-occupied France, nine-year-old Helen cannot understand why her Jewish friend, Lydia, must wear a yellow star and later disappears. A moving story of friendship complemented by powerful illustrations. Translated from the French.

448 Innocenti, Roberto and Christophe Gallaz. *Rose Blanche*. Illus.
     Roberto Innocenti. Mankato, MN: Creative Education, 1985. 32
     pp. (hc. 0-87191-994-X) $16.95; (pbk. 0-15200-971-5) $8.00
Gr. 2-4. Rose Blanche is a young German girl who witnesses and experiences the Holocaust and World War II without ever really understanding it. Innocenti's illustrations are vivid and powerful.

449 Klein, Gerda Weissmann. *Promise of a New Spring: The
     Holocaust and Renewal*. Illus. Vincent Tartaro. Chappaqua, NY:
     Rossel, 1981. 48 pp. (hc. 0-940646-50-1) $10.95;
     (pbk. 0-940646-51-X) $5.95
Gr. 1-4. Using an allegory of a forest fire, the author offers younger readers an introduction to the Holocaust and the meaning of survival. Illustrated with an odd, sometimes effective, assortment of black-and-white and color illustrations.

450 Lakin, Patricia. *Don't Forget*. Illus. Ted Rand. New York:
     Tambourine, 1994. 32 pp. (hc. 0-688-12075-X) $14.00
Gr. 2-4. While buying the ingredients for her first cake, a surprise for

her mother, Sarah learns from the Singers, friendly local shopkeepers, the secret of the blue numbers tattooed on their arms. Rand's watercolor illustrations are warm and appealing.

451 Nerlove, Miriam. *Flowers on the Wall.* New York: McElderry, 1996. 32 pp. (hc. 0-689-50614-7) $16.00
Gr. 2-4. Life is hard enough for Rachel , a young Jewish girl, and her family in Warsaw, but it becomes much worse when the Nazis occupy the city. As the family struggles to survive, Rachel maintains hope by painting flowers on her drab apartment walls. The story ends on a bleak but realistic note with Rachel and her family deported to Treblinka in the summer of 1942, where they perish. Includes a historical note by the author. Illustrated with expressive, often poignant, watercolors.

452 Oppenheim, Shulamith Levey. *The Lily Cupboard.* Illus. Ronald Himler. New York: Charlotte Zolotow, 1992. 32 pp. (hc. 0-06-024669-3) $14.89
Gr. 1-4. Miriam, a young Jewish girl from the city, is sent away by her parents to live with strangers in the country when the Germans occupy Holland. Beautifully illustrated with watercolor paintings.

453 Waldman, Neil. *The Never-Ending Greenness.* New York: Morrow, 1997. 32 pp. (hc. 0-688-14479-9) $16.00
Gr. 2-4. A small Jewish boy and his family leave their home in Vilna, Poland, when the Nazis come and make their way to Israel to begin a new life. Illustrated with stunning impressionistic paintings done in color acrylics.

454 Wild, Margaret. *Let the Celebrations Begin!* Illus. Julie Vivas. New York: Orchard, 1991. 30 pp. (hc. 0-531-05937-5) $14.95
Gr. 1-4. Based on a reference to a small collection of stuffed toys made by Polish women in Belsen for a children's party after liberation, this story depicts children in an unidentified, liberated concentration camp preparing for a celebration. Neither the text nor the illustrations do much of anything to convey the horrors of the Holocaust. The illustrations are simply dreadful. Vivas's choice to use pastel colors is utterly tasteless and her depictions of the characters are grotesquely absurd.

Poetry and Songs

In addition to anthologies and original collections of poetry, two collections of songs are cited here.

455 Berkowitz, Judith and Eve Edelman, Trans. *Young Voices from the Ghetto: A Collection of Children and Young People's Poetry Written in the Ghettos of World War II.* Waltham, MA: Brandeis University Department of Near Eastern and Judaic Studies, 1979. 60 pp.
Gr. 4-12. Poems by children and young adults who lived in various ghettos. With the exception of one in Polish, all of the poems were originally written in Yiddish and all are presented in the original along with the English translation. See also *I Never Saw Another Butterfly.*

456 Borenstein, Emily. *Night of the Broken Glass: Poems of the Holocaust.* Mason, TX: Timberline Press, 1981. 83 pp.
Gr. 7-12. A collection of honest, moving poems arranged by three themes: "I Must Tell My Story," "May It Never Be Forgotten," and "Psalm of Hope." Illustrated with serigraphs and linoleum block design.

457 Duba, Ursula. *Tales from a Child of the Enemy.* New York: Penguin, 1997. 153 pp. (pbk. 0-14-058787-X) $8.95
Gr. 9-12. The author grew up in postwar Germany, but a relationship with a Jewish boy awakened her to the atrocities committed by the Nazis. Each of these narrative poems is about some aspect of the Holocaust. A powerful collection written from an unusual, interesting perspective.

458 Fishman, Charles, ed. *Blood to Remember: American Poets on the Holocaust.* Lubbock, TX: Texas Tech University Press, 1990. 426 pp. (hc. 0-89672-214-7) $25.00; (pbk. 0-89672-215-5) $16.95
Gr. 9-12. An outstanding collection of Holocaust poetry from American poets, including such highly regarded authors as David Ignatow, Randall Jarrell, Denise Levertov, Philip Levine, and Yuri Suhl. The poems are arranged thematically. Includes reference notes on the

poems and biographical sketches of the poets. Indexed by author and title.

459 Florsheim, Stewart J. *Ghosts of the Holocaust: An Anthology of Poetry by the Second Generation.* Detroit: Wayne State University Press, 1989. 190 pp. (hc. 0-8143-2052-X) $19.95
Gr. 9-12. A thematically arranged anthology of poetry by children of Holocaust survivors. Includes brief biographical sketches of the poets and an author index.

460 Harrison, Michael and Christopher Stuart-Clark, comp. *Peace and War: A Collection of Poems.* New York: Oxford University Press, 1989. 208 pp. (hc. 0-19-276069-6) $17.95 (pbk. 0-19-276071-8) $13.95
Gr. 7-12. An excellent collection of poems about war, many of which concern the Holocaust.

461 Heifetz, Julie. *Oral History and the Holocaust: A Collection of Poems from Interviews with Survivors of the Holocaust.* New York: Pergamon, 1985. (pbk. 0-08-032657-9) $12.50
Gr. 9-12. Poems based upon survivor testimonies. Includes a glossary and explanation of the origin of each poem. Illustrated with black-and-white drawings. Available from the St. Louis Center for Holocaust Studies.

462 Heyen, William. *Erika: Poems of the Holocaust including The Swastika Poems.* New York: Vanguard, 1984. 128 pp. (hc. 0-8149-0875-6) $20.00
Gr. 9-12. Heyen, an American of German heritage, tries to make sense of the incomprehensible that was the Holocaust through this collection of provocative poetry.

463 Hyett, Barbara Helfgott. *In Evidence: Poems of the Liberation of Nazi Concentration Camps.* Pittsburgh University Press, 1986. 161 pp. (hc. 0-8229-3526-0); (pbk. 0-8229-5376-5) $10.00
Gr. 7-12. A collection of poems representing the voices of Allied troops who liberated Nazi concentration camps in Europe in the spring of 1945. An original, moving collection.

464 Kalisch, Shoshana with Barbara Meister. *Yes, We Sang! Songs of the Ghettos and Concentration Camps.* New York: Harper & Row, 1985. 160 pp. (hc. 0-06-015448-9); (pbk. 0-06-091236-7)

Gr. 4-12. A collection of twenty-five songs from the Holocaust, written and sung by Jews in the ghettos and concentration camps. Lyrics are presented in English and Yiddish, with the music and without. Each song is preceded with a historical anecdote, explaining its origin or when and where it was first performed. Includes a Yiddish pronunciation guide, the original Yiddish text of the songs, and a bibliography.

465 Klein, Cecilie. *Poems of the Holocaust.* Jerusalem: Geffen, 1985. 47 pp. (pbk. 965-229-020-3)
Gr. 10-12. Written by a survivor of Auschwitz, these poems are introspective and deeply personal.

466 Kovner, Abba. *My Little Sister and Selected Poems, 1965-1985.* Trans. Shirley Kaufman. Oberlin, Ohio: Oberlin College, 1986. 159 pp. (hc. 0-932440-20-7) $13.50; (pbk. 0-932440-21-5) $7.95
Gr. 9-12. When the Nazis invaded Poland, Kovner became a partisan leader who settled in Israel after the war. An accomplished poet, this collection of work focuses upon the Holocaust.

467 Melek, Jacob E. *Poems of the Holocaust.* Jaques Melek, 1996. 276 pp. (pbk. 0-61-495918-7) $24.00
Gr. 9-12. Autobiographical poems relating the author's own Holocaust experiences.

468 Mlotek, Eleanor and Malke Gottlieb, comp. *We Are Here: Songs of the Holocaust.* New York: The Educational Department of the Workmen's Circle and Hippocrene, 1983. 104 pp.
Gr. 7-12. A collection of forty songs from the Holocaust, written and sung by Jews in the ghettos and concentration camps. The songs reflect the whole scope of human emotion: courage, despair, hope, strength, and suffering. The lyrics are presented in English, Hebrew, and Yiddish. Each song's score follows the lyrics. Includes black-and-white drawings and a foreword by Elie Wiesel.

469 Pagis, Don. *Variable Directions: The Selected Poetry of Don Pagis.* Trans. Stephen Mitchell. San Francisco: North Point, 1989. 153 pp. (hc. 0-86547-383-8) $21.00; (pbk. 0-86547-384-6) $9.95
Gr. 10-12. Pagis spent his adolescence in a concentration camp and his experiences there serve as the subject for many of the poems in this collection.

470 Reznikoff, Charles. *Holocaust*. Los Angeles: Black Sparrow,
     1975. 111 pp. (hc. 0-87685-232-0) $14.00
Gr. 9-12. A collection of vivid, disturbing poems contemplating the
horrors of the Holocaust, based upon the United States government
publication, *Trials of the Criminals* before the Nuremberg Military
Tribunal and records of the Adolf Eichmann trial in Jerusalem.

471 Rosenfeld, Ruth. *Beyond These Shores, 1934-1940: Poems and
     Diary of a Jewish Girl Who Escaped from Nazi Germany*. Trans.
     Thomas Dorsett. Baltimore: Icarus, 1996. 79 pp.
     (pbk. 0-944806-09-0) $9.95
Gr. 7-12. Like Anne Frank, Ruth Rosenfeld was born in Germany and,
in 1934 at the age of fourteen, began writing poems and keeping a
diary, which commented upon the terrible times in which she lived. She
escaped to England in 1939, but both her parents perished in the
Holocaust. Recently discovered, the diary and poems offer a revealing
look at a devastating time in history. The poems are presented side-by-
side in the original German and English translation. The diary is
presented in English only.

472 Sachs, Nelly. *O the Chimneys: Selected Poems*. New York: Farrar,
     Straus & Giroux, 1967. 387 pp. (hc. 0-374-22380-7) $10.00;
     (pbk. 0-374-67651-8) $2.75
Gr. 10-12. Poems about the Holocaust by the winner of the 1966 Nobel
Prize for Literature. She was a German Jew who escaped to Sweden in
1940. "The chimneys" refer to the crematoriums. The poems are
presented in the original German and English translation side-by-side.
Translated from the German by several translators.

473 —. *The Seeker and Other Poems*. Trans. Ruth and Matthew Mead
     and Michael Hamburger. New York: Farrar, Straus & Giroux, 1970.
     339 pp. (hc. 0-374-2-5780-9) $12.50
Gr. 10-12. Poems written in tribute to the millions of Jews who were
victims of Nazi terror. The poems are presented in the original German
and English translation side-by-side. Translated from the German.

474 Schiff, Hilda, comp. *Holocaust Poetry*. New York: St. Martin's
     Griffin, 1996. 234 pp. (pbk. 0-312-14357-5) $12.00
Gr. 9-12. An outstanding anthology of 119 Holocaust poems by fifty-
nine poets. Includes brief biographical sketches of the poets. Indexed
by poet, translator, and first line. A must for collections.

Poetry and Songs   113

475 Stern, Menahem. *100 Poems plus . . .* New York: Star, 1994. 96 pp.
Gr. 9-12. A collection of 100 poems reflecting on various aspects of Jewish life, many pertaining to the Holocaust.

476 Torren, Asher. *Seven Portholes in Hell: Poems of the Holocaust.* 153 pp. Washington, D.C.: United States Holocaust Memorial Museum, 1991. (hc. 0-89604-150-6) $18.95; (pbk. 0-89604-151-4) $9.95
Gr. 9-12. On December 5, 1941, thirty-seven members of Asher Torren's family were killed when the Germans destroyed the Jewish community of Novaradock, Poland. This is a collection of powerful, disturbing images.

477 Volavkova, Hana, ed. *I Never Saw Another Butterfly: Children's Drawings and Poems from Terezin Concentration Camp, 1942-1944.* Expanded 2nd Ed. 106 pp. New York: Schocken, 1993. (hc. 0-8052--4115-9) $25.00; (pbk. 0-8052-1015-6) $14.00
Gr. 4-12. An incredibly poignant collection of art and poetry by children of the Terezin Ghetto in Czechoslovakia. Of the 15,000 children under the age of fifteen who passed through the camp, less than 100 survived. The drawings are reproduced in color. Includes a foreword by Chaim Potok and an afterword by Vaclav Havel.

478 Whitman, Ruth. *The Testing of Hanna Senesh.* Detroit: Wayne State University Press, 1986. 115 pp. (hc. 0-8143-1853-3) $15.00; (pbk. 0-8143-1854-1) $11.95
Gr. 9-12. Through poetry and prose, the author recreates the last nine months of the life of Hanna Senesh, the heroine who tried to save Hungarian Jews. Includes an introduction offering historical background by Livia Rothkirchen.

Reference

In addition to traditional reference books such as atlases, dictionaries and encyclopedias, I have included additional titles, which offer excellent general introductions to the Holocaust.

479 Arad, Yitzhak, ed. *The Pictorial History of the Holocaust*. New York: Macmillan, 1990.
Gr. 7-12. An exceptional collection of archival photographs documenting the Holocaust. A sensibly arranged and visually stunning book. As one would expect of such a volume, many of the photographs are quite horrific and disturbing. There is enough information text to put the pictures in context.

480 Edelheit, Abraham J. and Hershel Edelheit. *History of the Holocaust: A Handbook and Dictionary*. Boulder, CO: Westview, 1995. 524 pp. (pbk. 0-81332-240-5) $29.95
Gr. 9-12. An alphabetically arranged, useful guide for students to use as a beginning place for research on the Holocaust. The authors do a very good job of referring the reader to other excellent resources.

481 Gilbert, Martin. *Routledge Atlas of the Holocaust: Complete History*. 2nd Ed. London: Routledge, 1995. 282 pp. (hc. 0-460-86171-9) (pbk. 0-460-86172-7)
Gr. 4-12. Now that the United States Holocaust Memorial Museum has produced its own historical atlas of the Holocaust, Gilbert's has lost its place as best. The black-and-white maps are easy to read and richly detailed. Includes black-and-white photographs, an index to the maps, and index of individuals, and an index of places. Includes a bibliography.

482 Gutman, Israel, ed. *Encyclopedia of the Holocaust*. 5 vols. New York: Macmillan, 1996. (hc. 0-02-896090-4)
Gr. 9-12. Entries are alphabetically arranged. The articles are brief but informative, averaging between one and one half to three pages. Each article ends with a bibliography. There are numerous cross-references in the articles to related topics. Black-and-white photographs, diagrams, and maps accompany many articles. The last volume has a very

thorough index. An excellent resource for any public or senior high school library collection.

483 *Holocaust.* 8 vols. Woodbridge, CT: Blackbirch Press, 1997. Gr. 7-9. In lieu of individual annotations, here is a general overview of the contents of this multivolume series. The series offers students an excellent introduction to the Holocaust. Six volumes in the series approach the Holocaust chronologically, with each focusing upon a different period, beginning with historical context that looks at anti-Semitism in ancient history through 1935. The sixth volume concludes with a look at the aftermath of the Holocaust. Volume 7 is a collection of primary source documents, in whole and in part, and Volume 8 is an excellent resource guide educators will find most useful. Each volume is eighty pages in length, extensively illustrated, and includes a glossary, suggestions for further reading, source notes, a bibliography, and a subject index. The authors and titles of each volume are:

484 *Book 1: Forever Outsiders: Jews and History from Ancient Times to August 1935* by Linda Jacobs Altman. (1-56711-200-5) $18.95

485 *Book 2: Smoke to Flame: September 1935 to December 1938* by Victoria Sherrow. (1-56711-202-1) $18.95

486 *Book 3: The Blaze Engulfs: January 1939 to December 1941* by Victoria Sherrow and Stephen Greenstein. (1-56711-202-1) $18.95

487 *Book 4: A Firestorm Unleashed: January 1942 to June 1943* by Eleanor H. Ayer. (1-56711-205-6) $18.95

488 *Book 5: Inferno: July 1943 to April 1945* by Eleanor H. Ayer. (1056711-206-4) $18.95

489 *Book 6: From the Ashes: May 1945 and After* by Eleanor H. Ayer and Stephen D. Chicoine. (1-56711-206-4) $18.95

490 *Book 7: Voices and Visions: A Collection of Primary Resources* by William H. Shulman, comp. (1-56711-207-2) $18.95

491 *Book 8: Resource Guide: A Comprehensive Listing of Media for Further Study* by William L. Shulman, comp. (1-56711-208-0) $18.95

492 Rosen, Philip E. and Eric Joseph Epstein. *Dictionary of the Holocaust: Biography, Geography and Terminology*. Westport, CT: Greenwood, 1997. 384 pp. (hc. 0-31330-355-X) $49.95

493 Snyder, Louis L. *Encyclopedia of the Third Reich*. New York: Marlowe, 1994. 410 pp. (pbk. 1-56924-917-2) $16.95

494 United States Holocaust Memorial Museum. *Historical Atlas of the Holocaust*. New York: Macmillan, 1996. 252 pp. (hc. 0-02-897451-4)
Gr. 4-12. A historical atlas of the Holocaust is presented in nine subject sections: "Europe Before the War," "The Holocaust in Eastern Europe," "Nazi Extermination Camps," "The Holocaust in Western Europe," "The Holocaust in Central Europe," "The Holocaust in Southern Europe and Hungary," "Rescue and Jewish Armed Resistance," "Death Marches and Liberation," and "Postwar Europe, 1945-1950." The maps are large, in color, and beautifully detailed. This is a scrupulously researched, essential reference tool. An absolute must for all collections.

495 Wigoder, Geoffrey, ed. *The Holocaust: A Grolier Student Library*. 4 vols. New York: Grolier, 1997. (hc. 0-7172-7637-6) $169.00
Gr. 6-9. A thoroughly researched encyclopedia providing good introductory information about the Holocaust by examining a variety of incidents, events, and personalities in affected countries. The text is written in a clear, conversational style. The alphabetically arranged entries vary in length from one paragraph to several pages. Cross-references are provided. The information is attractively laid out with text in a two-column format and highlighted boxes frequently appear offering quotations, anecdotes, or further relevant information. Large photographs are offered on each page. Each volume has an individual index and the fourth volume contains a cumulative index, including an excellent subject index. An incomplete annotated bibliography is also offered. An excellent resource for any public or school library.

Making Connections

Anti-Semitism throughout History and the World

It is pointless to teach students about the Holocaust if we do not also teach them that anti-Semitism existed long before it and has persisted since. Without the long history of anti-Semitism that existed in Europe prior to the Holocaust, Hitler could not have carried out his "Final Solution" to its great extent. These are facts that must be impressed upon students if they are to truly understand the motives and meaning of the Holocaust.

496 Baram, Meir. *The Parnas*. Trans. Esther von Handel. Illus. Aharon
     Shevo. New York: Feldheim, 1987. 183 pp. (hc. 0-87306-393-7)
     (pbk. 0-87306-400-3)
Gr. 7-12. Upon hearing of the pogroms of the Christians of the First Crusade, The Parnas, head of the Cologne Jewish community, begins a selfless effort to save his people. Includes an introduction putting the story in historical context and a glossary of Hebrew terms. Illustrated with black-and-white drawings. Translated from the Hebrew.

497 Gray, Bettyanne. *Manya's Story*. Minneapolis: Lerner, 1978. 127
     pp. (hc. 0-8225-0762-5)
Gr. 4-8. A biography telling the story of how Manya Abramson and her family fought to survive the repeated pogroms and persecutions inflicted upon the Jews in the Russian Ukraine during the years 1917-1921. Includes a chronology of events relating to Manya's story, black-and-white photographs, and a glossary of Hebrew and Yiddish terms.

498 Hautzig, Esther. *The Endless Steppe: Growing Up in Siberia*. New
     York: HarperCollins, 1987. 256 pp. (pbk. 0-06-447027-X) $3.95
Gr. 5-9. The author relates the experiences of her and her family when, in June 1941, the Soviet government deports them from their home in Vilna, Poland, to Siberia. For five years, they lived in exile, struggling against hunger and the harsh elements. A vivid, moving account of one family's persecution and ultimate triumph. Inspiring and memorable.

499 Hesse, Karen. *Letters from Rifka*. New York: Puffin, 1992. 148
    pp. (pbk. 0-14-036391-2) $3.99
Gr. 4-8. In letters to her cousin, twelve-year-old Rifka chronicles her
family's flight from brutal persecution in Russia in 1919. An incredibly
moving story told with great sensitivity and simplicity. Includes a
historical note by the author, placing the story in context.

500 Lasky, Kathryn. *The Night Journey*. Illus. Trina Schart Hyman.
    New York: Warne, 1981. 150 pp. (hc. 0-7232-6201-2)
Gr. 4-8. Rachel secretly visits Nana Sashie's room to hear her great-
grandmother tell stories of how the Czar's army persecuted Jews in
Russia and how she devised a plan for her family to escape. Illustrated
with black-and-white drawings.

501 Lehmann, Marcus. *Between Two World*. Trans. Chani Feferkorn.
    New York: Feldheim, 1982. 175 pp. (hc. 0-87306-295-7)
Gr. 7-12. A young man is forced to choose between the conflicting
worlds of Christianity and Judaism. Translated from the German.

502 —. *The Royal Resident: A Historical Tale*. Trans. Chani
    Feferkorn. New York: Feldheim, 1981. 236 pp.
Gr. 9-12. The Polish Court of Augustus Saxony plots against Jews.
Originally published in 1964 by Honigson in London. Translated from
the German.

503 Phillips, Mildred. *The Sign in Mendel's Window*. Illus. Margot
    Zemach. New York: Macmillan, 1984. 24 pp. (hc. 0-02-774600-3)
Gr. 2-4. When a stranger comes to Kosnov, a small Russian village,
and accuses Mendel the butcher, a Jew, of stealing his money, the
whole town joins in to show the authorities who is really guilty.
Illustrated with very appealing watercolor paintings.

504 Pitt, Nancy. *Beyond the High White Wall*. New York: Charles
    Scribner's Sons, 1986. 135 pp. (hc. 0-684-18663-2)
Gr. 5-9. When thirteen-year-old Libby witnesses the murder of a
peasant outside her small village in the Russian Ukraine in 1903, she
triggers a wave of hate against her Jewish family that prompts them to
consider immigrating to America.

505 Sherman, Eileen Bluestone. *Monday in Odessa*. Philadelphia:
    Jewish Publication Society in America, 1986. 164 pp.
    (hc. 0-8276-0262-6) $10.95

Gr. 5-10. Twelve-year-old Marina Biger is devastated when her parents announce their plans to apply for an exit visa to leave the Soviet Union.

Apartheid in South Africa

The apartheid system in South Africa is the best modern example we have of institutionalized racism. South Africa's apartheid can be connected to Nazi Germany's racial laws passed in the 1930s, which stripped Jews of most of their civil rights, including holding government office, marrying Gentiles, or teaching in schools and universities. The institutionalized racism in apartheid South Africa and Nazi Germany can also be connected to the post-Civil War segregation laws imposed by the United States against its black citizens.

506 Gordon, Shelia. *Waiting for the Rain*. New York: Orchard, 1987.
     (hc. 0-531-05726-7) $12.95; (pbk. 0-553-27911-4) $3.99
Gr. 7-12. Two boys, white Frikkie and black Tengo, grow up on the same farm in South Africa but lead very different lives. Frikkie, nephew of the farm owner, joins the army. Tengo, son of the farm foreman, goes to the city where he desperately tries to get an education and is drawn into the struggle against the white apartheid government.

507 Isadora, Rachel. *At the Crossroads*. New York: Greenwillow,
     1991. (hc. 0-688-05270-3)
All Ages. Striking depictions of life in a South African shantytown are the setting for this story of painful family separations and joyful reunions to life. Isadora's simple text and stunning watercolor paintings are superb.

508 Lewin, Hugh. *Jafta: The Homecoming*. Illus. Lisa Kopper. New
     York: Knopf, 1994. (hc. 0-679-84722-7)
Gr. 4-8. A simple but moving story told from the point of view of young Jafta about the joyful reunion of a family separated by apartheid.

509 Mathabane, Mark. *Kaffir Boy: The True Story of a Black Youth's
     Coming of Age in Apartheid South Africa*. New York: NAL, 1986.
     354 pp. (pbk. 0-452-25943-6) $9.95
Gr. 9-12. *Kaffir* is the South African equivalent for *nigger* in the United States. This is an extraordinarily vivid and powerful autobiography that was banned until recently in South Africa. Mathabane tells of his growing up in an environment of fear and poverty in a Johannesburg

ghetto. He escaped to a better life when he came to the United States on a tennis scholarship.

510 Naidoo, Beverley. *No Turning Back*. New York: HarperCollins, 1997. (hc. 0-06-027505-7)
Gr. 5-10. When twelve-year-old Sipho can no longer stand the regular beatings from his stepfather, he runs away to the tough streets of Johannesburg where he learns to survive the hard way. This is a riveting story set in the confusing world of post-apartheid South Africa where longtime racial barriers are slowly collapsing.

511 Paton, Alan. *Cry, the Beloved Country*. New York: Simon & Schuster, 1995. 320 pp. (pbk. 0-684-81894-9) $12.00
Gr. 7-12. The classic story about the ordeal of Reverend Stephen Kumalo, a black country parson who goes to the city seeking his son Absalom only to find he is condemned to hang for the murder of a white man. A piercing, profoundly moving story.

512 Paton, Jonathan. *The Land and People of South Africa*. New York: HarperCollins, 1990. 288 pp. (hc. 0-397-32361-1) $14.95
Gr. 7-12. The son of author Alan Paton attacks white versions of South African history and offers a far more multicultural perspective.

513 Rochman, Hazel, ed. *Somehow Tenderness Survives: Stories of Southern Africa*. New York: HarperCollins, 1988.
(hc. 0-06-025022-4) $12.95; (pbk. 0-06-447063-6) $3.25
Gr. 7-12. A collection of ten stories and autobiographical accounts of prominent adult southern African authors who convey from many interesting perspectives what it is like to live under apartheid. Authors featured include: Nadine Gordimer, Doris Lessing, and Mark Mathabane.

The Armenian Genocide

The Turkish extermination of the Armenians, beginning in 1915 and ending in 1923, was the first instance of an organized, mass genocide. Over one and one-half million people are believed to have died. This genocide, as destructive and horrific as it was, has never been accorded the same attention or study as the Holocaust. To show students that genocide was not the exclusive invention of the Nazis, it is essential to examine this event.

514 Arlen, Michael J. *A Passage to Ararat*. New York: Farrar, Straus

& Giroux, 1975. 293 pp.
Gr. 9-12. Told in an engaging, dramatic style like that of a novel, Arlen looks at Armenia and what it was to be Armenian. A considerable portion of the book examines the Armenian genocide.

515   Balakian, Peter. *Black Dog of Fate: A Memoir.* New York: Basic Books, 1997. 289 pp. (hc. 0-465-00704-X) $24.00
Gr. 9-12. Balakian explores his Armenian past and discovers the personal effects genocide had upon his own family.

516   Bedoukian, Kerop. *Some of Us Survived: The Story of an Armenian Boy.* New York: Farrar, Straus & Giroux, 1978. 242 pp. (hc. 0-374-37132-6)
Gr. 6-12. Nine-year-old Kerop Bedoukian witnessed the horrors of genocide when Turks occupied his hometown of Sivas. With his father imprisoned and home destroyed, Kerop, his mother, and the rest of his family were forced to join over 30,000 other Armenians in the death march from Sivas to Aleppo. Kerop was one of the survivors. A vivid remembrance of the Armenian genocide. Includes a glossary.

517   Hovannisian, Richard G., ed. *The Armenian Genocide in Perspective.* New Brunswick, NJ: Transaction, 1986. 215 pp. (hc. 0-88738-096-4); (pbk. 0-88738-6360-9)
Gr. 9-12. A collection of scholarly investigations and analyses of various dimensions of the Armenian Genocide. Indexed by subject. For advanced students.

518   Kherdian, David. *The Road from Home: The Story of an Armenian Girl.* New York: Puffin, 1988. 238 pp. (pbk. 0-14-032524-7) $4.95
Gr. 5-9. From 1915-1923, the Turkish government committed mass genocide against its Armenian population. The author tells the story of his mother's childhood in Turkey on the eve of this holocaust. A poignant, revealing account of an often overlooked period in history. Compare to "ethnic cleansing" in the former Yugoslavia. A Newbery Honor Book. Originally published by Greenwillow in 1979.

519   Miller, Donald E. and Lorna Touryan Miller. *Survivors: An Oral History of the Armenian Genocide.* Berkeley: University of California Press, 1993. 242 pp. (hc. 0-520-0784-1)
Gr. 9-12. This book is the first comprehensive study of the Armenian genocide based on survivor testimony. Using these testimonies as a primary source, the authors recreate events of the Armenian genocide.

Includes black-and white photographs of some of the survivors interviewed, a map of past and present Armenia, an interview guide the authors used to collect their information, extensive chapter notes, and a subject index. An outstanding, informative work.

The Cambodian Genocide

Though not as organized as the Armenian genocide or the Holocaust, Pol Pot's Khmer Rouge regime managed to slaughter millions of their fellow Cambodians in the name of cultural purity in the 1970s. Despite the worldwide attention the Holocaust in Europe commanded, genocides like this still occurred. A very important point to impress upon students.

520 Criddle, Joan D. and Teeda Butt Mam. *To Destroy You is No Loss: The Odyssey of a Cambodian Family*. New York: Atlantic Monthly Press, 1987. 289 pp. (hc. 0-87113-116-1)
Gr. 7-12. The story of the harrowing ordeal of the Butt family in Cambodia. After four years in a forced labor camp, they made a daring escape from their country's holocaust to a refugee camp in Thailand and finally made their way to America.

521 Ngor, Haing with Roger Warner. *A Cambodian Odyssey*. New York: Macmillan, 1987. 478 pp. (hc. 0-02-589330-0) $19.95
Gr. 9-12. The incredible story of a man who lost his family and witnessed the total destruction of his homeland. He spent four years living under the brutal Khmer Rouge regime. A vivid, harrowing account offering great insight into this horrific period of Cambodia's history. Includes black-and-white photographs and a subject index.
Haing Ngor portrayed Dith Pran, whose experiences are chronicled in the motion picture *The Killing Fields*.

522 Pran, Dith, comp. *Children of Cambodia's Killing Fields: Memoirs by Survivors*. Ed. Kim DePaul. New Haven, CT: Yale University Press, 1997. 199 pp. (hc. 0-300-06839-5)
Gr. 7-12. An extraordinary collection of eyewitness accounts of life in Cambodia during Pol Pot's Khmer Rouge regime from 1975 to 1979. Survivors who were children at the time wrote all of the accounts. Dith Pran, whose own experiences are depicted in the film *The Killing Fields*, collected the accounts. Includes a glossary.

523 Szymusiak, Molyda. *The Stones Cry Out: A Cambodian*

Childhood, 1975-1980. Trans. Linda Coverdale. New York: Hill and Wang, 1986. 245 pp. (hc. 0-86-1310957) $17.95
Gr. 7-12. The author was twelve years old and the daughter of a high official when her peaceful life in Phnom Penh was shattered by the Khmer Rouge takeover. An especially vivid personal narrative. Translated from the French.

524 Welaratna, Usha. *Beyond the Killing Fields: Voices of Nine Cambodian Survivors in America.* Stanford, CA: Stanford University Press, 1993. 285 pp. (hc. 0-8047-2139-4)
Gr. 7-12. Cambodians of various ethnic and socioeconomic backgrounds recount their experiences living under the brutal Khmer Rouge regime.

The Enslavement of Africans

It will never be known for sure how many Africans were kidnapped and sold into a lifetime of slavery in the Americas, but over the hundreds of years it occurred, victims numbered in the millions. Europeans and Americans justified the institution of slavery with the belief that Africans were an inferior race and therefore suitable for exploitation by a superior master race. There is no difference between this view and that of Hitler and the Nazis, who believed all "non-Aryans" were inferior and worthy only of serving the Germans, the master race. This is an obvious and necessary connection to make to the Holocaust.

525 Berry, James. *Ajeemah and His Son.* New York: HarperCollins, 1992. 96 pp. (hc. 0-06-021044-3) $13.89; (pbk. 0-06-440523-0) $4.50
Gr. 4-9. Ajeemah and his eighteen-year-old son are kidnapped by fellow Africans and sold into slavery in Jamaica in the early nineteenth century. They are sold to separate owners and never see each other again. Each is affected differently and their experiences are told in alternating chapters. A powerful, unforgettable, and heartbreaking story. Berry is exceptional at revealing the utter inhumanity of slavery.

526 Feelings, Tom. *The Middle Passage: White Ships/Black Cargo.* New York: Dial, 1995. 80 pp. (hc. 0-8037-1804-7) $45.00
Gr. 5-12. An astonishing, profoundly moving chronicle of the cruel and terrifying journey of enslaved Africans across the Atlantic Ocean rendered in wordless, black-and-white illustrations. Feelings created the

artwork using pen and ink and tempura on rice paper. The illustrations are intensely emotional, haunting, and horrific. An introduction by Dr. John Henrik Clarke offers excellent historical background on the African slave trade.

527 Hurmence, Belinda. *Slavery Time: When I Was Chillun*. New York: Putnam, 1997. 98 pp. (pbk. 0-399-23194-3) $8.95
Gr. 5-12. A collection of twelve oral histories of former slaves selected from the 2,000 interviews archived in the Slave Narratives of the Library of Congress and collected by the Works Progress Administration in 1936. These are extraordinary first hand accounts of slaves from different parts of the southern United States. Generously illustrated with many black-and-white photographs. Includes a bibliography of suggestions for further reading.

528 Katz, William Loren. *Breaking the Chains: African-American Slave Resistance*. New York: Atheneum, 1990. (hc. 0-689-31493-0) $14.95
Gr. 7-12. A detailed account of the harshness of slavery and the many forms of resistance. Katz bases his text largely upon slave testimony, the recollections of slaveowners, and public records. See also *Rebels Against Slavery* by the McKissacks.

529 Lester, Julius. *From Slave Ship to Freedom Road*. Illus. Rod Brown. New York: Dial, 1998. 40 pp. (hc. 0-8037-1893-4) $17.00
Gr. 5-10. Lester's profound, passionate, and provocative meditations on slavery are perfectly complemented with Brown's striking illustrations. Compare the power of this book with that of Tom Feelings's *Middle Passage* and Lester's *To Be a Slave*.

530 —. *To Be a Slave*. Illus. Tom Feelings. New York: Dial, 1968. 160 pp. (hc. 0-8037-8955-6) $16.99
Gr. 5-10. An extraordinarily vivid, profoundly moving arrangement of selections of slave narratives. Lester succeeds in bringing the grim, horrific realities of slave life to light. The text is complemented with haunting black-and-white drawings. Includes a historical note by the author and a bibliography. A Newbery Honor Book.

531 McKissack, Patricia C. and Frederick L. McKissack. *Christmas in the Big House, Christmas in the Quarters*. Illus. John Thompson. New York: Scholastic, 1994. 68 pp. (hc. 0-590-43027-0) $15.95
Gr. 3-7. In the period just before the Civil War, a comparison and

contrast is depicted of how Christmas is celebrated in the big plantation house and the slave quarters. Well-researched and beautifully presented. The excellent text is complemented with colorful, expressive acrylic paintings. Includes historical notes on the text and a bibliography.

532 —. *Rebels Against Slavery: American Slave Revolts.* New York: Scholastic, 1996. 191 pp. (hc. 0-590-45735-7) $14.95
Gr. 6-12. A collection of scrupulously researched and well written profiles of men and women who heroically led slave rebellions and resistance movements in North America. Slaves profiled include: John Brown, Toussaint Louverture, Gabriel Prosser, Harriet Tubman, Nat Turner, and Denmark Vesey. Black-and-white reproductions of paintings, drawings, and documents appear throughout. Includes a chronology of important dates, bibliography, and a subject index.

533 Mellon, James, ed. *Bullwhip Days: The Slaves Remember.* New York: Avon, 1988. 460 pp. (pbk. 0-380-70884-1) $12.95
Gr. 7-12. An outstanding collection of oral slave narratives collected by the Federal Writer's Project in the 1930s. A superb primary historical source for students. See also Belinda Hurmence's *Slavery Time: When I Was Chillun.*

534 Paulsen, Gary. *Nightjohn.* New York: Delacorte, 1993. 92 pp. (hc. 0-385-30838-8) $14.00 (pbk.)
Gr. 5-9. Twelve-year-old Sarny's brutal life as a plantation slave in the 1850s Deep South becomes even more dangerous when she meets Nightjohn, a slave who offers to teach her to read. Paulsen vividly depicts the brutality and utter inhumanity of slave life. He also tells an inspiring story of a young girl willing to risk her life to learn to read. A powerful, moving story. Paulsen continues the story of Sarny's life in *Sarny: A Life Remembered* (Delacorte, 1997, hc. 0-385-32195-3).

535 Thomas, Velma Maia. *Lest We Forget: The Passage from Africa to Slavery and Emancipation.* New York: Crown, 1997. 32pp. (hc. 0-609-60030-3) $29.95
Gr. 5-10. An outstanding three dimensional interactive book chronicling the enslavement of Africans in the United States. The photographs and documents featured in the book are taken from the Black Holocaust Exhibit in Atlanta. The author is the creator and curator of the exhibit. The text is most informative and the interactive parts are beautifully designed and arranged. This is an outstanding book

for reluctant readers. The fragile contents of the book will mean a short circulation life, but this is a must for any collection. For older students, see James Mellon's *Bullwhip Days*.

Ethnic Cleansing in the Former Yugoslavia

Although not conducted on as vast a scale, "ethnic cleansing" in the former Yugoslavia has been aptly compared to the Holocaust. Mass graves continue to be unearthed, and there are conflicts in this region that have yet to be resolved. There is no better connection to make of the past to the present.

536 Filipovic, Zlata. *Zlata's Diary: A Child's Life in Sarajevo*. Trans. Christina Pribichevich-Zoric. New York: Viking, 1994. 200 pp. (hc. 0-670-85724-6) $16.95
Gr. 5-12. Thirteen-year-old Zlata offers vivid and compelling observations of life in war ravaged Sarajevo. Includes color photographs of Zlata and her family. Compare with Anne Frank's *Diary of a Young Girl*.

537 Gjelten, Tom. *Sarajevo Daily: A City and Its Newspaper Under Siege*. New York: HarperCollins, 1995. 270 pp. (hc. 0-060-19052-3) $20.00
Gr. 9-12. A correspondent for National Public Radio offers a vivid account of daily life in Sarajevo while it was besieged from 1992-1994. Includes black-and-white photographs and a subject index.

538 Mead, Alice. *Adem's Cross*. New York: Farrar, Straus & Giroux, 1996. 132 pp. (hc. 0-374-30057-7) $15.00
Gr. 5-9. Adem is a fourteen-year-old ethnic Albanian living in Kosovo of the former Yugoslavia. Occupied by the Serbian military, the Albanian population suffers the constant persecution and terror of "ethnic cleansing." Through Adem's experiences, Mead creates a graphic, intensely realistic portrait of a contemporary holocaust. Includes an author's note explaining the story's historical context. See also *Zlata's Diary*.

539 Open Society Fund. *Dear Unknown Friend, Children's Letters from Sarajevo*. New York: Open Society Fund, 1994. 67 pp. (pbk. 0-9641568-0-6)
Gr. 4-12. A collection of drawings and letters written by children in Sarajevo during the siege of that city to pen pals in America. These

children tell extraordinary stories of their experiences in the war. An incredibly moving and poignant collection. Compare this work to *I Never Saw Another Butterfly*.

540 UNICEF. *I Dream of Peace: Images of War by Children of Former Yugoslavia*. New York: HarperCollins, 1994. 80 pp. (hc. 0-06-251128-9) $12.95
Gr. 3-12. A moving collection of drawings and writings by children whose lives were shattered by the death and devastation of war in the former Yugoslavia. Includes a preface by Maurice Sendak. Compare to *I Never Saw Another Butterfly*.

Genocide and Prejudice

Studying the Holocaust, other genocides, or any other instances of prejudice must be done in more than their historical contexts. Students must confront the questions of what prejudice is, its causes and effects, how it is part of the human condition, the meaning of genocide, and other broader important issues. These issues can be examined by looking at the personal stories of individual victims.

541 Altman, Linda Jacobs. *Genocide: The Systematic Killing of a People*. Springfield, NJ: Enslow, 1995. 112 pp. (hc. 0-89490-664-X)
Gr. 5-12. Explores the meaning of genocide, and depicts some of the most brutal examples from history. Offers insight into the psychology of genocide from the perspectives of both victims and perpetrators. A brief, but informative and well-organized book. Includes black-and-white photographs, chapter notes, bibliography, and subject index. From the *Issues in Focus* series.

542 Adryszewski, Tricia. *The Militia Movement in America: Before and After Oklahoma City*. Brookfield, CT: Millbrook, 1997. 126 pp. (0-7613-0119-4)
Gr. 9-12. Explores the roots and growth of militia movements in the United States, their ideologies, and their legacies of hate and terrorism. A very good overview of the subject. Illustrated throughout with black-and-white photographs. Includes chapter notes, suggestions for further reading, and a subject index.

543 Augenbraum, Harold and Ilan Stavans, eds. *Growing Up Latino: Memoirs and Stories*. New York: Houghton Mifflin, 1993. (hc. 0-395-66124-2) $22.95; (pbk. 0-395-66124-2) $12.95

130 Making Connections

Gr. 9-12. Twenty-five selections from a diverse group of authors, including Sandra Cisneros, Edward Rivera, and Richard Rodriguez. A wonderful collection of varied, insightful voices.

544 Cook, Fred J. *The Ku Klux Klan: America's Recurring Nightmare.* New York: Julian Messner, 1989. 152 pp. (hc. 0-671-68421-3) Gr. 7-12. A concise, informative history of the Klan from its post-Civil War beginnings. Cook looks at the consistent pattern of the bigotry, intolerance, and violence of the Klan since its founding. Includes a bibliography and subject index.

545 Ezekiel, Raphael S. *The Racist Mind: Portraits of American Neo-Nazis and Klansmen.* New York: Penguin, 1996. 330 pp. (hc. 0-670-83958-2); (pbk. 0-14-023449-7) $12.95 Gr. 9-12. An in-depth, enlightening look at organized hate movements in America. Through detailed research and firsthand observations, the author has created a window into the terrifying world of racist movements like the Aryan Nation and Ku Klux Klan. This vivid, disturbing book is essential to understanding the ideologies of American racist movements. There is unfortunately no index, but there is an appendix of recommendations for further reading.

546 Gay, Kathlyn. *Neo-Nazis: A Growing Threat.* Springfield, NJ: Enslow, 1997. 112 pp. (hc. 0-89490-901-0) Gr. 7-12. A general but informative overview of neo-Nazism: its history, ideology, and organizations and activities connected with the movement. Special attention is given to ways in which individuals can help combat hate crimes and prejudice. Includes stock black-and-white photographs, chapter notes, suggestions for further reading, and a subject index. From the *Issues in Focus.*

547 Gillam, Scott. *Discrimination: Prejudice in Action.* Springfield, NJ: Enslow, 1995. 128 pp. (hc. 0-89490-643-7) Gr. 7-12. Examines the many forms of discrimination (e.g., age, disability, gender, race, sexual orientation), discusses its consequences and ramifications upon society, and suggests ways in which individuals can fight against it. Includes stock black-and-white photographs, chapters notes, a glossary, suggestions for further reading, and a subject index. An unremarkable but informative overview of the issue. From the *Multicultural Issues* series.

548 Landau, Elaine. *The White Power Movement: America's Racist*

Hate Groups. Brookfield, CT: Millbrook, 1993. 96 pp.
(hc. 1-56294-327-8)
Gr. 5-10. The author explores the origins and developments of white
supremacist groups in the United States. Certain factions such as the
Aryan Nation, Ku Klux Klan, and the Order are given special attention.
A good, general introduction to this topic. Illustrated throughout with
black-and-white photographs. Includes chapter notes, suggestions for
further reading, a directory of organizations, and a subject index.

549 Lee, Marie G. *Finding My Voice.* New York: Houghton Mifflin,
     1992. (hc. 0-395-62134-8) $13.95
Gr. 7-12. High school senior Ellen Sung is being pressured by her strict
Korean immigrant parents to go to Harvard, but she is more interested
in friends, romance, and fun in her small Minnesota town. To make
Ellen's life even more complicated and difficult is the racism she
encounters from some of her classmates, and even a teacher. Lee's
story is a bit too dense and awkward and tense at times, but her
characters are beautifully drawn and memorable.

550 McCuen, Gary E. *The Militia Movement and Hate Groups in
     America.* New York: GEM, 1996. 160 pp. (hc. 0-86596-135-2)
Gr. 9-12. A collection of articles examining such issues as domestic
terrorism, ethnocentrism, race bias, the militia movement, and white
supremacy. Each section concludes with suggested activities for
classroom discussion and further study. The goal of the book is to teach
students critical thinking skills through the study of these various
issues. Includes a bibliography and subject index. An excellent book to
use in the classroom.

551 McKissack, Patricia C. and Frederick L. McKissack. *Taking a
     Stand Against Racism and Racial Discrimination.* New York:
     Watts, 1990. 157 pp. (hc. 0-531-10924-0)
Gr. 6-10. The authors examine racism and racial discrimination in the
United States, from Revolutionary War days to contemporary times.
Individuals and organizations that have worked against racism and
discrimination are profiled. Attention is also given to ways with which
an individual can act against or cope with acts of racism. Illustrated
throughout with black-and-white photographs. Includes a directory of
civil rights organizations, chapter notes, a bibliography, and subject
index.

552 Muse, Daphne. *Prejudice: Stories about Hate, Ignorance,*

Revelation, and Transformation. New York: Hyperion, 1995. 212
   pp. (hc. 0-7868-0024-8) $16.95; (pbk. 0-7868-1057-2)
Gr. 7-12. An excellent collection of short stories and excerpts from
novels that deal with various dimensions of prejudice. Among the
authors represented are Chris Crutcher, Sandra Cisneros, Marie Lee,
and Jacqueline Woodson. Includes suggestions for further reading and
brief biographical profiles of the contributors.

553 Nye, Naomi Shihab. *Habibi.* New York: Simon & Schuster, 1997.
      260 pp. (hc. 0-689-80149-1)
Gr. 5-10. Fourteen-year-old Liyana is very unhappy when her father, a
native Palestinian, announces the family is leaving St. Louis to move to
Jerusalem. Liyana slowly adjusts and, when she meets Omer, a Jewish
boy, her homesickness disappears completely. Though mainly a
colorful coming of age story, the constant conflicts and violence
between Jews and Palestinians always figures prominently in the
background. A distinguished novel about a place and its people one
seldom sees depicted in young adult literature.

554 Pascoe, Elaine. *Racial Prejudice: Why Can't We Overcome?* New
      York: Watts, 1997. 128 pp. (hc. 0-531-11402-3)
Gr. 5-10. The author surveys the history of prejudice against minority
groups in the United States, discusses its causes, observes its damaging
effects upon society, and considers ways that we may go about
eliminating prejudice. A well-organized, highly readable introduction
to the subject. A good place to begin individual or classroom study of
the subject. Includes stock black-and-white photographs, source notes,
suggestions for further reading, a directory of organizations to contact,
and a subject index.

555 Tillage, Leon Walter. *Leon's Story.* Illus. Susan L. Roth. Farrar,
      Straus & Giroux, 1997. 112 pp. (hc. 0-374-34379-9) $14.00
Gr. 4-up. Leon Tillage grew up a sharecropper's son in a small North
Carolina town where he had to endure the terrorism of the Ku Klux
Klan and other common injustices before the Civil Rights Movement.
In a very simple, forthright prose, Leon remembers these days without
bitterness or malice, revealing the senselessness and stupidity of
racism. His simple honesty and sincerity is utterly charming.

556 Yep, Laurence. *The Star Fisher.* New York: Morrow, 1991.
      (hc. 0-688-09365-5) $12.95; (pbk. 0-440-20433-X) $3.50
Gr. 5-10. Set in the 1920s this is the story of fifteen-year-old Joan Lee

who was born in America, but when her family moves to Clarksburg, Virginia, to open a laundry, they are the first Chinese Americans the people in town have ever seen. Some of Joan's classmates cannot accept she is an American. Based upon stories about Yep's own grandparents, this is a poignant, often humorous, novel that explores prejudice.

Hiroshima and Nagasaki

Hundreds of thousands of innocent people were instantly annihilated in the dropping of a single bomb on each of these two cities. Thousands more died quickly and slowly afterward from its devastating after-effects. The justification for using the bombs was that it brought the surrender of Japan without invasion, which could possibly have cost the lives of tens of thousands of American soldiers. Some historians have questioned why the atomic bomb was used on Japan and not Germany. Was it a racially motivated decision? The bombing of Dresden was as costly in lives lost as either of the Hiroshima or Nagasaki bombings, so one can question the validity of such an argument. Looking at the human dimensions of these catastrophes will raise many questions and much discussion about the ethics of the decision to drop the bombs.

557 Coerr, Eleanor. *Sadako*. Illus. Ed Young. New York: Putnam,
       1993. 48 pp. (hc. 0-399-21771-1)
Gr. 2-6. Coerr tells the story of Sadako Sasaki in a new text illustrated with beautiful, haunting pastel paintings by Young.

558 —. *Sadako and the Thousand Paper Cranes*. Illus. Ronald Himler.
       New York: G.P. Putnam's Sons, 1977. 64 pp. (hc. 0-399-20520-9)
Gr. 2-4. The moving story of Sadako Sasaki, the heroine who died of leukemia at age twelve as a result of the radiation she was exposed to from the Hiroshima atomic bomb ten years earlier. The title refers to a Japanese legend that holds that if a person who is ill makes a thousand paper cranes, the gods will grant that person's wish to be well again. Illustrated with affecting black-and-white drawings.

559 Hersey, John. *Hiroshima*. New York: Knopf, 1985. 144 pp.
       (hc. 0-394-54844-2) $25.00; (pbk. 0-679-721037) $5.99
Gr. 7-12. Hersey recounts hour by hour what becomes of six human beings who were in Hiroshima when the atomic bomb was dropped. The author's brilliant, simple narrative is absolutely engrossing.

560 Maruki, Toshi. *Hiroshima No Pika*. New York: Lothrop, Lee and
     Shepard, 1980. 48 pp. (hc. 0-688-01297-3)
Gr. 2-6. A mother recounts what happened to her family during the
flash that destroyed Hiroshima in 1945. A stunning picture book full of
unforgettable horrific images.

561 Mattingly, Christobel. *The Miracle Tree*. Illus. Marianne
     Yamaguchi. San Diego: Gulliver/HBJ, 1985. 32 pp.
     (hc. 0-15-200530-7)
Gr. 3-6. After they are separated by the atomic bomb explosion, a
husband, wife, and mother carry on their lives in the ruins of Nagasaki
until they are reunited one Christmas. An inspiring story illustrated
with beautiful, sensitive charcoal drawings.

562 Yep, Laurence. *Hiroshima: A Novella*. New York: Scholastic,
     1995. 56 pp. (hc. 0-590-20832-2) $9.95
Gr. 3-6 A taut, engrossing tale of how the Hiroshima bombing affects
twelve-year-old Sachi and her older sister Riko. Based upon true life
accounts written by survivors of the Hiroshima bombing.

The Horrors of War

563 Attema, Martha. *A Time to Choose*. Victoria, B.C., Canada: Orca,
     1995. 166 pp. (pbk. 1-55143-045-2) $6.95
Gr. 7-12. In 1944 Holland, sixteen-year-old Johannes van der Meer has
had to endure the Nazi occupation for five long years. Now he has to
face the bitter fact that his father has turned collaborator and made
outcasts of the entire family. Johannes must make the tough choice of
whether to stay loyal to his father or to his country and join the
Resistance. This is a fast-paced, engrossing story of being forced to
make hard choices in very difficult times. Includes a historical note,
bibliography, and a pronunciation guide to the Dutch names.

564 Choi, Sook Nyul. *Year of Impossible Goodbyes*. Boston:
     Houghton Mifflin, 1991. 171 pp. (hc. 0-395-574-196) $13.95;
     (pbk. 0-440-40759-1) $4.50
Gr. 4-9. Ten-year-old Sookan and her family must endure the cruelties
of the Japanese military occupying Korea during World War II. A very
powerful, moving story of a young girl experiencing first hand the
horrors of war. Sookan's story continues in two sequels: *Echoes of the
White Giraffe* (Houghton Mifflin, 1993, hc. 0-395-64721-5, pbk. 0-
440-40970-5) and *Gathering of Pearls* (Houghton Mifflin, 1994, hc. 0-

395-67437-9).

565 Crane, Stephen. *The Red Badge of Courage*. New York: NAL/
      Dutton, 1997. (pbk. 0-451-52647-3) $3.95
Gr. 9-12. The classic psychological study of a young Civil War soldier
struggling to cope with the horrors of war. The novel remains as
powerful today as it was when first published in 1895.

566 Denenberg, Barry. *Voices from Vietnam*. New York: Scholastic,
      1995. 251 pp. (hc. 0-590-44267-8) $16.95
Gr. 7-12. Men and women who served in Vietnam tell of their
experiences in their own words. An extraordinary collection of personal
narratives. Includes a chronology, glossary, source notes, and
bibliography.

567 Fenkl, Heinz Isu. *Memories of My Ghost Brother*. New York:
      Plume, 1997. 271 pp. (hc. 0-525-94175-4); (pbk. 0-452-27717-5)
      $11.95
Gr. 10-12. A vivid and powerful autobiographical novel of an
Amerasian boy who comes of age in a Korea ripped apart by bloody,
devastating warfare with the Japanese, the Chinese, and the United
States.

568 Frank, Rudolf. *No Hero for the Kaiser*. Trans. Patricia Crampton.
      Illus. Klaus Steffens. New York: Lothrop, Lee and Shepard, 1986.
      222 pp. (hc. 0-688-06093-5)
Gr. 6-10. Jan, a fourteen-year-old Polish boy whose town is invaded
during World War I, joins a German battalion and experiences the
horrors of battle. Illustrated with occasional black-and-white drawings.

569 Heide, Florence Perry and Judith Heide Gilliand. *Sami and the
      Time of Troubles*. Illus. Ted Lewin. New York: Clarion, 1992. 32
      pp. (hc. 0-395-55964-2) $14.95
Gr. 2-6. Sami, a ten-year-old Lebanese boy living in Beirut suffers the
consequences of the civil war ripping apart his country. The text is
complemented perfectly with Lewin's realistic watercolor illustrations.

570 Lingard, Joan. *Tug of War*. New York: Lodestar, 1989. 194 pp.
      (hc. 0-525-67306-7)
Gr. 5-10. Fourteen-year-old Astra and her twin brother Hugo flee their
home in Latvia and become refugees in 1944 when Germany and
Russia battle for control of their country. Astra and Hugo's story

continues in *Between Two Worlds*, in which they go to Canada after the war as displaced persons (Lodestar, 1991, 0-525-67360-1).

571 Myers, Walter Dean. *Fallen Angels*. New York: Scholastic, 1988. 309 pp. (hc. 0-590-40942-5) $12.95; (pbk. 0-590-40943-3) $4.50
Gr. 7-12. Seventeen-year-old Richie Perry enlists in the army in 1967 and has a horrific tour of duty in Vietnam. This is one of the greatest anti-war novels ever written.

572 Ousseimi, Maria. *Caught in the Crossfire: Growing Up in a War Zone*. New York: Walker, 1995. 120 pp. (hc. 0-802-78363-5) $20.00; (pbk. 0-802-78364-3)
Gr. 7-12. A fascinating, powerful examination on the effects of war upon children. The author examines war zones in Bosnia-Herzegovina, El Salvador, Lebanon, Mozambique, and even Washington, D.C. neighborhoods ravaged by gang warfare. Illustrated with many vivid, sometimes horrific, black-and-white photographs. Includes a subject index.

573 Remarque, Erich Maria. *All Quiet on the Western Front*. Boston: Little, Brown, 1929. (hc. 0-316-73992-8) $22.95; Fawcett, 1996 (pbk. 0-449-911497) $12.00
Gr. 9-12. The horrors of World War I are vividly related through Paul Baumer, a young German soldier whose enthusiasm and patriotism are quickly diminished by the many horrific events he experiences.

574 Trumbo, Dalton. *Johnny Got His Gun*. New York: Bantam, 1984. 244 pp. (pbk. 0-553-27432-5) $6.50
Gr. 9-12. Another graphic novel about World War I told through the perspective of an American soldier. Trumbo is uncompromising in his utterly gruesome depictions of the horrors of war. This is a very interesting novel to compare and contrast with *All Quiet on the Western Front*.

575 Tsuchiya, Yukio. *Faithful Elephants: A True Story of Animals, People, and War*. Trans. Tomoko Tsuchiya Dykes. Illus. Ted Lewin. Boston: Houghton Mifflin, 1988. 32 pp. (hc. 0-395-46555-9)
Gr. 2-6. The heartbreaking, tragic story of John, Tonky, and Wally, three elephants at Ueno Zoo who had to be killed because of the danger of their escape during bombing raids. The moving text is complemented by poignant watercolor paintings. Read this aloud and

you will not have a dry eye in the classroom. Translated from the Japanese.

576 Wassiljewa, Tatjana. *Hostage to War: A True Story*. Trans. Anna Trenter. New York: Scholastic, 1997. 192 pp. (hc. 0-590-13446-9) $15.95
Gr. 5-10. The author was thirteen years old when the Nazis invaded the Soviet Union and Leningrad where she lived. She personalizes the suffering of the millions of Russian civilians during World War II. She tells of her experiences during the occupation, her deportation to Germany to work in forced labor camps, and her poignant homecoming. This is a strong personal narrative, full of detail and emotion. Includes a historical note on the author's life following the war. The English translation comes from a German translation of the original Russian.

577 Westall, Robert. *Gulf*. New York: Scholastic, 1996. 101 pp. (hc. 0-590-22218-X) $14.95
Gr. 5-10. Tom Higgins tells the bizarre story of how his younger brother Andy becomes obsessed with and assumes the role of an Iraqi soldier during the Persian Gulf War. A remarkable anti-war story told through a fascinating supernatural narrative.

578 —. *A Time of Fire*. New York: Scholastic, 1997. 172 pp. (hc. 0-590-47746-3) $15.95
Gr. 5-10. In World War II England, Sonny realizes the real horrors of war when he first loses his mother in a bombing raid and then his father when he goes off to fight in the war to seek revenge but is killed in action. Moving and powerful, as only Westall can make it.

Japanese-American Internment

The United States had its own concentration camps during World War II. They held not prisoners of war, but rather citizens whose only crime was their Japanese ancestry. Though they did not experience the horrors of the victims in Hitler's concentration camps, they did suffer the very indignities and injustices that their own country decried before the rest of the world. There is much to connect between the treatment of Japanese Americans by the United States government and that of the Jews by the Nazi regime.

579 Brimner, Larry Dane. *Voices from the Camps: Internment of*

Japanese Americans During World War II. New York: Watts, 1994.
110 pp. (hc. 0-531-11179-2)
Gr. 7-12. A straightforward, factual account of the events that lead up
to the internment of 110,000 persons of Japanese ancestry. Excerpts
from interviews with people interred appear throughout the book.
Includes many black-and-white photographs depicting life in the prison
camps, a bibliography, glossary, and subject index.

580 Bunting, Eve. *So Far from the Sea.* Illus. Chris K. Soentpiet. New
York: Clarion, 1998. 32 pp. (hc. 0-395-72095-8) $15.00
Gr. K-3. Laura Iwasaki visits the grave of her grandfather at Manzanar,
where thousands of Japanese-American families were interned during
World War II. Bunting's simple, straightforward text and Soentpiet's
finely detailed watercolor paintings complement each other to create a
poignant story about a family remembering a shameful time in
American history.

581 Davis, Daniel S. *Behind Barbed Wire: The Imprisonment of
Japanese Americans during World War II.* New York: Dutton,
1982. (hc. 0-525-26320-9) $15.95
Gr. 7-12. An excellent examination of the imprisonment of Japanese
Americans in internment camps during World War II. Davis's book
stands out among others on this subject because he looks at the broader
issues of Asian-American prejudice in the United States, and the roles
played by the media, public opinion, politicians, courts, and the
president in the wholesale suspension of civil rights on a such a grand
scale. In addition to detailed descriptions of conditions in the camps,
Davis also discusses the difficulties inmates encountered when they
tried to reenter society after the war.

582 Hamanaka, Shelia. *The Journey: Japanese Americans, Racism,
and Renewal.* New York: Orchard, 1990. (hc. 0-531-05849-2)
Gr. 6-12. Based upon the artists mural depicting the internment of
Japanese Americans, Hamanaka tells of the experiences of Japanese
Americans, placing particular emphasis upon their internment during
World War II. She was born after the war, but her parents and siblings
were all interned. It was not until she was much older that she learned
her grandfather had died in the camps. A personal story of prejudice
and injustice told with raw honesty and great passion.

583 Houston, Jeanne Wakatsuki and James D. Houston. *Farewell to Manzanar*. New York: Bantam, 1973. 145 pp. (pbk. 0-553-27258-6) $4.99
Gr. 7-12. Jeanne Wakatsuki was seven years old in 1942 when her family was forced to uproot their lives to go to live in the Manzanar internment camp along with 10,000 other Japanese Americans. This intensely personal and emotional account offers an extraordinary picture of what Japanese Americans were forced to endure during World War II.

584 Stanley, Jerry. *I Am an American: A True Story of Japanese Internment*. New York: Crown, 1994. 102 pp. (hc. 0-517-59786-1)
Gr. 5-12. A well-researched and highly readable account of the removal of Japanese Americans from their homes and their internment in concentration camps built by the United States government during World War II. Illustrated with many striking black-and-white photographs. Indexed by subject.

585 Takashima, Shizuye. *A Child in Prison Camp*. Montreal: Tundra, 1971. 100 pp. (hc. 0-88776-241-7)
Gr. 5-9. Like the United States, the Canadian government also interned its citizens of Japanese descent in concentration camps during World War II. The author describes what the internment was like for Japanese Canadians. No illustrations or index.

586 Tunnell, Michael O. and George W. Chilcoat. *The Children of Topaz: The Story of a Japanese-American Internment Camp*. New York: Holiday House, 1996. 74 pp. (hc. 0-8234-1239-3) $16.95
Gr. 5-9. Based upon the third grade classroom diary of Japanese-American children, the authors depict what life was like for the families forced to live in the internment camp in Utah called Topaz. Illustrated with many candid black-and-white photographs offering a very revealing look at life in the camp. Well-researched and most informative. Includes suggestions for further reading and a subject index.

587 Uchida, Yoshiko. *The Bracelet*. Illus. Joanna Yardley. New York: Philomel, 1993. 32 pp. (hc. 0-399-22503-X) $15.95
Gr. 2-4. In 1942, seven-year-old Emi doesn't want to leave her friends, her school, and her home, but the United States government forces her family to move to an internment camp. On her first day at the camp, Emi loses the bracelet given to her by her best friend Laurie Madison as

a going-away present. Emi comes to realize she does not need more
than her memory to remember her friend. Based upon the author's own
experiences, this poignant story is complemented perfectly with
Yardley's gentle watercolor paintings.

588 —. *Journey to Topaz: A Story of Japanese-American Evacuation.*
    Illus. Donald Carrick. New York: Charles Scribner's Sons, 1971.
    149 pp. (hc. 0-684-12497-1)
Gr. 4-8. When Pearl Harbor is attacked by the Japanese, eleven-year-
old Yuki and her family are declared "enemy aliens" by the FBI, forced
to leave their California home and go to Topaz, a concentration camp in
the Utah desert. A vivid, realistic story. Illustrated with black-and-
white drawings.

Jewish Cultural Heritage

589 Cahn-Lipman, David E. *The Book of Jewish Knowledge: 613
    Basic Facts about Judaism.* Northvale, NJ: Jason Aronson, 1994.
    478 pp. (pbk. 1-56821-182-1) $24.95
Gr. 5-up. A collection of brief, alphabetically arranged articles offering
general information about various facets of Jewish Culture and
Judaism. A fine starting place for research.

590 Dawidowicz, Lucy S. *The Golden Tradition: Jewish Life and
    Thought in Eastern Europe.* New York: Schocken, 1984. 502 pp.
    (pbk. 0-8052-0768-8) $15.95
Gr. 9-12. An anthology reflecting Jewish culture in Eastern Europe,
from the sixteenth century through 1939. An important resource that
shows the great loss to civilization suffered as a result of the Holocaust.

591 Gurko, Miriam. *Theodor Herzl, the Road to Israel.* Illus. Erika
    Weihs. Philadelphia: Jewish Publication Society of America, 1988.
    89 pp. (hc. 0-8276-0312-6)
Gr. 4-8. A biography of the Austro-Hungarian who became the founder
and leader of the Zionist movement. Illustrated with black-and-white
drawings. Includes a chronology of important dates in Herzl's life and a
subject index.

592 Mack, Stan. *The Story of the Jews: A 4,000 Year Adventure.* New
    York: Villard, 1997. 273 pp. (hc. 0-375-50130-4) $19.95
Gr. 5-up. A funny, original, and highly informative account of the
history of the Jewish people from the time of Abraham to contemporary

Israel. Mack combines comic strip-like, black-and-white illustrations with humorous text to create a wonderfully engaging narrative that will particular appeal to reluctant readers and young people who enjoy comics or graphic novels. This book is a terrific example of how history can be made engaging for young readers. It is strong on both appeal and content. Includes a subject index.

593 Potok, Chaim. *The Chosen.* New York: Knopf, 1967.
   (hc. 0-679-402225-5) $30.00; (pbk. 0-449-21344-7) $5.95
Gr. 7-12. This fine novel centers around the strong friendship between two Orthodox boys that begins with a fiercely competitive rivalry. The story is richly decorated in Jewish culture and traditions.

594 Reichwald, Faye. *18 Lives.* Illus. Daniela Rosenhaus Bar-Zion.
   New York: Board of Jewish Education of Greater New York, 1981.
   249 pp. (pbk. 0-88384-024-3)
Gr. 5-8. An intermediate-level reader for students of English as a second language. The stories present heroes and heroines from various periods of Jewish history. Each story is followed by suggested objective and expansive activities.

The Native American Experience in the Americas

It is particularly important to make the connection between the Holocaust and the systematic destruction of Native American tribes in North America. Americans have a tendency to think of themselves as morally superior to barbarians like the Nazis, but examining the treatment of our indigenous people will quickly deflate such notions. The United States succeeded in wiping many tribes completely out of existence and brought all of the others very close to the brink. Like the Nazis, the majority of whites in America were consumed with the ethnocentric belief that their racial superiority endowed them with the right to do whatever they liked at the expense of their "inferiors."

595 Brown, Dee. *Bury My Heart at Wounded Knee.* New York: Holt,
   1971. 512 pp. (hc. 0-805-01045-9) $27.50; (pbk. 0-805-01730-5)
   $14.95
Gr. 9-12. An eloquent and thoroughly researched and documented account of the systematic destruction of Native American tribes in North America during the second half of the nineteenth century. Brown's many sources include: autobiographies, council records, and eyewitness descriptions, letters, and oral histories. A fascinating,

powerful work that tells of the "winning of the west" from the Indian perspective. This is still the best work of its kind on this important subject.

596 Josephy Jr., Alvin, ed. *America in 1492: The World of the Indian Peoples before the Arrival of Columbus*. New York: Knopf, 1992. (hc. 0-394-56438-3) $35.00
Gr. 9-12. A collection of seventeen essays by authorities depicting the rich, diverse lives of the millions people living in the Americas in the late fifteenth century. The authors shatter many of the stereotypes, half truths, and false information about indigenous peoples that have persisted for centuries.

597 Nies, Judith. *Native American History: A Chronology of the Vast Achievements of a Culture and Their Links to World Events*. New York: Ballantine, 1996. 420 pp. (pbk. 0-345-39350-3) $13.95
Gr. 7-12. An excellent reference guide presenting its information through an interesting timeline format. Well-researched and thoughtfully presented. Includes a thorough subject index and occasional black-and-white illustrations.

598 Wright, J. Leitch. *The Only Land They Knew: The Tragic Story of the Indians in the Old South*. New York: Free Press, 1981. 372 pp. (hc. 0-02-935790-X) $16.95
Gr. 9-12. An excellent history of Indians in the southern United States from the arrival of Ponce de Leon in Florida in 1513 to the "Trail of Tears" in the 1830s. The author does a fine job of explaining the contributions, customs, and histories of such great tribes as the Catawba, Cherokee, Chickasaw, Creek, Powhatan, Seminole, and Yamasee. Includes extensive chapter notes, bibliography, and a thorough subject index.

Professional Resources for Educators

Curricular Resources for Teachers

Books

Avery, Patricia and Dorothy Hoffman. *Tolerance for Diversity of Beliefs: A Secondary Curriculum Unit.* Boulder, CO: Social Science Education Consortium, 1993.

Benamy, Avivah, comp. *Teacher's Guide for True Experiences of Children Who Survived the Holocaust.* Brooklyn, NY: Center for Holocaust Studies Documentation and Research, 1988.

Bolkosky, Sidney M., Betty Rotberg Ellias, and David Harris. *A Holocaust Curriculum: Life Unworthy of Life: An 18 Lesson Instructional Unit.* Farmington Hills, MI: Center for the Study of Child, 1987.

Freedman-Apsel, Joyce and Helen Fein. *Teaching About Genocide: A Guidebook for College and University Teachers: Critical Essays, Syllabi, and Assignments.* Ottawa, Canada: Human Rights Internet, 1995.

Gagnon, Kathleen and Dianne Ruxton. *Holocaust Literature: Study Guides to 12 Stories of Courage.* Portland, ME: J. Weston Walch, 1997.
A reproducible teacher's book offering guides to teaching twelve well known works of Holocaust literature for the middle and high school level. Includes cooperative activities that explore prejudice and put the Holocaust in historical context.

Garber, Zev, ed., with Alan L. Berger and Richard Libowtiz. *Methodology in the Academic Teaching of the Holocaust.* Lanham, MD: University Press of America, 1988.

Grobman, Alex and Joel Fishman. *Anne Frank in Historical Perspective: A Teaching Guide for Secondary Schools.* Los

Angeles: Martyrs Memorial and Museum of the Holocaust, 1995.
Suggestions for secondary educators on how to teach the Holocaust
through Anne Frank and her world. Includes a chronology of Anne
Frank's life and a very good bibliography of suggestions for further
reading.

Grobman, Gary. *The Holocaust: A Guide for Pennsylvania Teachers.*
Harrisburg, PA: Pennsylvania Department of Education, 1990.

"Guidelines for Teaching About the Holocaust." Washington, D.C.:
United States Holocaust Memorial Museum, 1993.
A useful resource to consult if designing a Holocaust studies
curriculum.

The Holocaust: A Modular Curriculum for Secondary Students. Los
Angeles: Martyrs Memorial and Museum of the Holocaust, Jewish
Federation Council of Greater Los Angeles, 1989.

"The Holocaust: A Study of Genocide." Curriculum Bulletin, no. 13.
New York: Board of Education of the City of New York, Division
of Curriculum and Instruction, 1979.

Littell, Marcia Sachs, ed. *Holocaust Education: A Resource Book for
Teachers and Professional Leaders.* Symposium series, vol. 13.
New York: E. Mellen Press, 1985.

Maxwell, Elisabeth. *Why Should the Holocaust Be Remembered and
Therefore Taught?* Oxford: The Yarnton Trust for the Oxford
Centre for Hebrew Studies, 1988.

Merti, Betty. *Understanding the Holocaust.* Portland, ME: J. Weston
Walch, 1982. Revised Edition, 1995.
A wonderful activity book teaching Holocaust history for grades 9-12.
Each chapter is full of review questions in objective and essay form to
test reading comprehension. Other activities include class discussion
questions, crossword puzzles, research topics, and vocabulary
exercises. The revised edition includes updated information and
expanded resource lists.

—. *The World of Anne Frank: A Complete Resource Guide.* Portland,
ME: J. Weston Walch, 1998.
A variety of reproducible activities to support a classroom reading of

Anne Frank's *Diary of a Young Girl*. Includes comprehension, discussion, vocabulary, and writing activities. This is a revised, updated version of a book by the same author entitled *The World of Anne Frank: Readings, Activities, and Resources* (Walch, 1984).

Model Curriculum for Human Rights and Genocide. Sacramento, CA: California State Board of Education, 1987.

Roskies, Diane K. *Teaching the Holocaust to Children: A Review and Bibliography*. New York: KTAV, 1975.

Scher, Linda. *South Carolina Voices: Lessons from the Holocaust*. Columbia, SC: South Carolina Department of Education and South Carolina Humanities Council, 1992.

Shimoni, Gideon, ed. *The Holocaust in University Teaching*. New York: Pergamon, 1991.

Stein, Leon and Judy Stein. *The Holocaust: A Turning Point of Our Time: A Five Day Holocaust Curriculum and Teacher's Guide for the Secondary Schools*. 2nd ed. Skokie, IL: The Holocaust Memorial Foundation of Illinois, 1991.

Stephens, Elaine C., et al. *Learning About the Holocaust: Literature and Other Resources for Young People*. North Haven, CT: Library Professional Publications, 1995.
An excellent resource guide for classroom teachers. The authors look at 300 works of Holocaust literature and offer practical suggestions for classroom application. Though by no means comprehensive in their coverage of children's and young adult literature, the book does cover a wide scope in a variety of genres. Indexed by author and title.

A Study of the Holocaust: Student Handbook. Des Moines, IA: Des Moines Independent School District, 1984.

Teaching About the Holocaust: A Resource Book for Educators. Washington, D.C.: United States Holocaust Memorial Museum, 1995.
A brief but useful resource guide for educators. Includes information about the museum and the services it offers, an annotated bibliography and videography, a historical summary of the Holocaust, and a chronology.

Teaching About the Holocaust and Genocide. Human Rights Series,
vol. 1-2. Albany, NY: University of the State of New York and
New York State Education Department, Bureau of Curriculum
Development, 1985.

*Teaching Holocaust Studies with the Internet: Internet Lesson Plans
and Classroom Activities.* Lancaster, PA: Classroom Connect, 1997.
A collection of fifteen activities for intermediate and high school
grades, which integrate the use of World Wide Web, sites into
Holocaust studies. The lessons offer exercises that can be used by
individual students or the whole class. The exercise sheets are
reproducible. There is an answer key for all of the activity sheets.
Includes an annotated directory of Internet sites, lists of print and video
resources teachers can integrate into their lessons, and a companion
CD-ROM. A particularly appealing feature of this book is that it ties
the Holocaust to other genocidal events, such as Bosnia-Herzegovina,
Cambodia, and Rwanda.

"Wall of Remembrance: Teaching Guide." Washington, D.C.:
Committee to Remember the Children, United States Holocaust
Memorial Council, 1988.

Zornberg, Ira. *Classroom Strategies for Teaching About the
Holocaust: Ten Lessons for Classroom Use.* New York: Anti-
Defamation League of B'nai B'rith, 1983.
Ten classroom lessons for use with high school students. The lessons
cover a broad scope of topics on anti-Semitism and the Holocaust.
Includes a bibliography.

ERIC Documents

Avery, Patricia
"Tolerance for Diversity: A Secondary Curriculum Unit."
ED365595

This document consists of a six-week curriculum unit designed to allow
secondary students to actively explore issues associated with freedom
of belief and expression. The curriculum includes eight lessons and
corresponding handouts. Each lesson is divided into eight parts:
objectives, estimated time, materials and equipment needed,
vocabulary, optional films and videos, set induction, learning sequence,

and closure. The lessons cover victims of intolerance, the origins of intolerance, basic human rights, censorship, political intolerance and United States courts, international rights and responsibilities, beliefs and believers, and developing a class declaration of rights and responsibilities.

Barton, Keith C. and Lynne A. Smith
"Historical Fiction in the Middle Grades."
ED383618

This research presents findings from a preliminary study of the use of historical fiction in the middle grades. Focusing on historical fiction related to World War II and the Holocaust, the researchers sought to examine the factors that influenced teachers' decisions to implement historical fiction in their classrooms and students' responses to its use. Issues addressed in the study include problems of scheduling, lack of available materials, reading levels of materials, and discomfort in allowing students to work in literature response groups.

Gorman, Michael J., ed.
"Crossroads: Integrated Models for Teaching Ethics and Spirituality."
ED349243

An anthology of seven articles focusing on the integration of ethical and spiritual concerns in the study of subjects such as literature, history, foreign languages and cultures, and science. One of the articles is entitled "The Holocaust: An Icon for Religious Education" by Julie A. Collins.

"The Holocaust: A Study of Genocide."
ED184912

This teaching guide presents lesson plans, activities, and readings about the Holocaust for use in the secondary grades. There are a total of thirty-seven lessons, each of which consists of a focus question, an introductory activity, an outline of content emphases, summary questions, and suggested readings.

Holt, Evelyn R.
"'Remember Our Faces'–Teaching About the Holocaust."
ED345990

This ERIC Digest presents a rationale for Holocaust education, discusses curriculum placement for inclusion of the topic, lists organizations and resources available to help educators in teaching about the Holocaust, and provides a bibliography of relevant materials in the ERIC database.

Lieberman, Marcus
"Teaching the Holocaust."
ED170204

This paper reports on the first year of an eighth grade social studies unit entitled "Facing History and Ourselves: Holocaust and Human Behavior." The unit focuses on the question of individual responsibility in society.

Presseisen, Barbara Z. and Ernst L. Presseisen
"The Authentic Lessons of Schindler's List."
ED368674

This document suggests ways in which the film *Schindler's List* can be used as an instructional resource.

Holocaust-Related Periodicals

The Journal of Holocaust Education
(formerly *The British Journal of Holocaust Education*)
London: Frank Cass, 1992-
ISSN: 1359-1371
3/yr. ($70 Inst./$36 Ind.)

Christian Jewish Relations
London: Institute of Jewish Affairs, 1968-1991. (Suspended)
Quarterly

History and Memory: Studies in Representations of the Past
Bloomington, IN: Indiana University Press, 1989-
Semiannual ($30.00 Inst./$15.00 Ind.)

Holocaust and Genocide Studies
New York: Oxford University Press, 1986-
ISSN:
3/yr. ($148.00 Inst./$39.00 Ind.)

Holocaust Studies Annual
New York: Garland, 1990-1992. (Discontinued)
Annual

Patterns of Prejudice
London: Institute of Jewish Affairs, 1967-
Quarterly ($60.00)

Simon Wiesenthal Center Annual
Los Angeles: Simon Wiesenthal Center, 1984-1990. (Suspended)
Annual

Yad Vashem Studies
Jerusalem: Yad Vashem, 1957-
Annual ($37.75)

Journal Articles

Alexander, William. "Teaching the Holocaust: A Conceptual Model."
   College English 39(5): 548-52
Describes a course on the Holocaust and Vietnam that encourages
students to feel a responsibility and a right to assert themselves as
critical citizens.

Avery, Patricia and Dorothy Hoffman. "Tolerance for Diversity of
   Beliefs: A Secondary Curriculum Teaching about the Holocaust as
   Part of a Genocidal Universe." *Social Studies* 72.3 (May-June
   1981): 107-110.
The authors suggest that if the concept of genocide is not integrated
into our mental and moral world, we may become passive or active
participants in processing people for destruction. Provides definitions
of the terms genocide and holocaust and eight classroom strategies to
help develop understanding.

Barclay, Susanne. "Teaching the Holocaust: A Unit for the Transition
   Years." *Canadian Social Studies* 29.4 (Summer 1995): 154-155.
Presents practical suggestions for resources and instructional strategies
for teaching the Holocaust to middle school students. Describes the
experiences of a classroom teacher working with an eighth grade class
on the topic of the Holocaust. Discusses the use of novels and includes
a list of eleven recommended titles.

Bialystok, Franklin. "The Holocaust: Pedagogical Considerations." *Canadian Social Studies* 29.4 (Summer 1995): 137-139.
Discusses content selection, skill development, appropriate resources, and student sensitivities.

Brabeck, Mary. "Human Rights Education through the 'Facing History and Ourselves' Program." *Journal of Moral Education* 23.2 (1994): 333-347.
Reports on a study examining the effects of the "Facing History and Ourselves" program on moral development and psychological functioning.

Carmon, Arye. "Toward a Methodology of Teaching about the Holocaust." *Curriculum Inquiry* 9.3 (Fall 1979): 208-209.
Through their confrontation with the meaning of the Holocaust, adolescent students are taught specific values that will prepare them for their initiation into a democratic society. The content and methodology of the program is examined and its success evaluated.

Carrier, Anne. "The Holocaust in Literature." *History and Social Science Teacher* 21.4 (Summer 1986): 214-216.
Provides an annotated list of instructional resources for teaching about the Holocaust in secondary schools. Included are textbooks, multidisciplinary units, eyewitness accounts, fiction, poetry, anthologies, and audiovisual materials.

Chartrock, Roselle. "A Holocaust Unit for Classroom Teachers." *Social Education* 42.4: 278-285.
Presents a social studies unit for ninth grade. Includes suggested readings, audiovisual materials, paper topics, and discussion questions.

Colt, Lisa. "Facing Ourselves: Student Journals." *Independent School* 40.3 (February 1981): 17-20.
Advocates the use of daily journal entries as a vehicle for student expression to chart the process and progress of the course, "Facing History and Ourselves: The Holocaust and Human Behavior." Cites examples of student journal entries and suggests procedures for keeping journals.

Cooper, Ruth Ann. "From Holocaust to Hope: Teaching the Holocaust in Middle School." *Middle School Journal* 25.4 (March 1994): 15-17.

This article explains several approaches to teaching the Holocaust, including literature about teenagers facing complex moral issues, interdisciplinary methods, interviews with survivors, field trips to synagogues, research reports, original poetry, and memorial displays and presentations.

Danks, Carol. "Using Holocaust Short Stories and Poems in the Social Studies Classroom." *Social Education* 59.6 (October 1995): 358-361.
The author maintains that most history textbooks contain little information on the Holocaust and asserts that short stories and poems should be added to nonfiction accounts to provide unique insights for students. Provides teaching suggestions and recommends two short stories and poetry selections on the topic.

—. "Using the Literature of Elie Weisel and Selected Poetry to Teach the Holocaust in the Secondary History Classroom." *Social Studies* 87.3 (May-June 1996): 101-105.
The author recommends teachers use the literature of Holocaust survivors to provide students with empathy and understanding not found in traditional historical texts.

Drabble, Margaret A. "Merging Literature and History in Teaching about Genocide." *Social Education* 55.2 (February 1991): 128-129.
Delineates the difficulties of teaching about genocide. Suggests literature to help students understand atrocities as real events affecting individuals. Includes recommended reading for children and young adults.

Drew, Margaret A. "Incorporating Literature into a Study of the Holocaust: Some Advice, Some Cautions." *Social Education* 59.6 (October 1995): 354-356.
The author maintains that any historical literature needs to be evaluated as both history and literature and asserts that no single book can convey the full story of true horror of that historical period.

Fine, Melinda. *Habits of Mind: Struggling Over Values in America's Classrooms.* San Francisco: Jossey-Bass, 1995. 227 pp. (hc. 0-7879-0061-3)
The author explores the politics and practice of programs designed to foster moral thinking and civic responsibility. She examines closely the "Facing History and Ourselves" curriculum which, uses the study of the

Holocaust to reflect upon contemporary issues of racism, violence, intolerance, and prejudice. A thoughtful, provocative book any educator will find fascinating.

Foster, Harold M. "Embracing *All But My Life* by Gerda Weissman Klein." *English Journal* 86.8 (December 1997): 56-59.
The author proclaims Klein's autobiography a "classic" and advocates making the book required reading. Not a particularly practical article, but Foster's arguments for using the book are interesting.

Fox, Ruth. "Exploring the Holocaust." *EL: Emergency Librarian* 24.5 (May/June 1997): 8-13.

Freedman-Apsel, Joyce and Helen Fein. *Teaching About Genocide: Guidebook for College and University Teachers: Critical Essays, Syllabi, and Assignments.* Ottawa, Canada: Human Rights Interest, 1992.

Freedman, Theodore. "Introduction: Why Teach the Holocaust?" *Social Education* 42.4: 263.
Presents a rationale for teaching about the Nazi era in social studies courses.

Friedman, Norman L. "Teaching about the Holocaust." *Teaching Sociology* 12.4 (July 1985): 449-461.
The author discusses how the study of the Holocaust can provide valuable historical and comparative perspectives for a largely American society oriented course in ethnic and racial relations. He maintains that, by studying the Holocaust, students can learn about the patterns and causes of, and minority reactions to, discrimination and prejudice.

Gabelko, Nina Hersch. "Prejudice Reduction in Secondary Schools." *Social Education* 52.4 (April-May 1988): 276-279.
Describes how a group of tenth grade teachers taught a unit on the Holocaust that actively engaged students' thinking skills and reduced their level of prejudice while increasing their self-esteem.

Gerrity, Thomas. "Holocaust Studies: An Approach to Peace." *Momentum* 14.4 (December 1983): 36-37.
Reports on a survey of the attitudes of 120 high school students, administrators, and teachers toward curricular coverage of the Holocaust and the best way to teach about the subject.

Goldman, Martin S. "Teaching the Holocaust: Some Suggestions for
Comparative Analysis." *Journal of Intergroup Relations* 6 (2): 22-
30.
The author suggests ways of comparing the Jewish Holocaust with
black slavery and the American Indian experiences.

Gorrell, Nancy. "Teaching the Holocaust: Light from a Yellow Star
Leads the Way." *English Journal* 86.8 (December 1997): 50-55.
A high school teacher gives an account of a five day Holocaust lesson
she taught and focuses on the use of Robert O. Fisch's book *Light from
a Yellow Star* in the lesson.

Hamilton, Paula. "Create a Character and Bring History to Life."
Learning 22.8 (April-May 1994): 61-62.
An eighth grade teacher describes how she taught her class about Anne
Frank, the Holocaust, and World War II by creating a character playing
the role of the character, and making history personal for the students.

Hirshfield, Claire. "Teaching the Holocaust: A Conceptual Model."
Improving College and University Teaching 29.1 (Winter 1981):
24-27.
A conceptual model of a course on the history of the Holocaust is
presented.

Holroyd, Peter R. "Lest We Forget: The Importance of Holocaust
Education." *NASSP Bulletin* 79 (March 1995): 16-25.
The author offers sound justifications for teaching the Holocaust and
considers theories and principles in developing a curriculum.

Holzman, Terry. "Facing History: Teaching the Holocaust."
Independent School 40.3 (February 1981) 8-15.
Describes the "Facing History and Ourselves: The Holocaust and
Human Behavior" curriculum designed for secondary social studies
students. Offers examples of student and teacher reactions to the
course.

Hurst, Carol Otis. "Escaping in Literature: Teaching in the
Library." *Teaching Pre-K-8* 24.1 (August-September 1993): 124-
129.
Explores the escape genre in children's literature. The author
recommends and describes several books that deal with such topics as
escape from prison camps, from slavery, from the Holocaust, from war,

and from Utopian societies.

Kalb, Virginia. "Literature as a Personal Approach to the Study of the Holocaust." *School Library Media Quarterly* 17.4 (Summer 1989): 213-214.

Kalfus, Richard. "Euphemisms of Death: Interpreting a Primary Source Document on the Holocaust." *History Teacher* 23.2 (February 1990): 87-93.
The author analyzes a primary source document in which German bureaucrats describe in euphemistic terms the murder of the Jews. He illustrates how the document can be used as a teaching aid by having students replace the euphemisms with words that convey their intended meaning, and reading it aloud in class.

Kleg, Milton. "Anti-Semitism: Background to the Holocaust." *Social Education* 59 (October 1995): 334-338.
Considers teaching the Holocaust in the larger context of anti-Semitism in European history.

Kunctz, Kim. "Beyond Anne Frank." *Educational Leadership* 51.3 (November 1993): 35.
A former junior high school teacher proposes that eighth graders are not too young to grasp the impact of the Holocaust. She explains how she went beyond *The Diary of Anne Frank* to explore topics of genocide, racism, prejudice, and persecution in-depth.

Marinak, Barbara. "Books in the Classroom: The Holocaust." *The Horn Book* 69.3 (May-June 1993): 368-374.
The author recounts her successful experiences introducing students to several Holocaust books and their reactions to the works. This article is interesting to read for the reactions of the students. I vehemently disagree with the author's praise for that dreadful picture book *Let the Celebrations Begin!*

Meisel, Esther. "'I Don't Want to Be a Bystander:' Literature and the Holocaust." *English Journal* 71.5 (September 1982): 40-44.
Describes in detail an elective unit that uses drama, fiction, film, and nonfiction to engage student interest in studying the Holocaust.

Miller, Scott. "Denial of the Holocaust." *Social Education* 59.6 (October 1995): 342-345.

Discusses the views of Holocaust deniers and categorizes them into two groups: hard deniers and soft deniers. The author maintains that Holocaust denial has no historical support and asserts that the United States Holocaust Memorial Museum is one of the best resources to counter the claims of Holocaust deniers.

Muallem, Miriam and Frances A. Dowd. "Model Criteria for and Content Analysis of Historical Fiction about the Holocaust for Grades Four through Twelve." *Multicultural Review* 1.2 (April 1992): 49-55.
Establishes components of high quality books about the Holocaust for children and young adults. Uses these criteria in a content analysis of six historical novels about the Holocaust. The authors recommend using these criteria as a model for future analysis of historical fiction.

Petropouos, Jonathan. "Confronting the 'Holocaust as Hoax' Phenomenon as Teachers." *The History Teacher* 28 (August 1995): 523-539.
Considers what history teachers can do to combat historical revisionists who deny the Holocaust.

Poll, Carol. "The Sociology of Genocide/The Holocaust: A Curriculum Guide." *Teaching Sociology* 23 (April 1995): 186-189.
A practical guide for teaching the sociological aspects of the Holocaust and other genocides.

Reed, Carole Ann. "Racism Today: Echoes of the Holocaust." *Canadian Social Studies* 29.4 (Summer 1995): 140-142.
The author explores the usefulness of employing an ant-racist framework to each Holocaust education. She maintains that different forms of discrimination are linked psychologically and asserts that Holocaust education can be used also to teach about disabled individuals, homosexuals, and other groups who suffer discrimination.

Ringelheim, Joan. "Women and the Holocaust: A Reconsideration of Research." *Signs* 10.4 (Summer 1985): 741-761.
Discusses general assumptions, hypotheses, and categories used to study the experiences of women during the Holocaust. Presents excerpts from interviews with three women who survived imprisonment in concentration camps.

Rochman, Hazel. "Bearing Witness to the Holocaust." *Book Links* 7.3

(January 1998): 8-14.
The first of three articles by Rochman on Holocaust literature for youth. This first discussion speaks to the necessity of Holocaust education and offers connections educators can make of the Holocaust to other accounts of prejudice and racism in other times and places. Also notable is a focus on Margaret Wild's *Let the Celebrations Begin!*, a dreadful "upbeat" story about the liberation of a concentration camp.

——. "Should You Teach *Anne Frank: The Diary of a Young Girl?*"
     Book Links 7.5 (May 1998): 45-49.
Rochman examines recent criticisms of Anne Frank's *The Diary of a Young Girl*, questioning its value as a piece of "significant" Holocaust literature. The article also considers the problem of students having their only exposure to the Holocaust through reading the book. Rochman recommends a number of other excellent Holocaust narratives to have students read in addition to *The Diary of a Young Girl*. This article is essential reading for any Holocaust educator.

Rosenberg, Alan and Jack Zevin. "Teaching about the Holocaust as
     Part of a Genocidal Universe." *Social Studies* 72.3 (May-June
     1981): 107-110.
The authors suggest that if the concept of genocide is not integrated into our mental and moral world, we become passive or active participants in processing people for destruction. Provides definitions of the terms genocide and holocaust and eight classroom strategies to help develop understanding.

Schwartz, Donald. "Who Will Tell Them after We're Gone?:
     Reflections on Teaching the Holocaust." *History Teacher* 23.2
     (February 1990): 95-110.
Explores the rationale for including the Holocaust in the social studies curriculum and analyzes how aspects can be introduced at elementary grade levels.

Schwartz, Eleanor E. "Mediaviews: Studying the Holocaust." *NJEA*
     Review 52.6 (February 1979): 15, 51, 54.
Offers key resource materials, background readings, and informative organizations teachers can utilize in planning units or courses on the Holocaust.

Short, Geoffrey. "Teaching the Holocaust: The Relevance of

Children's Perceptions of Jewish Culture and Identity."
British Educational Research Journal 20.4 (1994): 393-405.
The author examines the Jewish Holocaust component that is now part
of the history curriculum for 11- to 14-year-old students in England and
Wales. He argues that teachers need to know how children in this age
group perceive culture and identity.

Shur, Irene G., Franklin H. Littell, and Marvin E. Wolfgangs, eds.
"Reflections on the Holocaust: Historical, Philosophical and
Educational Dimensions." *Annals of the American Academy of
Political and Social Science*, vol. 450. Philadelphia: American
Academy of Political and Social Science, 1980.

Stotsky, Sandra. "Is the Holocaust the Chief Contribution of the Jewish
People to World Civilization and History?: A Survey of Leading
Literature Anthologies and Reading Instructional Textbooks."
English Journal 85 (February 1996): 52-59.

Strom, Margot Stern. "The Holocaust and Human Behavior."
Curriculum Review 22.3 (August 1983): 83-86.
Describes the comprehensive curriculum approach and teacher training
program on the Jewish Holocaust developed for adolescents by the
Facing History and Ourselves organization. The author discusses
course objectives, problems teachers may encounter, and student
responses.

Totten, Sam. "A Unit on the Holocaust." *Social Science Record* 22.1
(Spring 1985): 17-20.
Examines a unit of study on the Holocaust designed for use with senior
high school students. Includes social studies and language skills
objectives. Many learning activities are suggested.

—. "Teaching a Unit on Human Rights." *Georgia Social Science
Journal* 15.3 (Fall 1984): 12-17.
Examines the seven activities that comprise a unit of study on human
rights.

Totten, Samuel and Stephen Feinberg. "Teaching about the Holocaust:
Issues of Rationale, Content, Methodology, and Resources." *Social
Education* 59.6 (October 1995): 223-233.
Discusses key concerns regarding issues of rationale, methodology, and
resources when teaching about the Holocaust. Identifies twelve

objectives and five content criteria for the topic.

Weitzman, Mark. "Coming to Grips with Teaching the Holocaust."
    Momentum 19 (1) (February 1988): 55-57.

White-Stevens, Lillian. "On Teaching the Lessons of the Holocaust."
    NJEA Review 53.8 (April 1980): 18-20.
Citing recent events such as the Cambodian genocide, the author
stresses the importance of teaching students about genocide and the
Holocaust. She discusses curriculum developments in this area,
particularly a high school course developed by New Jersey teachers.

Other Professional Resources

Braham, Randolph L., ed. *The Treatment of the Holocaust in*
    Textbooks. New York: Columbia University Press, 1987. 333 pp.
    (0-88033-955-1) $30.00
A fascinating, informative study that teachers or anyone interested in
Holocaust education will want to consult. From the *Holocaust Studies
Series*.

Cargas, Harry James. *The Holocaust: An Annotated Bibliography*.
    2nd ed. Chicago: American Library Association, 1985. 196 pp.
    (0-8389-0433-5)
Though not as comprehensive as the Edelheit's *Bibliography on
Holocaust Literature*, this is still a valuable resource and all the entries
are annotated. Unfortunately, like the Edelheits, Cargas overlooks
Holocaust literature for children and young adults.

Drew, Margaret A. *Facing History and Ourselves: Holocaust and
    Human Behavior Annotated Bibliography*. New York: Walker,
    1988.
Excellent annotations of Holocaust literature, including a section on
books for children and young adults that is substantial but far from
comprehensive. Includes bibliographies on the Armenian and
Cambodian genocides.

Edelheit, Abraham J. and Hershel Edelheit. *Bibliography on Holocaust
    Literature*. Boulder, CO: Westview, 1986. 842 pp.
    (0-8133-7233-X)
A massive collection of citations of approximately 15,000 books,
pamphlets, periodicals, and dissertations pertaining to the Holocaust.

Unfortunately, the Edelheits have almost entirely overlooked literature for children and young adults. This is a useful resource to consult in preparation for teaching about the Holocaust or for any in-depth research. Most of the entries are not annotated. Includes an introduction, index of periodicals and abbreviations, and an author index. Citations are arranged by subject.

——. *Bibliography on Holocaust Literature: Supplement*. Boulder, CO: Westview, 1990. 684 pp. (0-8133-0896)
A supplement to the Edelheit's massive 1986 opus, this one containing 6,500 new entries. Once again, Holocaust literature for children and young adults is largely overlooked. The supplement contains new entries on Holocaust-related novels, short stories, drama, and poetry, as well as reviews of Holocaust literature. Works the Edelheits consider 'significant' are annotated. Includes an introduction, index of periodicals and abbreviations, author/title, and subject index.

——. *History of the Holocaust: A Handbook and Dictionary*. Boulder, CO: Westview Press, 1994.

——. *A World in Turmoil: An Integrated Chronology of the Holocaust and World War II*. New York: Greenwood Press, 1991.

Gutman, Yisrael and Chaim Schatzker. *The Holocaust and Its Significance*. Jerusalem: The Zalman Shazar Center, 1984. 248 pp. (hc. 965-277-022-9)
A textbook for middle and high school grades examining the Holocaust that begins with the major events occurring in Europe between the two world wars. Includes a selection of primary source readings, charts, graphs, maps, and a glossary. One major drawback is the absence of an index. Illustrated with black-and-white photographs. A teacher's guide to this book was also published by The Zalman Shazar Center.

Hilberg, Raul. *The Destruction of European Jews*. 2nd ed. 3 vols. New York: Holmes & Meier, 1985.

Immell, Myra H., ed. *Readings on Anne Frank*. New York: Greenhaven, 1998. 144 pp. (hc. 1-56510-661-X) $20.96; (pbk. 1-56510-660-1) $12.96
A collections of diverse viewpoints of survivors, writers, critics, and historians on the *Diary* since its publication. From the *Greenhaven Literary Companion* series.

Laska, Vera. *Nazism, Resistance and Holocaust in World War II: A Bibliography.* Metuchen: Scarecrow Press, 1985. 183 pp. (0-8108-1771-3)
This resource is unique in the attention it gives to women's experiences in the Holocaust and World War II. Unfortunately, children's and young adult literature is largely overlooked. Some entries are annotated. Includes an introduction and author index.

Mogilanski, Roman, ed. *The Ghetto Anthology: A Comprehensive Chronicle of the Extermination of Jewry in Nazi Death Camps and Ghettos in Poland.* Los Angeles: American Congress of Jews from Poland and Survivors of Concentration Camps, 1985.

Mokotoff, Gary and Sallyann Admur Sack. *Where Once We Walked: A Guide to the Jewish Communities Destroyed in the Holocaust.* Teaneck, NJ: Avotaynu, 1991.

Muffs, Judith Herschlag and Dennis B. Klein, eds. *The Holocaust in Books and Films: A Selected, Annotated List.* New York: Hippocrene, 1986. 158 pp. (0-87052-292-2)
An outstanding, invaluable resource for educators produced by the International Center for Holocaust Studies of the Anti-Defamation League of B'nai B'rith. Includes a preface by Elie Wiesel.

Rochman, Hazel. *Against Borders: Promoting Books for a Multicultural World.* Chicago: American Library Association, 1993.

Sable, Martin Howard. *Holocaust Studies: A Directory and Bibliography of Bibliographies.* Greenwood, FL: Penkeville, 1987.

Shulman, William L., ed. *Directory: Association of Holocaust Organizations.* Bayside, NY: Holocaust Resource Center and Archives, Queensborough Community College, 1993.

—. *Educational Resource Guide on the Holocaust: A Selected Bibliography and Audio-Visual Catalogue.* Bayside, NY: Holocaust Resource Center and Archives, Queensborough Community College, 1993.

Szonyi, David M., ed. *The Holocaust: An Annotated Bibliography and Resource Guide.* New York: KTAV, 1985.

United States Holocaust Memorial Council. *Directory of Holocaust Institutions*. Washington, D.C., 1988. 56 pp. (0-9616518-1-4)
An alphabetically arranged directory of Holocaust institutions in the United States and Canada. Includes a user's guide, a description of the U.S. Holocaust Memorial Council, and a listing of its members. Includes a geographical index of institutions and an index of institutions arranged by activity.

Electronic Holocaust Resources

CD-ROMs

The Complete Maus: A Survivor's Tale
Voyager, 1994.
$59.95

The Complete Maus contains Art Spiegelman's two graphic novels: *Maus: A Survivor's Tale: Part I: My Father Bleeds History* and *Maus: A Survivor's Tale: Part II: And Here My Troubles Began* (see the annotations of the works on page 94). The CD-ROM enhances the original works in many respects. In addition to the complete texts of both works, it includes most of the transcripts and sketches Spiegelman used to create *Maus*. One sees the painstaking attention Spiegelman paid to making the work accurate and authentic. This CD-ROM offers students an incredible opportunity to see this work's text and artwork evolve. It will teach students about the Holocaust and also give them an appreciation of how much work goes into producing a work like *Maus*. For Mac/Windows.

Requirements: 8MB RAM; Windows requires 486 or better.

Ordering Information:
The Voyager Company
574 Broadway, Suite 406
New York, NY 10012
(212) 431-5199
1-800-446-2001
http://www.voyagerco.com

Historical Atlas of the Holocaust
United States Holocaust Memorial Museum

Gr. 7-up. An outstanding interactive CD-ROM allowing the user to examine maps of countries, ghettos, and forests. Over 230 full-color maps are accompanied with text chronicling the history of the war from 1933 to the makeup of postwar Europe in 1949-1950. For Windows.

Holocaust
Quanta, 1994.

Gr. 9-up. Formerly titled *Images of the Holocaust*, this CD-ROM offers graphic documentation of the shocking conditions discovered by the Allied soldiers who liberated the concentration camps. Featured are photographs from fifteen camps. Each photograph is explained with a brief caption. Other features include: original Holocaust-themed artwork by contemporary artists; archival newsreel footage; a text reference section containing a wealth of original documents, including interviews with liberating soldiers; correspondence from camp prisoners, and the Nuremberg Trial Report; and a slide show of photographs illustrating "Jacob's Song," an original song about the Holocaust by Jerry Rau. All photographs and text can be printed out or copied to the clipboard. For Windows.

Lest We Forget: A History of the Holocaust
Logos Research Systems, 1996.

An outstanding interactive CD-ROM that offers a thorough historical perspective on the Holocaust in a highly accessible and thoughtfully presented format. Among the many features are: 250 pages of original text written specifically for this work; interactive charts, maps, and timelines; subtitled German audio documents and film footage, narrated video-montages as summaries of the main topics; a gallery of 500 photographs with accompanying captions; and an original soundtrack. This product's overall design is exceptional. The information is thoughtfully mapped and linked in a way that makes it both appealing and useful.

Requirements: Macintosh requires IIci or better, 5MB free RAM; Windows requires 486 or better, 8 MB RAM.

Return to Life
Yad Vashem

Tells the story of liberated concentration camp survivors through a multimedia production, which includes film footage, interviews, maps, and a variety of textual material. Includes a teacher's manual.

Holocaust Resources on the Internet: Electronic Discussion Lists

H-ANTIS (History of Anti-Semitism)

A member of the H-NET Humanities & Social Sciences Online initiative, this moderated discussion list encourages scholarly discussion of anti-Semitism in history and makes available bibliographies, teaching aids, and other valuable resources. Subscription information and access to the list's archives can on the World Wide Web at http://h-net2.msu.edu/~antis/.

H-GERMAN (German History)

Another member of the H-NET initiative, this moderated list discusses scholarly topics concerning German history. Submissions are accepted and posted in both English and German. It is recommended subscribers be competent in both languages. Subcription information and the list's archives are available on the World Wide Web at http:// hnet2.msu.edu/ ~german/.

H-HOLOCAUST (History of the Holocaust and Anti-Semitism)

Another member of the H-NET Online initiative, the purpose of this list is to provide scholars of the Holocaust an opportunity to communicate with one another in order to exchange ideas on research and teaching methodologies. Teachers will find this a valuable resource. Subscription information and access to the list's archives are located at http://h-net2.msu.edu/~holoweb/.

HLIST (Holocaust Information List)

This unmoderated discussion list is devoted to Holocaust research and to refuting those who deny the event. Among the many topic included in the scope of the list are: the world-wide activities of racial supremacy organizations, the activities of neo-Nazi organizations, and Holocaust denial via electronic networking. The subscription address is listserv@ONEB.ALMANAC.BC.CA. The submission address is HLIST@ONEB.ALMANAC.BC.CA.

Holocaust Resources on the Internet: World Wide Web

Anne Frank Online
http://www.annefrank.com

A wealth of information about Anne Frank is offered through this site. Information about Anne's life and the time in which she lived and died, The Anne Frank Center USA, the traveling exhibit "Anne Frank in the World: 1929-1945," and resources for classroom teachers are among the many resources available. Teachers will find this an essential tool.

Anti-Semitism
http://www.igc.apc.org/ddickerson/antisemitism.html

A wealth of information on historical and contemporary anti-Semitism throughout the world.

Anti-Semitism: The Holocaust, Neo-Facism, Anit-Zionism & Black Anti-Semitism
http://ucsu.colorado.edu/~jsu/antisemitism.html

Another outstanding collection of information on historical and contemporary anti-Semitism, including dozens of Holocaust links. An invaluable resource.

Association of Holocaust Organizations
http://www.ushmm.org/organizations/list.html

Maintained by the United States Holocaust Memorial Museum, this is an invaluable international directory of Holocaust organizations located throughout the world. The information is current and frequently updated. Users can search the database by keyword or phrase.

Auschwitz: A Layman's Guide to Auschwitz-Birkenau
http://www.almanac.bc.ca/faqs/auschwitz/index.html

An outstanding collection of background information on the most infamous of the Nazi death camps. Thorough and most informative.

Auschwitz Alphabet
http://www.spectacle.org/695/ausch.html

Created by Jonathan Blumen, this is a unique presentation of introductory information about Auschwitz and the Holocaust.

Auschwitz-Birkenau Photograph Archive
http://www.remember.org/jacobs/index.html

An archive of contemporary photographs of Auschwitz and Birkenau taken by Alan Jacobs in the years 1979-1981. The images are of excellent quality and captioned. Be patient because they can take some time to load.

The Beast Within: An Interdisciplinary Unit
http://www.fred.net/nhhs/html/beast.htm

A unit for a ninth grade government course that examines authoritarian governments and compares them with a democratic system. An interesting lesson that will be of interest to social studies teachers. Also included are links to poems ninth grade students wrote in response to visiting the Holocaust Memorial Museum.

C.A.N.D.L.E.S. Holocaust Museum
http://www.candles-museum.com

A museum in Indiana dedicated to educating the general public about the horrors of the Holocaust. The site includes information about the museum's facilities, its collections and programs, and links to other Holocaust sites.

Children of the Holocaust
http://www.wiesenthal.com/mot/children.html

Maintained by The Simon Wiesenthal Center, this site is devoted to profiling the life of each one of the 1.5 million Jewish children murdered by the Nazis and their collaborators during the Holocaust. If available, a photograph of the child appears with a brief text detailing the child's life and death.

Chronology of the Holocaust: 1933-1945
www.bxscience.edu/orgs/holocaust/edguide/4.html

An excellent chronology of major Holocaust events created by The Holocaust Studies Center at the Bronx High School for Science.

Cybrary of the Holocaust
http://www.remember.org

An outstanding site with a wealth of resources for educators and students. Includes an archive of photographs showing how the Holocaust developed, information from witnesses and children of survivors, lesson plans for teachers, and many links to other Holocaust resources on the Internet.

Dachau: Principal Distinguished Badges Worn by Prisoners
http://www.igc.apc.org/ddickerson/dachau-badges.html

An interesting site exhibiting full-color pictures of badges assigned to the various types of prisoners in the Dachau concentration camp. The badges are labeled.

El Paso Holocaust Museum and Study Center
http://www.huntel.com/~ht2/holocst.html

In addition to information about the museum's activities, facilities, a virtual exhibit is available covering various aspects of the Holocaust.

Ernest and Elizabeth Cassutto Memorial Pages:
  Survivors of the Holocaust
http://www.fred.net/nhhs/htm/3/dadmom.htm

An interesting memorial page created by a child of the Cassuttos, two people who miraculously survived the Holocaust. Of particular interest to educators is a lesson plan for teachers that relates the experiences of the Cassuttos to introduce students to the Holocaust from a personal perspective.

Facing History and Ourselves
http://www.facing.org/

The site provides information about this national educational and professional development organization whose mission is to educate educators and their students about anti-Semitism, prejudice, and racism.

Five Questions About the Holocaust
http://www.uhmm.org/education/5quest.html

Provided by the United States Holocaust Memorial Museum, this is a list of five basic questions about the Holocaust and their answers. The questions are: What was the Holocaust?; Who were the Nazis?; Why did the Nazis want to kill large numbers of innocent people?; How did the Nazis carry out their policy of genocide?; and How did the world respond to the Holocaust? The answers are concise and informative. An excellent introductory handout to give to students before beginning a Holocaust lesson.

Fortunoff Video Archive for Holocaust Testimonies
http://www.library.yale.edu/testimonies/

Information about the collection of over 3,700 videotaped interviews with witnesses to and survivors of the Holocaust. Links include excerpts from the testimonies, information about the archive, and affiliate projects.

The Frances and Jacob Hiatt Collection of Holocaust Materials
http://webster.holycro...rossway/library/hiatt/anbout.htm

Maintained by the College of the Holy Cross, this is a substantial collection of materials focusing on the role of the Roman Catholic Church and the Society of Jesus (Jesuits) in Holocaust events.

Genocide Links
http://cug.concordia.ca/~shac/1_gen.html

Compiled by history students at Concordia University, Montreal, this is an outstanding collection of sites about the Holocaust and other genocides that have occurred throughout the world. Links to information about Armenia, Cambodia, the Irish Potato Famine, Rwanda, and the former Yugoslavia are among the resources available.

Guidelines for Teaching About the Holocaust
http://www.ushmm.org/education/guidelines.html

Created by the United States Holocaust Memorial Museum, this is an essential guide for all Holocaust educators.

Hate on the Net
http://www.vir.com/Shalom/hatred.html

A notable site devoted to monitoring hate activity on the Internet. Not as polished or professional as the HateWatch site but useful nonetheless.

HateWatch
http://www.hatewatch.org

This site provides an online source of information about hate activity on the Internet. Provides many links to sites concerning Neo-Nazis and other anti-Semites, Holocaust deniers, White Supremacists, and many others. Frequently updated.

The Holocaust Album
http://www.wenet.net/user
Rare photographs relating to the Holocaust. Be patient here as files can take some time to load. It will be worth the wait.

A Holocaust Primer: Understanding and Prevention
http://haven.ios.com/~kimel19/

Created by Alexander Kimel, this is a very interesting collection of information concerning various Holocaust topics. Of particular interest is a link to a Holocaust prayer and links to original poetry about the Holocaust.

Holocaust Curriculum Resources
http://falcon.jmu.edu/~ramseyil/holo.htm

An excellent collection of bibliographies, guidelines, and lesson plans teachers will find invaluable. Offers access to ERIC resources on the Holocaust, including an AskERIC Infoguide and ERIC Digests on teaching the Holocaust.

Holocaust/Genocide Project
http://www.igc.apc.org/iearn/hgpl

Focusing upon the study of the Holocaust and other genocides, the Holocaust/Genocide Project (HPG) is an international, nonprofit organization promoting education and awareness. The organization offers assistance to educators working with students, ages 12-17.

Holocaust Glossary: Terms, Places, and Personalities

http://www.wiesenthal.com/resource/glass.htm

Created by The Simon Wiesenthal Center, this is an outstanding cross-referenced glossary. An essential resource for the classroom.

Holocaust Pictures Exhibition
http://modb.oce.ulg.ac.be/schmitzholocaust.html

An archive of thirty-seven photographs of concentration camps, gas chambers, and graphic scenes of brutality. All photographs have brief captions. The images are all disturbing and some quite gruesome. Many of the pictures, particularly the larger ones, can take some time to load so be patient.

Holocaust Resources
http://arginine.umdnj/edu/~swartz/holocaust.html

An outstanding collection of Holocaust resources offering bibliographies, links to museums and research institutions, teaching materials, and other Holocaust sites.

The Holocaust/Shoah Page
http://www.mtsu.edu/~baustin/holo.html

An excellent collection of many useful Holocaust sites that educators will find very valuable.

Holocaust Studies Center
http://www.bxscience.edu/orgs/holocaust/

Maintained by the Bronx High School of Science, this site offers information on the center housed in the school and provides links to a wealth of other Holocaust information.

Holocaust Timeline
http://www.historyplace.com/worldwar2/holocaust/timeline.html

A very thorough, extremely useful timeline located at *The History Place* web site. Students can jump to any year between 1938-1945. There are links to text from some events enhancing this already useful resource.

iEARN Holocaust/Genocide Project
http://www.igc.apc,org/learn/hgp/

iEARN is an international, nonprofit, telecommunications project focusing on the study of the Holocaust and other genocides. The purpose of the project is promote education and awareness among students, ages 12 to 17, and their teachers. Among the site's many features are complementary lesson plans for teachers.

Jewish Culture and History
http://www.igc.apc.org/ddickerson/judaica.html

An outstanding collection of sites devoted to Jewish culture and history from various places and times. This is an essential resource for educators teaching the Holocaust or any other subject in Jewish history.

Judaica Collection
http://www.cs.cmu.edu/afs/cs.cmu.edu/user/clamen/misc/Judaica/README.html

Like the "Jewish Culture and History" homepage, this collection is another outstanding information resource on many diverse subjects concerning Jewish culture and history. This page has the additional value of having many links concerning contemporary developments and issues in Jewish history. There are many links for Holocaust studies and for Israel.

L'Chaim: A Holocaust Web Project
http://www.charm.net/~rbennett/l'chaim.html

Another very good resource for educators. Many images of the Holocaust are available, some extremely disturbing.

Literature of the Holocaust
http://www.english.upenn.edu/Holocaust/holhome.html

Maintained at the University of Pennsylvania, this site is rich in many Holocaust sources that are likely to be of more interest to educators than students. There are many good links here.

Louisiana Holocaust Survivors
http://www.tulane.edu/~so-inst/laholmainwindow.html

A collection of testimonies from Holocaust survivors. Pictures of the survivors accompany their testimonies. An excellent introduction to personal Holocaust narratives for students.

March of the Living
http://www.bonder.com/march.html

An introduction to the origin and purpose of The March of the Living movement introducing thousands of teens each year to the legacy of the Holocaust. Includes links to further information about the movement.

The March of the Living Official Site
http://www.motl.org/

The official homepage for The March of the Living organization. Compare this one to the March of the Living site.

New Jersey Commission on Holocaust Education
  Holocaust and Genocide Curriculum
http://www.remember.org/hist.root.holo.html

An outline of the outstanding Holocaust curriculum designed by the New Jersey Commission on Holocaust Education for grades K-12. An essential resource to consult before preparing a curriculum for one's own school.

The Nizkor Project
http://www2.ca.nizkor.org/index.html

Another rich source of Holocaust information that is updated frequently and has many links. An extremely valuable site.

The Pink Triangle Pages
The History of Nazi Persecution of Gay Men and Lesbians
http://www.cs.cmu.edu/...s/bulgarians/pink.html

An excellent source for introductory information on how homosexuals were persecuted by the Nazis.

Raoul Wallenberg
http://www.algonet.se/~hatikva/wallenberg/

An excellent introductory site to Raoul Wallenberg, the diplomat who helped save the lives of thousands of Jews and then later mysteriously disappeared. A wonderful introduction for students.

Reach & Teach Worldwide Holocaust Education Group
http://rio.com/~holcaust/

An organization of Holocaust survivors, their children, and educators located throughout the country who offer free educational outreach to schools and other institutions. Their homepage offers background and contact information.

Responses to the Holocaust: A Hypermedia Sourcebook for the
    Humanities
http://jefferson.village.virginia.edu/holocaust/response.html

A wealth of information is collected here to introduce the viewer/reader to various disciplines that have produced significant discussions concerning the Jewish Holocaust. The critical works collected here are scholarly and are likely to be useful only for older high school students engaged in advanced Holocaust studies or for educators seeking to broaden their own knowledge of the subject.

The Rise of Adolf Hitler
http://www.historyplace.com/worldwar2/rise of hitler/index.htm

Located at *The History Place* web site, this is an excellent online, hypertext biography of Adolf Hitler. There are twenty-four chapters covering Hitler's life, from birth to death.

Shamash: The Internet Consortium Holocaust Home Page
http://shamash.nysernet.org/holocaust/

A small but interesting collection of important Holocaust information. The contents include: documents refuting Holocaust denial, excerpts from original Nazi documents, statistics, Holocaust photographs, and a historical discussion of the "Protocols of the Elders of Zion."

The Simon Wiesenthal Center
http://www.wiesenthal.com

The Simon Wiesenthal Center is an international organization devoted to Holocaust remembrance, the defense of human rights, and combating contemporary anti-Semitism. The Center's homepage is another outstanding Internet source for Holocaust information, as well as current resources relating to anti-Semitism, prejudice, and racism in the world today.

Survivors of the Shoah Visual History Foundation
http://www.vhf.org/

Provides information about this nonprofit organization's efforts to create an archive of videotaped interviews with Holocaust survivors from around the world.

Teaching the Holocaust by Means of Stamps, Pictures, Text, and Children's Paintings
http://mofet.macam98.ac.il/~ochayo/einvert.htm

A wonderful collection of some very innovative Holocaust lesson plans. Teachers of both elementary and secondary grades will find these resources useful.

36 Questions about the Holocaust
http://www.wiesenthal.com/resource/36qlist1.htm

Created by the Simon Wiesenthal Center, this is an excellent tool to use with a class that is beginning study of Holocaust literature or the event itself. All teachers should consult this most useful document.

To Save a Life: Stories of Jewish Rescue
http://sorrel.humboldt.edu/~rescuers/

A collection of personal narratives and photographs of individuals who helped rescue Jews during the Holocaust. Countries represented include: Czechoslovakia, Holland, and Poland. Synopses of the narratives are also available for quick browsing.

United States Holocaust Memorial Museum
http://www.ushmm.org

Another essential Holocaust resource on the Internet. Information about the museum's facilities and collections is offered, as well as a wealth of resources for classroom teachers and their students to utilize.

Waco Holocaust Electronic Museum Library
http://www.dabney.com/WacoMuseum/library/library.html

Information about the history and holdings of the museum is included, as well as links to other resources.

Wannsee Protocol
http://www.english.upenn.edu/~afilreis/Holocaust/wansee-transcript.html

An English translation of the Wannsee Protocol, the blueprint the Nazis created for the systematic extermination of Europe's Jews. There is a link to the original German text as well.

World War Two in Europe: Timeline with Photos and Text
http://www.historyplace.com/worldwar2/timeline/ww2time.htm

Another excellent, extensive online timeline located on *The History Place* web site. Students can jump to any year between 1939-1945. Links to photos and text for certain events enhance the already useful resource even more.

YAD VASHEM
http://yad-vashem.org.il/

YAD VASHEM is The Holocaust Martyrs' and Heroes' Remembrance Authority. This homepage offers a great deal of information about the institution and about the people who have been declared "The Righteous Among the Nations."

Other Web Sites of Interest

Amnesty International
http://www.amnesty.org

Amnesty International is a nonprofit organization which monitors human rights violations around the world and acts as an advocate on behalf of victims of injustice. Of particular interest to educators will be Amnesty's resources on human rights education.

The Armenian Genocide
http://www-scf.usc.edu/~khachato/index1.html

This site offers some very introductory information about the Armenian Genocide.

Basic Facts on the Nanjing Massacre
http://www.cnd.org:8020/njmassacre/nj.html

An excellent source of general information about the Nanking Massacre and the Tokyo War Crimes Trial where many of its perpetrators were brought to justice. There are detailed facts about the atrocities committed, and an examination of the Japanese versions of the massacre. Includes a list of references.

Cambodian Genocide Page
http://www.cybercambodia.com/dachs/

This site offers a wealth of information on the Cambodian genocide committed under Pol Pot's Khmer Rouge regime. Included is information about the Cambodian "killing fields" and collections of survivors stories. Information on contemporary Cambodia is also available.

Exploratorium: Hiroshima/Nagasaki Links
http://www.exploratorium.edu/nagasaki/Library/Lin.html

Fact Sheet: Armenian Genocide
http://www.calpoly.edu/~pkiziria/pub-files/FACTS.html

Genocide: Also Known as Federal Indian Policy
http://mercury.sfsu.edu/~cypher/genocide.html

A historical overview of how the United States government has worked to systematically destroy indigenous peoples.

Genocide in Rwanda
http://MediaFilter.org/MFF/CAQ/CAQ52Rwanda.html

An informative site examining the tribal conflict in Rwanda that has devastated the nation and caused the death of hundreds of thousands of people on both sides. There is excellent historical background on Rwanda's colonial history and information on the tribal differences that escalated to create this conflict. The site also condemns the United States and the United Nations for their inadequate response to the conflict to a point of accusing both of complicity.

Human Rights Watch
http://www.hrw.org/home.html

Like Amnesty International, Human Rights Watch is a nonprofit, international organization monitoring human rights abuses around the world and acting on behalf of victims. Teachers interested in human rights education will find this site a valuable resource.

Human Rights Web
http://www.hrweb.org/

This site offers an excellent collection of resources on the history of the human rights movement and many documents pertaining to human rights issues and legislation. Biographies of prisoners of conscience are also available. Teachers interested in human rights education will want to use this site as a basic resource and beginning place with students.

Japanese War Crimes
http://www.cs.umn.edu/~dyue/wiihist/history.htm

A great deal of interesting information here, including: the rape of Nanking and other atrocities; the use of chemical and germ warfare by the Japanese army; and confessions of Japanese war criminals.

National Civil Rights Museum
http://www.mecca.org/~crights/ncrm.html

This site offers an introduction to the National Civil Rights Museum, located at the site of Dr. Martin Luther King's assassination at the Lorraine Motel, in Memphis, Tennessee. Included is information about the museum's events and exhibits, and a virtual tour is available as well.

The Native American Peoples: A History of Genocide
http://www.africa2000.com/BNDX/BAO320.htm

Another good historical overview of the treatment of Native Americans in colonial America and the United States.

The Other Holocaust: Nanjing Massacre
http://www.interlog.com/~yuan/japan.html

Reports on War Crimes in the Former Yugoslavia
http://www.haverford.edu/relg/sells/reports.html

Detailed reports of "ethnic cleansing operations," massacres, and other atrocities committed in the Bosnian conflict.

SAGE: Students Against GEnocide
http://www-leland.stanford.edu/group/SAGE

SAGE was formed in 1993 with the mission of uniting students around the world to work toward bringing peace to the people of Bosnia-Herzegovina. They are associated with the American Committee to Save Bosnia. The site offers a great deal of good information about war crimes committed in the former Yugoslavia, and serves as an excellent example of student activism.

Southern Poverty Law Center
http://www.splcenter.org

The Southern Poverty Law Center, located in Montgomery, Alabama, is a nonprofit organization that combats hate, intolerance, and discrimination through education and litigation. Included in this site is information about the Center's activities and resources. Of particular interest to educators will be the Center's "Teaching Tolerance" program.

U.N. Convention on the Prevention and Punishment of Genocide
http://hawaii-shopping.com/~sammonet/genocide.html

International Directory of Holocaust Memorials, Museums, Organizations, and Other Institutions

ADL Braun Holocaust Institute
823 United Nations Plaza
New York, NY 10017
(212) 885-7804
adlbraun@mindspring.com
http://www.adl.org

The Anti-Defamation League is an important watchdog organization devoted to exposing and combating anti-Semitic propaganda and actions through a variety of means. The ADL closely monitors the activities of militias and reports on all types of hate crimes. They offer resources of various kinds to educators, produce many valuable educational materials, and maintain a frequently updated site on the World Wide Web.

Allentown Jewish Archives
Holocaust Resource Center
702 North 22nd Street
Allentown, PA 18104
(215) 821-5500

American Friends of the Ghetto Fighter's House
P.O. Box 2153
765 Queen Anne Road
Teaneck, NJ 07666
(201) 836-1910
http://www.amfriendsgfh.org

The American Friends of The Ghetto Fighters' House is the American affiliate of The Ghetto Fighters' House, a leading Holocaust and Jewish Resistance museum and educational center, located in northern Israel. The founders of the institution are survivors of the Holocaust, many of whom were active in the Jewish Resistance.

American Gathering of Jewish Holocaust Survivors
122 West 30th Street
New York, NY 10001
(212) 239-4230

American Jewish Archives
3101 Clifton Avenue
Cincinnati, OH 45220
(513) 221-1875

The American Jewish Archives is an internationally recognized institution dedicated to the study of the Jewish experience in America and the rest of the Western Hemisphere. The Archives serves as a repository for World Jewish Congress papers, including two million pages of documentation highlighting rescue and relief efforts the WJC conducted during the Holocaust.

American Jewish Historical Society
2 Thorton Road
Waltham, MA 02154

American Society for Yad Vashem
500 Fifth Avenue
New York, NY 10110-1699
(212) 220-4304

Anne Frank Center, U.S.A.
584 Broadway
New York, NY 10012
(212) 431-7993
e-mail: 72550.3225@compuserv.com

Auschwitz Study Foundation, Inc.
P.O. Box 2232
Huntington Beach, CA 92647
(714) 848-1101

Baltimore Jewish Council
5750 Park Heights Avenue
Baltimore, MD 21215
(410) 542-4850
e-mail: baltjc@cje.noli.com

Beit Lohamei Haghetaot (The Ghetto Fighter's House)
Kibbutz Lochamei-Haghetaot
D.N. Western Galilee
Israel
(04) 995-8080

Founded in April 1949 by Holocaust survivors, many of whom were members of the Jewish Resistance, The Ghetto Fighters' House is one of Israel's leading museum and educational centers dedicated to commemorating and teaching people about the Holocaust and the Jewish Resistance. Among the institution's many features are historical exhibits, an art museum, an extensive film and documentation archive, and a teacher's training institute.

Beit Theresienstadt
Kibbutz Givat hayim-ihud
Mobile Post Emek Hefer
38935 Israel
972-6-636515
e-mail: bterezin@inter.net.il
www.cet.ac.il/terezin/terezin.htm

Located at Kibbutz Chaym Ichud, Beit Theresienstadt was opened in 1975 in memory of the Jews who perished in the ghetto and concentration camp. Among the many activities of Beit Theresienstadt are: an educational center that prepares Holocaust curricula for students and teachers from Israel and abroad; exhibitions of works by the artists of Terezin; archives and collections of documents, testimonies, and artifacts concerning Ghetto Theresienstadt; and a newsletter published twice a year in English, German, and Hebrew.

Beth Shalom Holocaust Memorial and Educational Centre
Laxton, Newark
NG22 0PA Nottinghamshire, UK
(+44) 1623-836627

Canadian Centre for Studies of the Holocaust and Genocide
2787 Bathurst Street
Toronto, Ont. M6B 3A2
Canada

Center for Holocaust Awareness and Information
Jewish Community Federation of Greater Rochester
441 East Avenue
Rochester, NY 14607
(716) 461-0290
e-mail: JESD@eznet.net (Subject: ATTN: Barbara Applebaum)

Center for Holocaust Studies
Brookdale Community College
765 Newman Spring Road
Lincroft, NJ 07738
(908) 224-2769

A resource center serving the college community and local schools.
The center has a collection of approximately 1,000 volumes.
Volunteers are largely responsible for running the Center and its
programs and the budget is primarily financed through budgets and
fundraising.

Center for Holocaust and Genocide Studies
Ramapo College Library
505 Ramapo Valley Road
Mahwah, NJ 07430
(201) 529-7409

The purpose of the Center for Holocaust and Genocide Studies at
Ramapo College is to instruct and sensitize educators to the lessons and
tragedies of the Holocaust and other genocides. The Center conducts
seminars for educators and also sponsors lectures and film series. Oral
histories are also collected by the Center. The collection now holds
over 100 testimonies. The original tape is deposited with the Fortunoff
Collection at Yale University and a copy is kept at the Center. The
Center houses a collection of over 700 print and film materials.

Center for Holocaust Education
St. Cloud State University
Stewart Hall 125
St. Cloud, MN 56301
(320) 255-3293

Center for Holocaust Studies, Documentation and Research
1605 Avenue J

Brooklyn, NY 11230
(718) 338-6494

The Center administers a major oral history project, which involves
interviewing survivors and American soldiers who participated in the
liberation of the concentration camps. The tapes are transcribed,
verified, and catalogued. The Center also collects documents,
Photostats of letters, artifacts, etc., from the period 1939-1945.

Community Relations Committee of the United Jewish Federation of
   Greater San Diego
5511 El Cajon Boulevard
San Diego, CA 92115

The Dallas Memorial Center for Holocaust Studies
7900 Northaven Road
Dallas, TX 75230
(214) 750-4654

Dayton Holocaust Resource Center
100 East Woodbury Drive
Dayton, OH 45415
(513) 278-7444

Drew University Center for Holocaust Study
Rose Memorial Library/301
Madison, NJ 07940
(201) 408-3600

El Paso Holocaust Museum and Study Center
405 Wallenberg Drive
El Paso, TX 79912
(915) 833-5656
http://www.huntel.com

The purpose of The El Paso Holocaust and Study Center is to combat
prejudice and bigotry and to remind the world of the value and dignity
of human life through remembrance of and education about the Nazi
Holocaust. Resources of the museum include a large collection of
artifacts and an educational facility, which has a referral service
providing speakers.

Facing History and Ourselves
16 Hurd Road
Brookline, MA 02146
(617) 232-1595
http://www.facing.org

A national educational and professional development organization, the mission of Facing History and Ourselves is to engage students of diverse backgrounds in an examination of anti-Semitism, prejudice, and racism in order to promote a more humane and informed citizenry. To meet that end, the organization offers opportunities to study the historical development and lessons of the Holocaust, and other forms of genocide, to enable students to make connections between history and the moral choices they will confront in their own lives. The organization provides teachers with staff development in the form of institutes, seminars, and workshops. It also makes available to teachers an assortment of books, periodicals, speakers, and videotapes for classroom use. The national headquarters of the organization is in Brookline, Massachusetts. There are regional offices in Chicago, Los Angeles, Memphis, New York City, and San Francisco.

Fortunoff Video Archive for Holocaust Testimonies
P.O. Box 802840
Sterling Memorial Library
Yale University
New Haven, CT 06520-8240
(203) 432-1879
e-mail: loren.burns@yale.edu
http://www.library.yale.edu/testimonies/homepage.html

The Archive holds a collection of over 3,700 videotaped interviews with witnesses and survivors of the Holocaust. The Archive is part of Manuscripts and Archives at Stirling Memorial Library, Yale University.

Fred R. Crawford Witness to the Holocaust Project
Emory University
Atlanta, GA 30322
(404) 329-6428

Friends of Le Chambon
8033 Sunset Boulevard
Suite 784
Los Angeles, CA 90064
(213) 650-1774

An organization dedicated to exploring why the people of Le Chambon, France, and others like them aided victims of the Holocaust while the rest of the world looked away. Holdings include documents, photographs, and other materials related to righteous conduct during the Holocaust.

Fundacion Memoira Del Holocausto
Montevideo 919
1019 Buenos Aires, Argentina
54-1-811-3537

Georgia Commission on the Holocaust
330 Capitol Avenue, S.E.
Atlanta, GA 30334
(404) 651-9273

Greater Cincinnati Interfaith Holocaust Foundation
3101 Clifton Avenue
Cincinnati, OH 45220
(513) 221-1875

Halina Wind Preston Holocaust Education Center
P.O. Box 2193
Wilmington, DE 19899
(302) 478-2100

Hatifvah Holocaust Education and Resource Center
1160 Dickinson Street
Springfield, MA 01108
(413) 737-4313

The Hawaii Holocaust Project
W. S. Richardson School of Law
University of Hawaii, Moanoa
2515 Dole Street
Honolulu, HI 96822

(808) 956-6994

Holocaust and Education Center of Central Florida
851 North Maitland Avenue
Maitland, FL 32751

Holocaust Awareness Institute
University of Denver
2199 South University Boulevard
Denver, CO 80208
(303) 871-3013
e-mail: dmichael@dn.edu

Coordinates Holocaust Days of Remembrance observances in the Denver area and has other community programming throughout the year.

Holocaust Awareness Museum
Gratz College
7611 Old York Road
Melrose Park, PA 01960
(215) 635-6480

Holocaust Center for the North Shore Jewish Foundation
McCarthy School
70 Lake Street, Room 108
Peabody, MA 01960
(508) 535-0003

Holocaust Center of the United Jewish Federation of Greater Pittsburgh
242 McKee Place
Pittsburgh, PA 15213
(412) 682-7111
ujf.pgh.lhurwitz@globalaccess.net

A full service educational resource center with a library collection and offering teacher training, curriculum development, speaking engagements, exhibits, and other educational programs.

The Holocaust Center of Northern California
639 14th Avenue
San Francisco, CA 94118

(415) 751-6041

The Center offers a library, some documents, and an exhibit.

Holocaust Child Survivors of Connecticut
2658 Albany Avenue
W. Hartford, CT 06117
(860) 523-5600

The Holocaust Documentation and Education Center at Florida International University
3000 N.E. 145 Street
North Miami, FL 33181
(305) 919-5690
e-mail: xholocau@servak.fiu.edu

Opened in 1979 and located at the North Miami Campus of Florida International University, the major purpose of The Holocaust Documentation and Education Center was to interview Holocaust survivors, liberators, and rescuers. Over the year's the Center's objectives and programs have expanded and diversified. The Center is now recognized as the international prototype for Holocaust documentation and education. Its oral history collection of over 1,000 interviews is renowned for being the largest, self-produced, standardized archive of Holocaust testimonies in the United States. The Center also includes a large reference library and memorabilia display. The Center sponsors teacher seminars and institutes, and offers curricular support to educators. The Center also has an active, heavily used speaker's bureau.

Holocaust Education and Memorial Centre of Toronto
4600 Bathurst Street
North York, Ontario
Canada M2R 3V2
(416) 631-5689
e-mail: pzilberman@feduja.org
http://www.feduja.org

Holocaust Education Center and Memorial Museum of Houston
2425 Mountainview Drive, Suite 270
Houston, TX 77057

Holocaust Education Center/Hiroshima Japan
866 Nakatsuhara
Miyuki Fukuyama-City
Hiroshima Pref.
Japan 720
(81) 849-55-0552
hecjpn@urban.or.jp

Holocaust Education Foundation
P.O. Box 6153
Newport News, VA 23606-1617

Holocaust Education Resource Center
College of St. Elizabeth
2 Convent Road
Morristown, NJ 07960
(201) 605-351
e-mail: sepinwall@liza.st-elizabeth.edu

Holocaust/Genocide Studies Center
Plainview/Old Bethpage
John F. Kennedy High School
5 Kennedy Drive
Plainview, NY 11803
(516) 937-6382

Holocaust-Genocide Studies Project
Monroe Community College
1000 East Henrietta Road
Rochester, NY 14623
(716) 292-3228

Holocaust Human Rights Center of Maine
P.O. Box 4645
Augusta, ME 04330-1644
(207) 993-2620
e-mail: nicholssk@juno.com

Incorporated since 1985, the mission of the Holocaust Human Rights
Center of Maine is to foster public education about the Holocaust and
issues of human rights, which grow out of study of and reflection upon
that event. The Center's goal is to teach lessons that can be learned

from the Holocaust about what can happen when basic human rights are destroyed. A cooperative agreement exists between the Center, the Maine Department of Education, and the University of Maine System to assist the Center in developing and promoting curricular materials dealing with the Holocaust and human rights issues.

Holocaust Learning Center
David Posnack Jewish Center
5850 South Pine Island Road
Davie, FL 33328

Holocaust Library and Research Center of San Francisco
639 14th Avenue
San Francisco, CA 94118

Holocaust Memorial Center
Jewish Community Center
6600 West Maple Road
West Bloomfield, MI 48033
(313) 661-0840

The Center holds a library and archives concentrating on documentation and literature of the Holocaust, destroyed communities in Europe, Jewish life and culture in pre-war Europe, and Jewish-Christian relations in historical perspective.

Holocaust Memorial Committee of Brooklyn
1405 Avenue Z
Box 265
Brooklyn, NY 11235
(718) 934-3500

Holocaust Memorial Foundation of Illinois
4255 West Main Street
Skokie, IL 60067-2063
(847) 677-4640
e-mail: 75557.1427@compuserv.com

Holocaust Memorial Resource and Education Center of Central Florida
851 North Maitland Avenue
Maitland, FL 32751
(407) 628-0555

Founded in 1980, The Holocaust Memorial Resource and Education Center acts upon the philosophy that genocide is the product of hatred, prejudice, ignorance, and indifference, and can only be prevented through education. The Center's primary mission is to provide educators with resource materials, including extensive multimedia holdings, a large book collection, and other important archival and documentary materials. All materials are provided free of charge. The Center also sponsors many community programs including lectures, dramatic performances, and educational conferences.

Holocaust Memorial and Educational Center of Nassau County
Welwyn Preserve
100 Crescent Beach Road
Glen Cove, NY 11542
(516) 571-8040

Holocaust Museum and Learning Center
12 Millstone Campus Drive
St. Louis, MO 63146
(314) 432-0020

Holocaust Museum Houston
5401 Caroline Street
Houston, TX 77004
(713) 942-8000
e-mail: laura@hmh.org
http://www.hmh.org

The mission of Holocaust Museum Houston is to promote awareness of the dangers of prejudice, hatred, and violence. The museum meets that end through a variety of educational activities.

Holocaust Oral History Archive of Gratz College
Old York Road and Melrose Avenue
Melrose Park, PA 19027
(215) 635-7300, ext. 30

Holocaust Oral History Project
P.O. Box 77603
San Francisco, CA 94107
(415) 882-7092

Holocaust Resource Center
Bureau of Jewish Education
441 East Avenue
Rochester, NY 14607

Holocaust Resource Center
Jewish Welfare Federation of Greater Toledo
6505 Sylvania Avenue
Sylvania, OH 43650

Holocaust Resource Center
Kean College of New Jersey
Nancy Thompson Library
Morris Avenue
Union, NJ 07208
(908) 527-3049

The Holocaust Resource Center at Kean College is a joint venture of
Kean and the Holocaust Resource Foundation, a private philanthropic
organization founded by a group of survivors who live in neighboring
communities. Among its many activities, the Center cooperates with
the School of Education on teaching multiculturalism and collects
materials on prejudice, racism, and ethnic diversity. The Center also
offers scholarships to educators participating in graduate courses on
"Teaching the Holocaust" and "Teaching Prejudice Reduction."

Holocaust Resource Center
Keene State College
Mason Library
Box 3201, 229 Main Street
Keene, NH 03431
(603) 358-2490
e-mail: childebr@keene.edu

Holocaust Resource Center
Stockton State College
Pomona, NJ 08240
(609) 652-1776

The Holocaust Resource Center at Stockton State College is a joint
project of Stockton and the Jewish Federation of Atlantic and Cape
May Counties. The Center focuses on the study of the Holocaust and

serves as a repository for Holocaust materials. Awareness programs and workshops to train educators teaching the Holocaust are sponsored through a variety of activities.

Holocaust Resource Center and Archives
Queensborough Community College
222-05 56th Avenue
Bayside, NY 11364
(718) 225-1617
e-mail: hrcaho@dorsai.org

Holocaust Resource Center of Buffalo
1050 Maryvale Drive
Cheektowaga, NY 14225
(716) 634-9535

Holocaust Resource Center of Minneapolis
8200 West 33rd Street
Minneapolis, MN 55426
(612) 935-0316

Holocaust Resource Center of the JCRC of South Jersey
2393 W. Marlton Pike
Cherry Hill, NJ 08002
(609) 665-6100

Holocaust Resource Center of the Jewish Federation of Greater Clifton-Passaic
199 Scoles Avenue
Clifton, NJ 07012
(201) 777-7031

Holocaust Resource Center of Toledo
6465 Sylvania Avenue
Sylvania, OH 43560
(419) 885-4485

Holocaust Studies Center
The Bronx High School of Science
75 West 205th Street
Bronx, NY 10468
(718) 367-5252

Holocaust Survivors and Friends in Pursuit of Justice
800 New Loudon Road
Suite 400
Latham, NY 12100
(518) 785-0035

Holocaust Survivors Memorial Foundation
350 Fifth Avenue
Suite 3508
New York, NY 10118
(212) 594-8765

The Foundation is devoted exclusively to the funding of Holocaust-related projects, including the Institute for Holocaust Studies, survivor and oral history conferences, and other educational events. The Foundation also offers grants to researchers, playwrights, filmmakers, and writers.

House of the Wannsee Conference
AmGroBen Wannsee 56-58
14109 Berlin
Germany
030/80-50-00-10

Institute for Holocaust Studies
Graduate Center of the City University of New York
33 West 42nd Street
New York, NY 10036

The Institute sponsors free seminars and in-service courses on teaching about the Holocaust for elementary and secondary school teachers.

Interfaith Council on the Holocaust
125 South 9th Street
Suite 300
Philadelphia, PA 19107
(215) 922-7222

The International Center for Holocaust Studies
Anti-Defamation League of B'nai B'rith
823 United Nations Plaza
New York, NY 10017

(212) 490-2525

The Center produces and distributes films and publications primarily for educational institutions. *Dimensions*, a journal of Holocaust studies, is also published by the Center. Local, national, and international staff development programs are also conducted. The Center works through 30 regional offices in the United States.

International Network of Children of Jewish Holocaust Survivors
Florida International University
N.E. 151st Street and Biscayne Boulevard
North Miami, FL 33181
(305) 940-5690

Jewish Federation of Las Vegas Holocaust Education Committee
3909 Maryland Parkway
Suite 400
Las Vegas, NV 89119-7520
(702) 732-0556

Jewish Foundation for the Righteous
165 East 56th Street, Suite 301
New York, NY 10022
(212) 421-1221
e-mail: jfrnyc@worldnet.att.net

Jewish Holocaust Museum and Research Centre
13 Selwyn Street
Elsternwick
Melbourne, Victoria
Australia 3185
(03) 9528-1985

JIR–Holocaust Museum and Raoul Wallenberg Operation Truth and Brotherhood to Prevent Genocide Center
1453 Levick Road
Philadelphia, PA 19149

Joseph Meyerhoff Library
Baltimore Hebrew University
5800 Park Heights Avenue
Baltimore, MD 21215

Julius and Dorothy Koppelman Holocaust/Genocide Resource Center
Rider University
2083 Lawrenceville Road
Lawrenceville, NJ 08648
(609) 896-5345
e-mail: holctr@rider.edu

Kharkov Holocaust Center
P.O.B. 4756
Kharkov 310002
Ukraine
0572-436887

Leo Baeck Institute
129 East 73rd Street
New York, NY 10021

Lillian and A. J. Weinberg Center for Holocaust Education of the
William Breman Jewish Heritage Museum
The Spring Center
1440 Spring Street N.E.
Atlanta, GA 30309-2837
(404) 873-1661

A Living Memorial to the Holocaust
Museum of Jewish Heritage
342 Madison Avenue, Suite 706
New York, NY 10173

Mania Nudel Holocaust Learning Center
Jewish Community Center
5850 Pine Island Road
Davie, FL 33328
(954) 434-0499

The Holocaust Learning Center is dedicated to promoting remembrance
and understanding of the Holocaust by offering the community an
extensive Holocaust library that includes young adult literature and
multimedia resources for use in classroom instruction. The Center also
hosts a lecture and film series and presents continuous exhibitions of
Holocaust artifacts and photographs.

March of the Living (Canada)
4600 Bathurst Street
Suite 315
Willowdale, ONT M2R 3V3
Canada
(416) 636-7655

March of the Living (International)
6 Laskov Street
Tel Aviv
Israel 64736
03-696-6161

March of the Living (USA)
136 East 39th Street
New York, NY 10016
(212) 252-0900

Martyrs Memorial and Museum of the Holocaust
of the Jewish Federation Council
6505 Wilshire Boulevard
Los Angeles, CA 90048
(213) 852-3242

Massuah Institute for the Study of the Holocaust
Kibbutz tel Yitzhak
45805 Tel Aviv, Israel
972-9-69965
massuah@netvision.net.il

Memorial Center for Holocaust Studies
7060 Brookshire Drive
Dallas, TX 75230
(214) 750-4654

The holdings of the Memorial Center include memorabilia, weapons, camp uniforms, passports, yellow armbands, barbed wire, and other artifacts. The study center has a large library of materials pertaining to anti-Semitism and the Holocaust, including rare and out-of-print publications and magazines.

Memorial Committee for the Six Million Jewish Martyrs
260 South 15th Street
Philadelphia, PA 19102

Metrowest Holocaust Education and Remembrance Council
901 Route 10
Whippany, NJ 07981
(201) 884-4800, ext. 178

Miami Holocaust Center
Greater Miami Jewish Federation
4200 Biscayne Boulevard
Miami, FL 33137

Midwest Center for Holocaust Education
5801 West 115th Street
Suite 106
Shawnee Mission, KS 66211-1800
(913) 327-8190
e-mail: SHOAHED@A.CRL.COM

The Montreal Holocaust Memorial Centre
5151 Cote Street
Catherine Road
Montreal, Quebec
Canada H3W 1M6
(514) 345-2605
e-mail: mhmc@accent.net

The Centre has a collection of documents, photographs, and artifacts
ranging from the nineteenth century to post-World War II. Educational
programs are offered for elementary and secondary school, and
university audiences.

National Catholic Center for Holocaust Education
Seton Hill College
Greensburg, PA 15601
(412) 830-1033
e-mail: ncche@setonhil.edu

National Conference of Christians and Jews
43 West 57th Street
New York, NY 10019

National Holocaust Remembrance Committee
Canadian Jewish Committee
1590 Avenue Drive Penfield
Montreal, P.Q. H3W 1H2
Canada

National Institute on the Holocaust
P.O. Box 2147
Philadelphia, PA 19103

Nevada Governor's Advisory Council on Education Relating to the
Holocaust
3909 South Maryland Parkway
Suite 400
Las Vegas, NV 89119-7520
(702) 732-0556

New Jersey Commission on Holocaust Education
New Jersey Department of Education
240 West State Street CN500
Trenton, NJ 08625-0500
(609) 292-9274

New York City Commission on the Holocaust
111 West 40th Street
New York, NY 10018
(212) 221-1573

The goal of the Commission is to establish a museum, library, and
archival center and lecture facility as a memorial to the victims of the
Holocaust.

New York State Museum Holocaust Center/Exhibit
New York State Cultural Education Center
Albany, NY 12230
(518) 474-5801

The Museum offers a permanent exhibit area of the history of the

Holocaust, United States inaction, and the "temporary haven" for 982 Jewish refugees in Oswego, N.Y.

North Carolina Council on the Holocaust
Department of Human Resources
101 Blaire Drive
Raleigh, NC 27603
(919) 733-2173

Oregon Holocaust Resource Center
2043 College Way
Warner 2S
Forest Grove, OR 97116
(503) 244-6284
e-mail: boasjl@PACIFICU.EDU

Rhode Island Holocaust Memorial Museum and Educational Outreach
   Center
4041 Elmgrove Avenue
Providence, RI 09206

Rockland Center for Holocaust Studies
17 South Madison Avenue
Spring Valley, NY 10977
(914) 356-2700

Rosenthal Institute for Holocaust Studies
Graduate School and University Center of the City University of New
York
33 West 42nd Street, Room 1516 GB
New York, NY 10036
(212) 642-2183

Russian Holocaust Research and Educational Center
Bulatnikovsky pas. 14-4-77
Moscow, Russia 113403
(095) 383-6242
e-mail: altman@glas.apc.org

Sanford L. Ziff Jewish Museum of Florida
301 Washington Avenue
South Miami Beach, FL
(305) 672-5044

Simon Wiesenthal Center
9760 West Pico Boulevard
Los Angeles, CA 90035
(310) 553-9036
e-mail: library@wiesenthal.com
http://www.wiesenthal.com

The Simon Wiesenthal Center is an international organization devoted
to Holocaust remembrance, the defense of human rights, and combating
contemporary anti-Semitism. Headquartered in Los Angeles, the Center
provides a variety of educational activities, including a library,
museums, and many publications. The Center's frequently updated
homepage is an outstanding Internet source for Holocaust information,
as well as current resources relating to anti-Semitism, prejudice, and
racism in the world today.

Sonoma State University Holocaust Studies Center
1801 East Cotai Avenue
Rohnert Park, CA 94928
(707) 664-4076/2160

South Carolina Council on the Holocaust
2352 Two Notch Road
Columbia, SC 29204
(803) 413-3819
e-mail: mwalden@scsn.net

South Florida Holocaust Memorial
1933-1945 Meridian Avenue
Miami Beach, FL 33139
(305) 538-1663

The South Florida Holocaust Memorial Museum is dedicated to
remembering and paying tribute to the Jews of the Holocaust whose
dreams did not come true. The Memorial features a sculpture by
Kenneth Triester.

Southern Institute for Education and Research at Tulane University
Tulane University
MR Box 1692
31 McAlister Drive
New Orleans, LA 70118-5555
(504) 865-6100
e-mail: so-inst.mailhost.TCS.Tulane.Edu
http://www.tulane.edu/~so-inst

Southern Poverty Law Center
400 Washington Avenue
Montgomery, AL 36104

Standing Committee on the Holocaust
950 West 41st Avenue
Vancouver, B.C. V52 2N7
Canada

Stiftung Topography des Terrors
Budapester Strasse 40
D-10787 Berlin
Germany
49-30-25 45 090

St. Louis Center for Holocaust Studies
12 Millstone Campus Drive
St. Louis, MO 63146
(314) 432-0020

Founded by the Jewish Federation, the Center offers a community
lecture series, commemorative programs, art exhibits, and a book and
film library.

Survivors of the Shoah Visual History Foundation
P.O. Box 3168
Los Angeles, CA 90078-3168
(800) 777-7802 (U.S. and Canada) (818) 777-7802 (Other)
e-mail: daisy@vhf.org
http://www.whf.org

Founded by motion picture director and producer Steven Spielberg in

1994, the Shoah Visual History Foundation is a nonprofit organization dedicated to videotaping and archiving interviews of Holocaust survivors all over the world. The goal of the Foundation is to compile the most comprehensive library of survivor testimony to be used as a tool for global education about the Holocaust, and to teach racial, ethnic, and cultural tolerance.

Tampa Bay Holocaust Memorial Museum and Educational Center
5001 Duhme Road
Madeira Beach, FL 33708-2700
(813) 392-4678
e-mail: 102477.1162@compuserve.com
http://zipmall.com/holocaust.htm

The Tampa Bay Holocaust Memorial Museum hosts visiting exhibits, provides teacher-training programs, features   lectures of Holocaust authors and scholars, and records eyewitness testimony of Holocaust survivors, liberators, and rescuers, which are part of a permanent archive located at the Center as well as at the United States Holocaust Memorial Museum in Washington, D.C.

Tauber Institute
Brandeis University
Waltham, MA 02254

Temple Judea of Manhasset Holocaust Resource Center
333 Searingtown Road
Manhasset, NY 11030

Tennessee Holocaust Commission on Education
2417 West End Avenue
Nashville, TN 37240
(615) 343-2563
e-mail: tnhol.com@ctrvax.vanderbilt.edu

United States Holocaust Memorial Council
425 13th Street, N.W. Suite 832
Washington, D.C. 20004

United States Holocaust Memorial Museum
100 Raoul Wallenberg Place, Southwest
(15th Street and Independence Avenue)

Washington, D.C. 20024-2150
(202) 488-0400
e-mail: education@ushmm.org, or research@ushmm.org
http://www.uhmm.org

Vancouver Holocaust Centre for Education and Remembrance
#50-950 West 41st Avenue
Vancouver, BC
Canada V5Z 2N7
(604) 264-0499
e-mail: holedctr@cybestore.ca
The Vancouver Holocaust Centre Education Society for Educational
Remembrance (VHC) exits to combat prejudice and racism by
educating the citizens of British Columbia, especially teachers and
students, about the events and implications of the Holocaust.
Incorporated since 1985, the center makes available many
interdisciplinary programs.

The Vanderbilt University Holocaust Art Collection
Vanderbilt University
402 Sarratt Student Center
Nashville, TN 37240
(615) 322-2471
e-mail: LOGIUDICE@vansvz.vanderbilt.edu

Washington State Holocaust Education Resource Center
2031 Third Avenue
Seattle, WA 98121
(206) 441-5747

Westchester Holocaust Commission
2900 Purchase Street
Purchase, NY 10577
(914) 696-0738
e-mail: WestHoloComm@MSN.COM

William Wiener Oral History Library
American Jewish Committee
165 East 65th Street
New York, NY 10022

Witness to the Holocaust Project
Emory University
Atlanta, GA 30322
(404) 329-7525

Focuses on recording the testimony of persons who witnessed the camps during the liberation period (e.g., military personnel, relief agency workers, and the press corps).

Yad Vashem
The Holocaust Martyrs' and Heroes' Remembrance Authority
P.O.B. 3477
Jerusalem, Israel 91034
972-2-6751611
http://www.yad-vashem.org.il

YIVO Institute for Jewish Research
1048 Fifth Avenue
New York, NY 10028
(212) 535-6700

YIVO does not deal exclusively with the Holocaust, but it has an outstanding library on the Holocaust and particularly strong is its photograph collection.

Zachor Holocaust Center
1753 Peachtree Road, Northeast
Atlanta, GA 30309

ZACHOR: The Holocaust Research Center
National Jewish Resource Center
250 West 57th Street
New York, NY 10107

Zell Center for Holocaust Studies
Spertus Institute of Jewish Studies
618 South Michigan Avenue
Chicago, IL 60605
(312) 922-9012

Booktalks, Classroom Activities, and Lesson Plans

Booktalks

Any good librarian will tell you booktalking is a marvelous means of introducing young people to books. The purpose of the booktalk is to "sell" a book to a reader. Booktalks are typically used for young adult audiences, but there are plenty of books for older children that can also be booktalked. When booktalking, the most important thing to remember is tell the reader just enough about the book to make them interested enough in it that one will want to read it for oneself. The booktalker must be careful not to give too much away in the talk. Collected here are several good examples of tested booktalks for books cited in the bibliographies. Use them as models for creating your own. For more information on the art of booktalking and tips on how to create your own, see the many editions of Joni Brodart's *Booktalk!* series available from H.W. Wilson.

Children of Bach by Eilis Dillon

"No matter what comes next, there will always be music." That's what Peter's father told him, before he and his mother disappeared.

Pali was the first to get home that day. It was his turn to use the music room to practice. The music room, which also happened to be the dining room, was big and cool, with a long parquet floor for walking up and down while practicing the violin; Pali loved to play there. Suzy, his sister, would be using the living room to practice her cello. Mama and Papa did their practicing in the morning while the rest of the family was at school.

As he walked through the streets of Budapest, Pali noticed that there were few people around, except for the German soldiers. The light reflecting off the windows of the apartment buildings gave him a feeling of being watched by hundreds of eyes. In the last few days at school, he noticed some of the boys whispering secrets to one another, which stopped when Jewish boys came close enough to hear. Pali always felt better at home. But today he would learn that home had totally changed.

He was about to ring the doorbell when he noticed that the door was standing open about an inch or so. He pushed it gently and slid into the hall. It was very quiet. Only Minna the cat rubbed against his ankles with a gentle purr. He went to the kitchen, filled her saucer with milk and noticed the breakfast dishes still in the sink. Aunt Eva must have heard there was something good in the shop and rushed out to try to get it. Yet he had an odd feeling that something was different. Mama must be in the music room practicing–this was a concert day. Both his parents were prominent musicians. But no–and they were not in their bedrooms either. When he looked in the closet, both suitcases were gone, as well as their coats. Both their violins were there. Tonight they were supposed to play the Bach Double Concerto together before a huge audience. They shouldn't have gone out. Something was wrong, and he suddenly felt like he might begin to cry. He decided to practice–there was nothing else to do–and playing the scales and his exercises gradually brought a sort of calmness. Then the bell rang. But it was his sister Suzy and her friend David. A little later, Peter arrived and Pali told his story again, of no one being home. Peter was not surprised. He had already heard the frightening news: everyone was being arrested–taken to the brickyard behind a high wall, just because they were Jews. The younger children started to get upset and looked toward Peter.

"You think they'll come for us?"

"Who knows? But I know what we'll do next–exactly what we do every day."

"You mean practice, like on an ordinary day?"

"Yes. If Papa were here, he'd say: 'Remember, you are children of Bach. You must play some Bach every single day. That's how you make a musician.'"

So life went on, almost as usual, at least for a little while. Except then it becomes too dangerous for even children to stay and Peter, Pali, Suzy, and David must find their way away from the danger, away from the Holocaust.

Contributed by Beryl Eber, Supervising Young Adult Specialist
The New York Public Library
Manhattan Borough Office

The Diary of a Young Girl by Anne Frank

Thirteen-year-old Anne Frank does not belong, hidden away in her father's office building that became known as the Secret Annex. Yet she feels she lives in a paradise compared to others and assumes at some point all will return to normal.

Here is the expanded version of Anne's diary, originally published in 1947. It had been edited by her father, and this definitive edition contains about 30% more material. It reveals not only her talents as a writer, and her capacity for self-evaluation, her doubts as well as her strength, but also that, above all, Anne Frank was a teenager. She's concerned about her awakening sexuality. Boys are attracted to her and she knows it. She feels her mother treats her like a baby.

Here's an example of typical teenage angst. (Read aloud the four complete paragraphs on p. 64.) If you haven't read *The Diary of a Young Girl*, it's time to take a look.

Contributed by Beryl Eber, Supervising Young Adult Specialist
The New York Public Library
Manhattan Borough Office

Smoke and Ashes by Barbara Rogasky

This is a book about terrible things, the kinds of things that appear in nightmares. But unlike a bad dream, this really happened. In twelve years almost six million people were deliberately murdered. They were not killed because they were soldiers, or spies, or guilty of any crime—only because they were Jews. How did it happen, and why? This book, *Smoke and Ashes* by Barbara Rogasky, tries to answer these questions. Reading about the Holocaust is not easy; the details are unpleasant, cruel, and even painful to read. But it is a story that needs to be told.

Adolf Hitler promised the people of Germany a way to restore their pride. They had lost World War I, and he told them the reason was their chief enemy: the Jews. He was appointed chancellor and within two years took absolute power for himself. The Nazi Party ran the country. To the Nazis, the Jews were automatically "enemies of the people and the state." At first, Jews were kept out of certain jobs. Then books of an "un-German spirit" were removed from libraries and burned. Later, Jews were forced out of towns where their families had lived for generations. In Poland, they were moved into ghettos, located in the oldest, most run-down sections of town, where thousands died of starvation.

Then, there were the special action groups. These were specially trained firing squads. They would enter a village and order all of the Jews to assemble. They had to hand over all their valuables. Then they had to dig a long, deep ditch, and they were shot and thrown into the ditch. In other words, they had to dig their own graves. It is estimated that two million Jews were killed this way. But this way was too slow.

So the Nazis proceeded with the "Final Solution": the establishment of death camps, like Auschwitz, so that large groups could be killed at one time. The chilling description of the horror and death of those camps I will leave for you to read in *Smoke and Ashes*. Once you read it, you will never forget it.

Contributed by Beryl Eber, Supervising Young Adult Specialist
The New York Public Library
Manhattan Borough Office

The Journey by Ida Fink

They had talked about escaping several times. People had been disappearing from the ghetto–some to hiding places, most never to return. But that had been just talk. This time, she knew for certain that the decision had been made. Father found documents for her and her sister, saying they were Aryan, not Jewish–identity cards with made-up names. She was not to be Katarzyna and her sister Elzbieta.

The day of their departure, they each spent a long time in front of the mirror, fixing their kerchiefs on their heads, the most important item of clothing in their travel wardrobe because their kerchiefs were what peasant girls wore–not Jewish girls. She tied the knot under her chin and forced a smile as she looked at her face among the roses and leaves of the scarf. The suitcase contained their new wardrobe–neutral, gray. The pocketbook held the documents–fake birth certificates, identity cards, letters from sponsors who would be giving them jobs in Germany. Unlike those who'd been rounded up on the street or those who'd been taken away for forced labor, they were volunteers. They knew where they were going and what sort of work they'd be doing.

That night, they walked across an endless plain. Later, they slept on straw in a peasant's attic. They tried not to think about Father in the ghetto, about mother who was no longer alive. They were silent all night. She didn't know it yet, but from now on, it would always be like this. At difficult moments, they would always be silent. Not until daybreak did Elzbieta ask, "What do you think?" and she answered, "I think it will work out somehow." Then the farmer harnessed the horses for the two hour drive. Then they would arrive in the provincial capital, alone, with only their cleverness to rely on, and their luck.

This is the story of their journey; constantly changing their names, hidden traps and close escapes are routine. Will they be discovered? Will the Nazis learn that the sisters are not Polish peasant girls, but Jews who they want to exterminate? The journey through hell is their only hope of survival.

Contributed by Beryl Eber, Supervising Young Adult Specialist
The New York Public Library
Manhattan Borough Office

Fragments by Binjamin Wilkomirski

Think back to your earliest memory. Is it your mother's face, or your first day of school? For Binjamin, there are only pieces of memories–fragments of a childhood, because his growing up was filled with such horror, his mind buried a lot of it deep inside. It was World War II, the Holocaust. His early childhood was on a farm in Poland with his brothers. He remembers seeing his father killed in front of him. Separated from his brothers, he finds himself in a death camp–with fears both inhuman–of bugs and rats–and human–the uniforms, with the blows, the kicks, the whip. Many of the images are shocking. (Read aloud from pp. 69-71 in the hardcover edition.) These fragments will slice into your soul.

Contributed by Beryl Eber, Supervising Young Adult Specialist
The New York Public Library
Manhattan Borough Office

Summer of My German Soldier by Bette Greene

The setting is World War II in rural Arkansas. Patty is a twelve-year-old girl who lives with her two abusive parents. Patty's father is a volatile man who has fits of rage. He beats her mercilessly. His past demons haunt him. And Patty's mother does not like her because she thinks that Patty's just not cute enough. Patty is also Jewish, which means she cannot go to the Baptist summer camp that all the other kids in town attend. Patty's summer just sucks in every way.

Patty has a five-year-old sister who is cute, perky, and has fits of "the giggles," and her parents just adore her. If only Patty was less serious and more like her sister, if she just had a little of that "cute" in her, then maybe her parents would like her too.

But don't feel too bad for Patty because she does have one ally in the house, and her name is Ruth. Ruth does all of the cooking and cleaning for the family and she has lovingly taken over the role of mother and protector to Patty. Their bond is strong and Patty will rely upon Ruth as the danger she encounters this summer unfolds.

One day, while working in her father's department store, Patty meets Anton, a German prisoner of war. He was sent to the store to buy things he needs to work in the hot southern sun. Anton speaks perfect English because his mother is from England. His father is a university professor, and Anton was a medical student before he was forced to drop out to join the German army and fight in the war.

It's instant attraction between Patty and Anton. He sees qualities in her that no one in her family can see–or refuses to see.

A couple of days later Patty is in a field behind her house just killing time when she notices a man running to catch the train, the train that goes north. She realizes the man running is her beloved Anton. He has escaped from the prisoner of war camp and he's trying to make his escape on the train. Patty yells out: "ANTON ANTON." She runs to him. He turns and grabs her arm. He does not board the train. Instead ....

Contributed by Nancy Zink, Supervising Project Librarian
The New York Public Library
Connecting Libraries and Schools Project

Classroom Activities

The ten classroom activities listed below center around many of the books cited in the bibliographies and are suitable for elementary and middle grade students. Feel free to use these activities as they are and as models for creating your own.

Group Discussion Questions and Activities

1. Ask students how the genocide of eleven million people during the Holocaust can be compared with the persecution of African Americans and other minorities by the Ku Klux Klan. Can they name any recent events that might lead them to suspect that this type of killing could occur again?

2. Have students discuss the Jewish resistance, and ponder why so many persecuted people did not join forces to overthrow Hitler. Have students also discuss why Hitler was so popular with the German people, especially since he had been such a failure during his youth. Did his "coming from nowhere" help him win support?

3. Using current newspapers and magazines, draw comparisons between the "ethnic cleansing" happening in Bosnia today and the Holocaust. Some students might also write about or discuss the "skinhead riots" in Germany today.

4. Suggest that students research newspapers and magazines and discuss how the reunification of Germany has affected the Jews and other minority populations there.

5. Read Innocenti and Gallaz's *Rose Blanche* and Wild's *Let the Celebrations Begin!* aloud to your class, and ask the students to compare and contrast the two books, focusing on theme, mood, illustrations, and viewpoint.

6. There are Holocaust survivors living in all areas of the United States. Contact your local synagogue to engage a survivor to speak to the class about his or her experience.

7. Many accounts of the Holocaust are autobiographical. Have

students read two autobiographies and write short ones of their own, as if they were Jews growing up in German-occupied territory. Their autobiographies may recount reactions to Hitler's rise to power, or may enter the world of Jewish hiding, deportation, and concentration camp experiences.

8. Several novels and autobiographical accounts of the Holocaust can be grouped together and used in a book discussion group for ages 11-14. Below is a list of books that, when grouped together, can lead to thought-provoking discussions. Appropriate for a public or school library setting, these discussion groups work well when they are limited to fifteen children who read the same books and then meet to discuss them.

Saving the Fragments	all by Isabella Leitner–
Fragments of Isabella	autobiographical account of her
The Big Lie	capture and rescue from camps

The Hidden Children by Howard Greenfeld	
Behind the Secret Window by Nelly Toll	all have to do with
The Upstairs Room by Johanna Reiss	Jewish children in
Anne Frank: The Diary of a Young Girl	hiding

Sheltering Rebecca by Mary Baylis-White	characters end up in
Kindertransport by Olga Levy Drucker	New York and have
Journey to America by Sonia Levitin	varying experiences there

Lisa's War by Carol Matas	deal with the resistance
The Man From the Other Side by Uri Orlev	groups and underground
Sky by Hanneke Ippisch	during the war
A Time to Fight Back by Jayne Pettit	

Don't Say a Word by Barbara Gehrts	a look at the

Borrowed House by Hilda van Stockum	Nazi occupation from a German child's perspective
Life in the Warsaw Ghetto by Gail B. Stewart *Child of the Warsaw Ghetto* by David A. Adler	specifically address life in the Warsaw Ghetto
The Shadow Children by Steven Schnur *After the War* by Carol Matas	deal with ghosts and survivors after the war

9. Students in an art class can study illustrated books that deal with the Holocaust and analyze the illustrations in each book, commenting on their realism, effectiveness, and mood conveyed. Books to be used could include:

> *Flowers on the Wall* by Miriam Nerlove
> *The Lily Cupboard* by Shulamith Levey Oppenheim
> *The Feather-Bed Journey* by Paula Kurzband Feder
> *Star of Fear, Star of Hope* by Jo Hoestlandt
> *Let the Celebrations Begin* by Margaret Wild
> *The Number on My Grandfather's Arm* by David A. Adler
> *The Children We Remember* by Chanya Abells
> *One Yellow Daffodil* by David A. Adler
> *My Brother's Keeper* by Israel Bernbaum

10. For a poetry project in a classroom setting, students can read and study "The Most Unbelievable Part" by Marjorie Agosin and "Refugee Blues" by W. H. Auden, both found in *Breaking Free: An Anthology of Human Rights Poetry*, selected by Robert Hull. Have students write poems about the Holocaust and share them with the class.

Contributed by Leslie Barban, Children's Services Manager
Richland County Public Librar
Columbia, South Carolina

Lesson Plans

These lesson plans are structured a little more formally than the preceding suggested classroom activities. They are examples of how one or a series of lessons can be centered around the reading of one particular title. Feel free to use these lesson plans exactly as they are or adapt for your own needs, and do use them as models for creating your own lesson plans around other Holocaust books.

The Number on My Grandfather's Arm by David A. Adler

Aim: To recognize what we give of ourselves to others.
       To understand the effects our words and actions can have upon others.

Preparation: For background information, the teacher should read Milton Meltzer's *Never to Forget* and Bea Stadtler's *The Holocaust: A History of Courage and Resistance.*

Introduction to the lesson: To prepare students for the lesson, engage students in a discussion about their grandparents. Some questions to ask could include: How do your grandparents help you?; Where do your grandparents live?; Where did your grandparents grow up?; and Did your grandparents ever tell you what it was like for them growing up? You could also ask students to write some descriptions of their grandparents or to draw a picture of them.

Activity: The teacher will read aloud *The Number on My Grandfather's Arm* to the class.

Questions for Discussion: When you finish reading the book to the class, engage them in discussion with some of these questions:

What does Grandfather do for a living?
Where was Grandfather born?
What was life like in his village?
Where does Grandfather live now?
Why does Grandfather wear a shirt with long sleeves?
How did he get the number on his arm?
What kind of place is Auschwitz? How does he describe it?

How did Grandfather feel about telling his story?
How did the granddaughter feel about his story?
What does she tell her Grandfather about the number?

Summary Activity: Ask students to create a family tree.

7th Grade
Rescue: The Story of How Gentiles Saved Jews in the Holocaust by
Milton Meltzer

Aim: To recognize various types of human behavior (e.g. positive,
      negative, bystander)
      To understand how behavior reflects an individual's choices and
      decisions.
      To analyze and understand why people, governments, and
      nations act in the following roles: bystander, collaborator, hero,
      rescuer.
      To understand the consequences of certain choices in terms of
      human pain and destruction.
      To evaluate the impact of the Holocaust on our lives today.

Activities: Read aloud to students or have them read for themselves
selected stories from part or all of Milton Meltzer's *Rescue: The Story
of How the Gentiles Saved Jews in the Holocaust.*

Discussion Questions:

What were the motivations of Gentiles like Countess Marushka, Oskar
Schindler, and Raoul Wallenberg to help the Jews? Why were they
willing to risk their lives for Jews when so many other people were
not?

Andrew Shepitsky, the Orthodox Archbishop of L'vov, the villagers of
Le Chambon in France, and Father Rurino Niccacci of Assisi in Italy,
all felt obligated to help Jews because of their religious convictions.
Although they are from different religious backgrounds, what
convictions did they share that made them want to help Jews?

Describe the qualities of righteous person?

Why is the Avenue of the Righteous at Yad Vashem so important?

Would you have been willing to help Jews? Why or why not? What
would you have done? Would you be willing to risk your own life as
well as the lives of your family and friends in order to help Jews?

Grade 6, 7, 8
The Devil in Vienna by Doris Orgel

Aim: To evaluate the personal values in making choices and decisions.
     To understand the impact of group dynamics on individual
     choices and actions.
     To recognize the difference one can make through individual
     choices and actions.

Preparation: Invite a survivor of the *Kristallnacht* to speak to your class
about his or her experiences. Read other stories about *Kristallnacht*
experiences (e.g., Hans Peter Richter's *Friedrich*) and compare them.

Introduction: Ask the class to cite the qualities of a best friend. List
them on the board. Ask each student to write a brief essay in class on
his or her "best friend," one who helped in a time of danger or in a time
of serious need.

Activities: Read Doris Orgel's *The Devil in Vienna*.

Discussion Questions:

How did Inge and Lise become best friends?
What happened in Austria in 1939 that changed the entire country?
Describe how Inge's world changed so drastically.
Describe how Inge and Lise's friendship is so unusual for the time.
What are the consequences of Lise's choice to help Inge and her
family?
What are the key factors that help Lise make this decision to help?
What does Inge's treasure chest symbolize?
What would you have done if you were Lise?

Grades 6, 7, 8

I Never Saw Another Butterfly by Hana Volavkova

Aim: To recognize that every person has unique attributes and traits in
which we take pride.
To understand that each of us must face making very difficult
choices.
To understand that all choices have consequences beyond oneself,
for other individuals and the group.

Activity: Read aloud and discuss the three poems in class.

"The Butterfly" by Pavel Friedman

What symbols does the poet use for beauty and freedom?

Following the discussion, ask students write a poem expressing his or
her feelings about the butterfly and to draw their own butterfly.

"Homesick" by Anonymous

Who are the people in your family? (You may want to list the responses
on the board)

How would you feel if someone took you away from your family and
told you that you could no longer live with them? What would you do?

Following the discussion, ask students to write a short story about the
importance of their family, how they feel about them, and to draw an
illustration of them.

"On a Sunny Evening" by Anonymous

What is your favorite activity or game? (You may want to list the
responses on the board)

How would you feel if you were told you could no longer do these
activities or play these games?
How does the poet use nature as a symbol of freedom?

Grades 11, 12, or Advanced Younger Students

Euphemisms, Doublespeak, and other Manipulations of Language

Aim: To understand that language can be manipulated to distort and obscure the truth.
To recognize that Nazis were masters of manipulating language, particularly in regard to the documents planning and recording of the Holocaust.
To be able to recognize when language is being manipulated in order to distort or obscure the truth.

Preparation: Teachers should read *The New Doublespeak: Why No One Knows What Anyone's Saying Anymore* by William Lutz. Select passages from Nazi documents that illustrate the use of doublespeak. The documents of the Wannsee Conference are an excellent source with which to begin.

Introduction: Have students take Lutz's "Doublespeak Quiz", appendixed in the book cited above.

Activity: Read George Orwell's "Politics and the English Language" Discuss examples of doublespeak from Nazi documents and how they relate to what Orwell says in his essay. Have students try to recognize the true meaning of words like: dispatched, evacuation, liquidation, protective custody, final solution, Jewish problem, relocation, resettlement, special action, special treatment, transport, etc. Discuss why the Nazis chose these particular words to describe their activities. From whom were they trying to disguise the truth?

Building a Core Holocaust Collection in Your School Library

Libraries, particularly school libraries, are typically underfunded and always have to make difficult selection choices due to inadequate materials budgets. Below are lists of "must have" titles for elementary, middle, and high school collections. Check the list against your holdings and make sure you purchase immediately the titles you do not have in your collection. For most of the books, two reviews are cited for each work. The titles of the journals in which the reviews appear are abbreviated. In some cases, I was unable to find any reviews or only one in *Book Review Digest* or *Book Review Index*.

Key to Journal Abbreviations

BCCB = Bulletin of the Center for Children's Books
BL = Booklist
CSM = Christian Science Monitor
HB = The Horn Book Magazine
LATBR = Los Angeles Times Book Review
LJ = Library Journal
NYTBR = New York Times Book Review
PW = Publishers Weekly
SLJ = School Library Journal
T = Teacher
VOYA = Voice of Youth Advocates

Elementary School (K-5)

Adler, David A. *A Child of the Warsaw Ghetto*
BCCB 48 (May 1995): 298; SLJ 41 (July 1995): 71
Adler, David A. *Hiding from the Nazis*
BL 94.5 (November 1, 1997): 463; SLJ 44.2 (February 1998): 94
Adler, David A. *The Number on My Grandfather's Arm*
PW 232 (Oct. 30, 1987): 71; SLJ 34 (April 1988): 93
Bachrach, Susan D. *Tell Them We Remember: The Story of the Holocaust*
SLJ 40 (November 1994): 110; VOYA 17 (December 1994): 292
Bishop, Claire Huchet. *Twenty and Ten*

LJ 95 (February 15, 1970): 741; *T* 96 (October 1978): 176
Bunting, Eve. *Terrible Things*
SLJ 26.8 (April 1980): 91; *PW* 20 (May 23, 1980): 71
Greenfeld, Howard. *The Hidden Children*
HB 70 (March 1994): 216; *VOYA* 17 (June 1994): 108
Innocenti, Roberto. *Rose Blanche*
NYTBR 90 (July 21, 1985): 14; *SLJ* 32 (October 1985): 172
Lowry, Lois. *Number the Stars*
HB 65.3 (May/June 1989): 371; *SLJ* 35.7 (March 1989): 177
Nerlove, Miriam. *Flowers on the Wall*
BCCB 43 (March 1996): 237; *HB* 72 (May/June 1996): 333
Richter, Hans. *Friedrich*
HB 47.2 (April 1971): 173-174; *NYTBR* (January 10, 1997): 26
United States Holocaust Memorial Museum. *Historical Atlas of the Holocaust*
BL 92 (May 1, 1996): 1528
Volavkova, Hana, ed. *I Never Saw Another Butterfly*
CSM (October 1, 1964): 11; *HB* 40 (December 1964): 632
Yolen, Jane. *The Devil's Arithmetic*
BCCB 42.2 (October 1988): 23-24; *SLJ* 35.3 (November 1988): 114

Middle School (6-8)

Bachrach, Susan D. *Tell Them We Remember: The Story of the Holocaust*
SLJ 40 (November 1994): 110; *VOYA* 17 (December 1994): 292
Bitton-Jackson, Livia. *I Have Lived a Thousand Years: Growing Up in the Holocaust*
HB 73.4 (July/August 1997): 472-473; SLJ 43.5 (May 1997): 142-143
Dillon, Eilis. *Children of Bach*
SLJ 38 (December 1992): 133; *VOYA* 15 (February 1993): 338
Frank, Anne. *The Diary of a Young Girl: The Definitive Edition*
BL 91 (April 15, 1995): 1476; *NYTBR* (March 5, 1995): 1
Hartmann, Erich. *In the Camps*
BL 91.7 (May 1, 1995): 1557; *LATBR* (May 28, 1995): BR8
Matas, Carol. *After the War*
VOYA 19.3 (August 1996): 158; *SLJ* 42.5 (May 1996): 135
Matas, Carol. *Lisa's War*
SLJ 34 (August 1988): 110; *VOYA* 11 (August 1988): 148
Meltzer, Milton. *Never to Forget: The Jews of the Holocaust*
BCCB 30.1 (September 1976): 14; *NYTBR* (May 2, 1976): 25, 42

Meltzer, Milton. *Rescue: The Story of How Gentiles Saved Jews in the Holocaust*
SLJ 34 (August 1988): 110; *VOYA* 11 (August 1988): 148
Nieuwsma, Milton J. *Kinderlager: An Oral History of Young Holocaust Survivors*
BL 95.5 (November 1, 1998): 480
Nolan, Han. *If I Should Die Before I Wake*
BCCB 47 (April 1994): 267; SLJ 41 (April 1994): 152
Pausewang, Gudrun. *The Final Journey*
HB 73.1 (January/February 1997): 66
Reiss, Johanna. *The Upstairs Room*
HB 49.1 (February 1973): 50-51; SLJ 19.4 (December 1972): 62
Rochman, Hazel and Darlene Z. McCampbell, eds. *Bearing Witness: Stories of the Holocaust*
HB 72 (March/April 1996): 232; SLJ 41 (September 1995): 228
Rogasky, Barbara. *Smoke and Ashes: The Story of the Holocaust*
BCCB 41 (June 1988): 215; SLJ 34 (June 1988): 28
United States Holocaust Memorial Museum. *Historical Atlas of the Holocaust*
BL 92 (May 1, 1996): 1528
Volavkova, Hana, ed. *I Never Saw Another Butterfly*
CSM (October 1, 1964): 11; HB 40 (December 1964) 632

High School (9-12)

Adelson. Alan, ed. *The Diary of Dawid Sierakowiak: Five Notebooks from the Lodz Ghetto*
BL 92.22 (August 1996): 1890; SLJ 43.6 (June 1997): 152-153
Bernstein, Sara Tuvel. *The Seamstress: A Memoir of Survival*
LJ 122.15 (September 15, 1997): 92; PW 224.34 (August 18, 1997): 77
Boas, Jacob. *We Are Witnesses: Five Diaries of Teenagers Who Died in the Holocaust*
PW 242.26 (June 26, 1995): 109; SLJ 41.7 (July 1995): 97
Dawidowicz, Lucy S. *The War Against the Jews, 1933-1945*
Del Calzo, Nick. *The Triumphant Spirit: Portraits and Stories of Holocaust Survivors*
BL 93.14 (March 15, 1997): 1223
Fuchs, Elinor, ed. *Plays of the Holocaust: An International Anthology*
SLJ 34.5 (January 1988): 37
Hartmann, Erich. *In the Camps*
BL 91.7 (May 1, 1995): 1557; *LATBR* (May 28, 1995): BR8

Nolan, Han. *If I Should Die Before I Wake*
BCCB 47 (April 1994): 267; SLJ 41 (April 1994): 152
Rochman, Hazel and Darlene Z. McCampbell. *Bearing Witness: Stories of the Holocaust*
HB 72 (March/April 1996): 232; SLJ 41 (September 1995): 228
Roubickova, Eva. *We're Alive and Life Goes On: A Theresienstadt Diary*
PW 244.45 (November 3, 1997): 86-87; SLJ 44.2 (February 1998): 124
Schiff, Hilda, comp. *Holocaust Poetry*
BL 91.18 (May 15, 1995): 1628; PW 242.17 (April 24, 1995): 66
Shevelev, Raphael with Karine Schomer. *Liberating the Ghosts: Photographs and Text from The March of the Living*
BL 93 (April 1, 1997): 1288
Shirer, William L. *The Rise and Fall of the Third Reich*
BL 57 (November 1, 1960): 142; LJ 85 (October 1, 1960): 3442
Spiegelman, Art. *Maus: A Survivor's Tale I: My Father Bleed's History*
NYTBR (December 7, 1986): 71; SLJ 33 (May 1987): 124
Spiegelman, Art. *Maus: A Survivor's Tale II: And Here My Troubles Began*
LJ 116 (December 1991): 160; NYTBR (November 3, 1991): 17
Taylor, Kressman. *Address Unknown*
PW 242.8 (February 20, 1995): 198
ten Boom, Corrie. *The Hiding Place*
United States Holocaust Memorial Museum. *Historical Atlas of the Holocaust*
BL 92 (May 1, 1996): 1528
Wiesel, Elie. *Night*
LJ 85 (September 1, 1960): 2932; NYTBR (November 13, 1960): 20
Wilkomirski, Binjamin. *Fragments: Memories of a Wartime Childhood*
NYTBR (January 12, 1997): 9; PW 243.27 (July 1, 1996): 47

Author Index

The numbers refer to entries, not pages.

Aaron, Chester 153
Abells, Chanya Byers 296
Ackerman, Karen 154
Adelson, Alan 009, 297
Adler, David A. 010, 011,
   298, 299, 300, 444
Admur, Richard 012, 286,
   294, 295
Adryszewski, Tricia 542
Almagor, Gila 155
Altman, Linda Jacobs 484,
   541
Altshuler, David A. 301
Ambrose, Kenneth 156
Appel, Benjamin 013
Appelfeld, Aharon 157, 158
Appleman-Jurman, Alicia 014
Arad, Yitzhak 479
Arlen, Michael J. 514
Arnold, Elliott 159
Arnothy, Christine 015
Arrick, Fran 160
Ashrawi, Hanan
Atkinson, Linda 016
Attema, Martha 563
Auerbacher, Inge 017
Augenbraum, Harold 543
Ayer, Eleanor H. 018, 302,
   303, 487, 488, 489

Bachrach, Deborah 304
Bachrach, Susan D. 305
Baer, Edith 161
Balakian, Peter 515

Baldwin, Margaret 019
Banet, Chana Marcus 020
Baram, Meir 496
Bar Oni, Bryna 021
Bartoszewski, Wladyslaw 022
Bauer, Yehuda 306
Bauman, Janina 023
Bauminger, Arieh L. 307
Baylis-White, Mary 162
Bedoukian, Kerop 516
Beller, Ilex 308
Benchley, Nathaniel 163
Benisch, Pearl 024
Benjamin, Ruth 164
Berenbaum, Michael 309
Bergman, Tamar 165, 166
Berkowitz, Judith 455
Bernard, Kenneth 135
Bernbaum, Israel 310
Bernheim, Mark 025
Bernstein, Sara Tuvel 026
Berry, James 525
Berwick, Michael 311
Bestic, Alan 124
Bezdekova, Zdenka 167
Bierman, John 027, 312
Bishop, Claire Huchet 168
Bitton-Jackson, Livia 028,
   029
Blatter, Janet 313
Bloch, Marie Halum 169
Block, Gay 314
Blum, Howard 315
Blume, Judy 170

Boas, Jacob 316
Borenstein, Emily 456
Brecher, Elinor J. 317
Brecht, Bertolt 138
Breznitz, Shlomo 030
Brimner, Larry Dane 579
Brown, Dee 595
Brown, Gene 031
Buchignani, Walter 032
Bunting, Eve 445, 580
Bush, Laurence 172
Butterworth, Emma Macalick
  033

Cahn-Lipman, Miriam 480,
  589
Chaikin, Miriam 318
Charney, Ann 173
Chicago, Judy 319
Chicoine, Stephen D. 489
Chilcoat, George W. 586
Choi, Sook Nyul 564
Coerr, Eleanor 557, 558
Cohen, Barbara 174
Conot, Robert E. 320
Cook, Fred J. 544
Cormier, Robert 175
Costanza, Mary S. 321
Cowan, Lore 322
Crane, Stephen 565
Criddle, Joan D. 520
Czarnecki, Joseph P. 323

Dank, Milton 176
David, Kati 324
Davis, Daniel S. 581
Dawidowicz, Lucy S. 325,
  326, 590
Degens, T. 177
Del Calzo, Nick 327
Demetz, Hannah 178
Denenberg, Barry 566

Borkas-Nemetz, Lillian 171
Boyarin, Jonathan 369
Deschamps, Helene 034
De Silva, Cara 328
Deutschkron, Inge 035
Dillon, Eilis 179
Dobroszycki, Lucjan 329
Dolan, Jr., Edward F. 330, 331
Douglas, Kirk 180
Dribben, Judith A. 036
Drucker, Malka 181, 314
Drucker, Olga Levy 037
Duba, Ursula 457

Eckman, Lester 332
Edelheit, Abraham J. 480
Edelheit, Herschel 480
Edelman, Eve 455
Edelstein, Dov Beril 038
Edvardson, Cordelia 039
Eisenberg, Azriel 333
Eisner, Jack 040
Eliach, Yaffa 334, 335
Eliav, Arie L. 336
Emmerich, Elisabeth 041
Epstein, Eric Joseph 492
Epstein, Helen 041, 337
Epstein, Rachel 042
Evenhuis, Gertie 182
Ezekiel, Raphael S. 545

Feder, Paula Kurzband 446
Feelings, Tom 526
Feinermann, Emmanuel 434
Feinstein, Stephen C. 338
Fenelon, Fania 043
Fenkl, Heinz Insu 567
Ferson-Osten, Renee 044
Fest, Joachim C. 339
Field, Hermann H. 183
Filipovic, Zlata 536
Fink, Ida 184, 185, 186

Finkelstein, Norman H. 340
Firer, Benzion 187
Fisch, Robert O. 045
Fisher, David 402
Fishman, Charles 458
Flender, Harold 341
Flinker, Moshe 046
Florsheim, Stewart J. 459
Forman, James 188, 189, 190,
    191, 192, 193
Forman, James D. 342
Frank, Anne 047, 343
Frank, Rudolf 568
Friedman, Carl 194
Friedman, Ina R. 048, 344,
    345
Friedman, Philip 346
Frielander, Albert 001
Fry, Varian 049
Fuchs, Elinor 139

Gallaz, Christophe 448
Ganor, Solly 050
Gay, Kathlyn 546
Gehrts, Barbara 195
Geve, Thomas 051
Gies, Miep 052
Gilbert, Martin 347, 348, 349,
    350, 481
Gillam, Scott 547
Gille, Elisabeth 196
Gilliand, Judith Heide 569
Ginsburg, Marvell 197
Gissing, Vera 053
Gjelten, Tom 537
Glatstein, Jacob 002, 459
Gold, Alison Leslie 052, 054
Goldreich, Gloria 198
Goldstein, Lisa 199
Goodrich, Francis 140
Gordon, Shelia 506
Gotfryd, Bernard 200
Gottlieb, Malke 468

Grafstein, Jerry S. 003
Gray, Bettyanne 497
Gray, Ronald 351
Green, Gerald 349
Greene, Bette 201, 202
Greene, Carol 055
Greenfeld, Howard 352
Greenstein, Stephen 486
Grossman, Joan Adess 062
Grossman, Mendel 351
Gruber, Ruth 353
Grunfeld, Frederic V. 354
Gurdus, Luba Krugman 460
Gurko, Miriam 591
Gutman, Israel 482

Haas, Gerda S. 355
Hackett, Albert 140
Hallie, Philip 356
Halperin, Michael 181
Hamanaka, Shelia 582
Handler, Andrew 357
Harrison, Michael 460
Hart, Kitty 056
Hartmann, Erich 358
Haugaard, Erik Christian 203
Hautzig, Esther 498
Heartfeild, John 359
Heck, Alfons 303
Heide, Florence Perry 569
Heifetz, Julie 461
Heller, Fanya Gottesfeld 057
Hellman, Peter 360
Henry, Clarissa 363
Herman, Agnes 204
Herman, Erwin 204
Hersey, John 205, 559
Hesse, Karen 499
Heydecker, Joe J. 361
Heyen, William 462
Heyes, Eileen 362
Hillel, Marc 363
Hochhuth, Rolf 141

Hoestlandt, Jo 447
Hoffman, Judy 058
Holliday, Laurel 004
Holm, Anne 206
Houston, James D. 583
Houston, Jeanne Wakatsuki
    583
Hovannisian, Richard G. 517
Hull, Robert 041
Hurmence, Belinda 527
Hurwitz, Johanna 059
Hyams, Joseph 060
Hyett, Barbara Helfgott 463

Innocenti, Roberto 448
Ippisch, Hanneke 061
Isaacman, Clara 062
Isaacson, Judith Magyar 063
Isadora, Rachel 507
Isherwood, Christopher 207

Joffo, Joseph 064
Josephs, Jeremy 364
Josephy, Jr., Alvin 596
Judd, Denis 365
Jules, Jacqueline 208
Justman, Stuart 366

Kalisch, Shoshana 464
Kanfer, Stefan 209
Karlin, Wayne 065
Katz, William Loren 367, 528
Kay, Mara 210
Keneally, Thomas 211
Kent, Evelyn Julia 103
Keren, Nili 306
Kerr, Judith 212, 213
Kerr, M. E. 214
Kherdian, David 518
Kirshenblatt-Gimblett,
    Barbara 329
Klein, Cecilie 066, 465
Klein, Gerda Weissmann 449

Klein, Rivkah Leah 067
Kluger, Ruth 368
Koehn, Ilse 068
Kohn, Nahum 069
Kovner, Abba 466
Krall, Hanna 070
Kranzler, Gershon 215
Kugelmass, Jack 369
Kuper, Jack 071
Kurzman, Dan 370

Lace, William W. 371
Laird, Christina 216, 217
Lakin, Patricia 450
Landau, Elaine 372, 373, 374,
    548
Lang, Daniel 375
Langbein, Hermann 376
Langer, Lawrence L. 005, 377
Lapides, Robert 297
Larsen, Anita 072
Lasky, Kathryn 218, 500
Lawliss, Charles 378
Lazan, Marian Blumenthal
    092
Lazar, Chaim 332
Leder, Sharon 008
Lee, Marie G. 549
Lehman, Marcus 501, 502
Leitner, Irving A. 074, 075,
    076
Leitner, Isabella 073, 074,
    075, 076
Lengyel, Olga 077
Lester, Elenore 078
Lester, Julius 529, 530
Levi, Primo 079, 080
Levin, Jane Whitebread 216
Levine, Gail 249
Levitin, Sonia 220, 221
Levoy, Myron 222
Lewin, Hugh 508
Lindwer, Willy 379

Linenthal, Edward T. 380
Lingard, Joan 570
Linnea, Sharon 081
Lowry, Lois 223
Lowy, Edith Pick 149
Lustig, Arnost 224
Lyttle, Richard B. 381

Mace, Elisabeth 225
Mack, Stan 592
Madison, Winifred 226
Mam, Teeda Butt 520
Mann, Gertrude 400
Mann, Peggy 368
Marks, Jane 382
Marrin, Albert 082
Maruki, Toshi 560
Matas, Carol 227, 228, 229, 230, 231, 232
Mathabane, Mark 509
Mattingly, Christobel 561
Mayer, Milton 383
Mazer, Harry 233
McCampbell, Darlene Z. 006
McCuen, Gary E. 550
McKissack, Frederick L. 531, 532, 551
McKissack, Patricia C. 531, 532, 551
Mead, Alice 538
Meister, Barbara 464
Melek, Jakob E. 467
Mellon, James 533
Meltzer, Milton 384, 385, 386, 387
Meschel, Susan V. 357
Miller, Arthur 142, 143, 144
Miller, Donald E. 519
Miller, Lorna Touryan 519
Milton, Sybil 313, 388
Mlotek, Eleanor 468
Moran, Thomas 234
Morin, Isobel V. 389

Morpurgo, Michael 235
Moskin, Marietta 236
Mosse, George L. 390
Muchman, Beatrice 083
Mueller, Filip 084
Murray, Michele 237
Muse, Daphne 552
Myers, Sondra 404
Myers, Walter Dean 571

Naidoo, Beverley 510
Napoli, Donna Jo 238
Neimark, Anne E. 085
Nerlove, Miriam 451
Neshamit, Sarah 239
Ngor, Haing 521
Nies, Judith 597
Noble, Iris 086
Nolan, Han 240
Nomberg-Przytyk, Sara 391
Noren, Catherine Hanf 392
Novac, Ana 087
Nye, Naomi Shihab 553
Nyiszli, Miklos 088

Oberski, Jona 089
Open Society Fund 539
Oppenheim, Shulamith Levey 452
Orenstein, Henry 090
Orgel, Doris 241, 242
Orlev, Uri 243, 244, 245
Ossowski, Leonie 246
Ousseimi, Maria 572
Ozick, Cynthia 247

Pagis, Don 469
Pascoe, Elaine 554
Paton, Alan 511
Paton, Jonathan 512
Patterson, Charles 393
Paulsen, Gary 534
Pausewang, Gudrun 248

Author Index

Perel, Solomon 091
Perl, Lila 092
Pettit, Jayne 394, 395
Phillips, Mildred 503
Pitt, Nancy 504
Plant, Richard 396
Poltawska, Wanda 093
Potok, Chaim 593
Prager, Arthur 397
Prager, Emily 397
Prager, Moshe 398
Pran, Dith 522
Proktor, Richard 399
Provost, Gary 249

Rabinovici, Schoschana 094
Rabinsky, Leatrice 400
Ramati, Alexander 095, 250
Rashke, Richard 401
Ray, Karen 251
Read, Anthony 402
Reichel, Sabine 096
Reichwald, Faye 594
Reisman, Arnold 099
Reisman, Ellen 099
Reiss, Johanna 097, 098
Remarque, Erich Maria 573
Rembrandt, Elaine 145
Reznikoff, Charles 470
Rice, Earle J. 403
Richter, Hans Peter 252, 253
Rigenblum, Emmanuel 100
Rittner, Carol 404, 405
Roberts, Jack L. 101
Rochman, Hazel 006, 513
Rogasky, Barbara 406
Roiter, Howard 069
Romm, J. Leonard 254
Rose, Anne 255
Roseman, Kenneth 256
Rosen, Philip E. 492
Rosenberg, Maxine B. 407
Rosenfeld, Alvin H. 146, 470

Rossel, Seymour 408
Roth, John K. 405, 412
Rothchild, Sylvia 409
Roth-Hano, Renee 257
Roubickova, Eva 102
Rubenstein, Eli 410
Rubin, Arnold P. 411
Rubinstein, Richard L. 412

Sachs, Nelly 472, 473
Samuels, Gertrude 258
Schiff, Hilda 474
Schleimer, Sarah M. 259
Schloss, Eva 103
Schnabel, Ernst 104
Schnur, Steven 260
Schomer, Karen 415
Schur, Maxine Rose 105, 261
Schwartz-Bart, Andre 262
Schweifert, Peter 106
Segal, Lore 263
Sender, Ruth Minsky 107, 108, 413
Senesh, Hannah 109
Serrailier, Ian 264
Shaw, Robert 147
Shemin, Margaretha 265, 266
Sherman, Eileen Bluestone 505
Sherrill, Elizabeth 116
Sherrill, John 116
Sherrow, Victoria 414, 485, 486
Shevelev, Raphael 415
Shirer, William L. 416, 417
Shulman, William H. 490, 491
Sichrovsky, Peter 418
Siegal, Aranka 267, 268
Silver, Eric 419
Singer, Isaac Bashevis 110, 111
Skloot, Robert 148
Smith, Carter 598

Snyder, Louis L. 420, 421, 493
Sommerfelt, Aimee 269
Spiegelman, Art 422, 423
Stadtler, Bea 424
Stance, Alaine 112
Stanley, Jerry 584
Stavans, Ilan 543
Stein, Andre 425
Stein, R. Conrad 426, 427, 428
Steiner, Jean-Francois 429
Steinhorn, Harriett 149
Stern, Ellen Norman 113
Stern, Menahem 475
Stiles, Martha Bennett 270
Strahinich, Helen 430
Stuart-Clark, Christopher 460
Suhl, Yuri 271, 272, 431
Switzer, Ellen 432
Sylvannus, Erwin 150
Szambelan-Strevinsky, Christine 273
Szymusiak, Molyda 523

Takashima, Shizuye 585
Tames, Richard 114
Tatelbaum, Itzhak B. 433
Taylor, Kressman 274
Tec, Nechama 115
Teichman, Milton 008
ten Boom, Corrie 116
Tene, Benjamin 275
Thalmann, Rita 434

Thomas, Velma Maia 535
Tillage, Leon Walter 555
Toll, Nelly S. 117
Torren, Asher 476
Tresder, Terry Walton 276
Trumbo, Dalton 574
Tsuchiya, Yukio 575
Tunnell, Michael O. 586

Tyler, Laura 118

Uchida, Yoshiko 587, 588
Uhlman, Fred 277
UNICEF 540
United States Holocaust Memorial Museum 494
Uris, Leon 278, 279

Van Dijk, Lutz 280
van Stockum, Hilda 281
Vegh, Claudine 435
Verhoeven, Rian 437
Vinke, Hermann 119
Vishniac, Roman 436
Vivier, Colette 282
Vogel, Ilse-Margaret 120
Voigt, Cynthia 283
Volavkova, Hana 477
Von der Grun, Max 121
von der Rol, Ruud 122, 437
Vos, Ida 123, 284, 285
Vrba, Rudolf 124

Waldman, Neil 453
Warner, Roger 521
Wassiljewa, Tatjana 576
Waterford, Helen 303
Weinstein, Frida Scheps 125
Weiss, Peter 151
Weitz, Sonia, Schreiber 126
Welaratna, Usha 524
Werstein, Irving 286, 438, 439
Westall, Robert 577, 578

Whitman, Ruth 152, 478
Wiesel, Elie 127, 287, 288
Wiesenthal, Simon 289, 440
Wigoder, Geoffrey 495
Wild, Margaret 454
Wilkomirski, Binjamin 128
Willenberg, Samuel 129
Williams, Laura E. 290

Williamson, David 441
Wolf, Jacqueline 130
Woolf, Marion Freyer 131
Wright, J. Leitch 598
Wuorio, Eva-Lis 291, 292

Yep, Laurence 556, 562
Yolen, Jane 293, 294

Zar, Rose 132
Zassenhaus, Hiltgunt 133
Zei, Alki 295
Zeinert, Karen 442
Ziemian, Joseph 443
Zucker-Bujanowska, Liliana
    134
Zuckerman, Abraham 135
Zyskind, Sara 136, 137

Geographic Index

The numbers refer to entries, not pages.

Armenia 514, 515, 516, 517, 518, 519
Austria 004, 018, 033, 154, 192, 226, 241, 242, 263, 324, 344, 374
Belgium 004, 032, 062, 083, 255, 286, 314, 316, 324, 344, 346, 431
Belorussia 332, 342, 346
Bosnia-Herzegovina 536, 537, 572
Bulgaria 314, 346, 404
Cambodia 520, 521, 522, 523, 524
Canada 171, 410, 585
Czechoslovakia 004, 030, 039, 053, 102, 167, 178, 197, 224, 312, 314, 322, 328, 337, 344, 345, 374, 431, 477
Denmark 004, 159, 163, 200, 206, 219, 223, 228, 231, 292, 324, 341, 394, 404, 438
El Salvador 572
England (see United Kingdom)
Estonia 324, 346
France 034, 044, 049, 064, 125, 130, 139, 144, 168, 176, 196, 232, 235, 255, 257, 282, 304, 314, 322, 324, 344, 346, 356, 364, 397, 404, 431, 435, 447,

573
Germany 004, 017, 026, 035, 041, 048, 068, 093, 120, 128, 136, 139, 156, 161, 169, 180, 188, 189, 195, 201, 203, 207, 210, 220, 224, 225, 243, 246, 251, 252, 253, 255, 259, 270, 274, 277, 290, 286, 303, 311, 318, 320, 322, 324, 331, 339, 342, 344, 345, 351, 354, 358, 367, 374, 375, 383, 385, 389, 390, 396, 399, 402, 403, 408, 416, 417, 418, 420, 421, 426, 434, 441, 447
Great Britain (see United Kingdom)
Greece 295, 346
Holland (see The Netherlands)
Hungary 004, 015, 016, 027, 028, 029, 038, 045, 063, 066, 067, 072, 078, 080, 081, 105, 109, 127, 209, 264, 314, 316, 324, 344, 346, 357, 374, 478
Israel (Palestine) 036, 050, 109, 139, 147, 155, 166, 187, 189, 230, 278, 287, 307, 312, 336, 344, 359, 366, 452, 553
Italy 095, 238, 322, 324, 346, 394, 404, 431

Jamaica 525
Japan 389, 557, 558, 559, 560,
    561, 562, 575
Korea 564, 567
Latvia 346, 570
Lebanon 569, 572
Lithuania 004, 050, 094, 112,
    239, 316, 332, 346
Mozambique 572
The Netherlands (Holland)
    004, 047, 058, 061, 097,
    098, 116, 122, 123, 182,
    191, 194, 236, 265, 266,
    281, 284, 285, 298, 303,
    322, 324, 344, 346, 374,
    404, 414, 452, 563
Norway 269, 322, 404
Palestine (see Israel)
Poland 004, 009, 010, 020,
    021, 022, 023, 024, 025,
    056, 057, 060, 065, 069,
    070, 071, 091, 099, 100,
    110, 111, 115, 117, 126,
    132, 134, 135, 139, 150,
    153, 158, 165, 171, 173,
    183, 184, 185, 186, 187,
    204, 205, 208, 216, 217,
    240, 264, 271, 273, 275,
    276, 279, 280, 287, 291,
    293, 294, 297, 299, 303,
    308, 310, 314, 316, 318,
    323, 324, 329, 337, 344,
    345, 361, 369, 373, 374,
    391, 404, 415, 422, 423,
    429, 431, 436, 439, 442,
    443, 444, 446, 451, 453,
    454, 476
Romania 026, 324
Russia 004, 099, 431, 499,
    500, 503, 576
Siberia 498
South Africa 164, 506, 507,

508, 509, 510, 511, 512,
    513
Soviet Union 165, 304, 310,
    314, 324, 397, 428, 505
Sweden 139, 219, 267, 269
Switzerland 154, 213, 324
Transylvania 087, 374
Turkey
Ukraine 036, 168, 272, 314,
    344, 346, 497, 504
United Kingdom 004, 037,
    139, 151, 162, 212, 259,
    260, 324, 347, 578
United States 139, 160, 170,
    174, 175, 179, 198, 202,
    205, 206, 214, 218, 220,
    221, 222, 236, 237, 254,
    274, 302, 315, 353, 380,
    527, 528, 530, 531, 532,
    533, 534, 535, 542, 543,
    544, 545, 546, 548, 549,
    550, 552, 554, 555, 556,
    579, 580, 581, 582, 583,
    584, 586, 587, 588, 593,
    595, 596, 597, 598, 599
Vietnam 566, 571
Yugoslavia 109, 314, 322,
    345, 346, 536, 537, 538,
    539, 540

Grade Index

The numbers refer to entries, not pages.

Elementary School, K-5

010, 011, 013, 016, 017, 018, 019, 025, 029, 031, 032, 033,
037, 041, 042, 046, 048, 053, 054, 055, 058, 059, 062, 068,
072, 073, 084, 085, 086, 092, 097, 098, 101, 105, 114, 117,
118, 122, 123, 125, 149, 154, 156, 159, 162, 165, 166, 167,
168, 170, 171, 172, 173, 174, 179, 180, 181, 182, 190, 197,
198, 200, 201, 202, 203, 204, 206, 208, 210, 212, 213, 215,
221, 222, 223, 226, 227, 228, 229, 231, 235, 238, 241, 242,
243, 245, 246, 249, 251, 252, 254, 255, 258, 259, 260, 261,
264, 265, 266, 267, 268, 269, 271, 272, 273, 275, 276, 281,
282, 284, 285, 286, 290, 291, 292, 294, 295, 296, 297, 298,
300, 305, 313, 327, 336, 338, 339, 340, 346, 347, 348, 350,
353, 354, 357, 358, 365, 366, 378, 381, 389, 391, 392, 394,
396, 403, 407, 411, 413, 421, 423, 424, 425, 430, 432, 434,
437, 439, 441, 442, 444, 445, 446, 447, 448, 449, 450, 451,
452, 453, 454, 455, 464, 477, 481, 494, 497, 498, 499, 500,
503, 504, 505, 507, 508, 510, 518, 525, 526, 527, 529, 530,
531, 534, 535, 536, 538, 539, 540, 541, 548, 553, 554, 555,
556, 557, 558, 560, 561, 562, 564, 569, 575, 576, 577, 578,
580, 584, 585, 586, 587, 588, 591, 594

Middle School, 6-8

001, 004, 006, 010, 011, 012, 013, 015, 016, 017, 018, 019,
021, 022, 023, 025, 029, 032, 033, 034, 035, 037, 041, 042,
045, 046, 048, 049, 058, 059, 061, 062, 066, 068, 072, 073,
074, 081, 082, 083, 084, 085, 086, 089, 091, 092, 093, 094,
095, 097, 098, 101, 102, 104, 105, 106, 110, 114, 115, 116,
117, 118, 119, 121, 122, 123, 125, 131, 134, 136, 137, 149,
155, 156, 157, 158, 159, 161, 162, 163, 165, 166, 167, 170,
171, 172, 173, 174, 175, 176, 179, 180, 181, 182, 189, 190,
191, 192, 195, 196, 198, 199, 201, 202, 203, 206, 210, 212,
213, 214, 215, 216, 217, 218, 220, 221, 222, 223, 224, 226,
227, 228, 229, 230, 231, 232, 233, 235, 236, 237, 238, 240,
241, 242, 243, 244, 245, 246, 248, 249, 251, 252, 253, 254,

255, 256, 257, 258, 259, 260, 261, 264, 265, 266, 267, 268,
269, 270, 271, 272, 273, 274, 275, 276, 277, 281, 282, 283,
284, 285, 286, 290, 291, 292, 293, 294, 296, 297, 298, 299,
302, 303, 304, 305, 306, 308, 311, 313, 314, 315, 319, 320,
322, 325, 326, 327, 331, 334, 338, 339, 340, 341, 342, 346,
347, 348, 350, 351, 353, 354, 356, 357, 358, 360, 361, 363,
364, 365, 366, 369, 371, 375, 378, 381, 382, 383, 385, 386,
387, 389, 391, 392, 394, 396, 397, 402, 403, 404, 407, 408,
410, 411, 412, 413, 417, 419, 420, 421, 423, 425, 427, 430,
431, 432, 433, 434, 436, 437, 439, 440, 441, 455, 456, 460,
463, 464, 468, 471, 477, 479, 480, 481, 483, 484, 485, 486,
487, 488, 489, 490, 491, 494, 495, 496, 497, 498, 499, 500,
501, 504, 505, 506, 507, 508, 510, 511, 512, 513, 516, 518,
520, 523, 524, 525, 526, 527, 528, 529, 530, 531, 532, 533,
534, 535, 536, 538, 539, 540, 541, 544, 546, 547, 548, 549,
551, 552, 553, 554, 555, 556, 557, 559, 560, 561, 562, 563,
564, 565, 566, 568, 569, 570, 571, 572, 573, 574, 575, 576,
577, 578, 579, 584, 585, 586, 588, 589, 591, 592, 593, 594,
597, 598, 599

High School, 9-12

001, 002, 003, 004, 005, 006, 007, 008, 009, 013, 014, 015,
016, 018, 020, 021, 022, 023, 024, 025, 026, 027, 028, 029,
030, 033, 034, 035, 036, 038, 039, 040, 043, 044, 045, 046,
047, 048, 049, 050, 051, 052, 053, 054, 056, 057, 060, 061,
063, 064, 065, 066, 067, 068, 069, 070, 071, 072, 073, 074,
075, 076, 077, 078, 079, 080, 081, 082, 083, 084, 085, 086,
087, 088, 089, 090, 091, 092, 093, 094, 095, 096, 097, 098,
099, 100, 101, 102, 103, 104, 105, 106, 107, 108, 109, 110,
111, 112, 113, 115, 116, 117, 119, 120, 121, 122, 124, 125,
126, 127, 128, 129, 130, 131, 132, 133, 134, 135, 136, 137,
138, 139, 140, 141, 142, 143, 144, 145, 146, 147, 148, 149,
150, 151, 152, 153, 155, 157, 158, 159, 160, 161, 163, 164,
165, 166, 169, 171, 172, 173, 175, 176, 177, 178, 183, 184,
185, 186, 187, 188, 189, 190, 191, 192, 193, 194, 195, 196,
198, 199, 200, 201, 202, 203, 205, 206, 207, 209, 210, 211,
214, 215, 216, 217, 218, 219, 224, 225, 227, 228, 229, 230,
231, 232, 233, 234, 235, 236, 237, 238, 239, 240, 241, 242,
243, 244, 245, 246, 247, 248, 250, 251, 254, 255, 256, 257,
258, 259, 260, 261, 262, 263, 267, 268, 270, 271, 273, 274,
276, 277, 278, 279, 280, 282, 283, 284, 286, 287, 288, 289,

293, 294, 296, 298, 299, 300, 301, 302, 303, 304, 305, 306,
307, 308, 309, 310, 311, 312, 313, 314, 315, 316, 317, 318,
319, 320, 321, 322, 323, 324, 325, 326, 327, 328, 329, 330,
331, 332, 333, 334, 335, 337, 338, 339, 340, 341, 342, 343,
344, 345, 346, 347, 348, 349, 350, 351, 352, 353, 354, 355,
356, 357, 358, 259, 360, 361, 362, 363, 364, 367, 368, 369,
370, 371, 372, 373, 374, 375, 376, 377, 378, 379, 380, 381,
382, 383, 384, 385, 386, 387, 388, 389, 390, 391, 392, 393,
395, 396, 397, 398, 399, 400, 401, 402, 404, 405, 406, 407,
408, 409, 410, 411, 412, 413, 414, 415, 416, 417, 418, 419,
420, 422, 426, 427, 428, 429, 431, 432, 433, 434, 435, 436,
437, 438, 440, 441, 455, 456, 457, 458, 459, 460, 461, 462,
463, 464, 465, 466, 467, 468, 469, 470, 471, 472, 473, 474,
475, 476, 477, 478, 479, 480, 481, 482, 483, 484, 485, 486,
487, 488, 489, 490, 491, 492, 493, 494, 495, 496, 498, 501,
502, 504, 505, 506, 507, 508, 509, 510, 511, 512, 513, 514,
515, 516, 517, 518, 519, 520, 521, 522, 523, 524, 525, 526,
527, 528, 529, 530, 532, 533, 534, 535, 536, 537, 538, 539,
540, 541, 542, 543, 544, 545, 546, 547, 548, 549, 550, 551,
552, 553, 554, 555, 556, 559, 563, 564, 565, 566, 567, 568,
570, 571, 572, 573, 574, 576, 577, 578, 579, 581, 582, 583,
584, 585, 586, 589, 590, 592, 593, 595, 596, 597, 598, 599

Subject Index

The numbers refer to entries, not pages.

African Slave Trade 525, 526, 529, 535

Anne Frank House 122, 400, 437

Anti-Semitism 143, 160, 172, 175, 218, 236, 254, 261, 305, 306, 318, 330, 365, 385, 390, 393, 408, 496, 497, 498, 499, 500, 501, 502, 503, 504, 505,

Apartheid 506, 507, 508, 509, 510, 511, 512, 513

Armenian Genocide 514, 515, 516, 517, 518, 519

Art 005, 045, 305, 313, 315, 321, 323, 328, 359, 388

Assisi Underground 095, 394

Auschwitz-Birkenau 029, 038, 046, 051, 056, 066, 073, 074, 075, 076, 077, 079, 080, 084, 087, 088, 103, 107, 108, 124, 127, 128, 137, 196, 299, 303, 318, 337, 379, 384, 391, 400, 412, 416, 423, 444, 465

Avenue of the Righteous 360

Baeck, Leo 085

Barbie, Klaus 372

Baum, Froim 010

Bawnik, Nachama

Bergen-Belsen 054, 089, 092, 236, 244, 267, 379, 454

Bormann, Martin 381

Buchenwald 051, 127, 227, 375

Cambodian Genocide 520, 521, 522, 523, 524

Christians 021, 055, 056, 057, 093, 346

Civil War, American 565

Concentration Camps 017, 026, 028, 029, 039, 040, 094, 102, 126, 135, 224, 229, 206, 321, 343, 358, 376, 408, 410, 415, 454, 463, 464, 468, 469

Dachau 010, 050

Eichmann, Adolf 147, 372, 381, 403, 470

Ethnic Cleansing 536, 537, 538, 539, 540, 572

Final Solution 301, 325, 357, 385

Fortunoff Video Archives for Holocaust Testimonies 377

Frank, Anne 011, 012, 031, 042, 047, 052, 054, 057, 059, 104, 114, 118, 122, 140, 343, 379, 437

Genocide 541

Gies, Miep 052, 394

Goebbels, Joseph 390

Gypsies 250

Hidden Children 030, 032, 044, 097, 098, 117, 122, 125, 168, 181, 183, 196, 284, 298, 352, 425

Himmler, Heinrich 403

Hiroshima and Nagasaki 557, 558, 559, 560, 561, 562

Hitler, Adolf 013, 018, 082, 146, 170, 193, 311, 339, 342, 351, 354, 371, 399, 416, 417, 420, 421

Hitler Youth Movement 068,
Homosexuals 280, 396
Hoss, Rudolf 403
Israeli War of Independence
   050, 166, 278, 287
Japanese-American Internment
   579, 580, 581, 582, 583,
   584, 585, 586, 587, 588
Jewish-Christian Relations
   407, 411, 496
Khmer Rouge
   521, 522, 523, 524
The Killing Fields (motion
   picture) 521, 522
Korczak, Janusz 010, 025,
   058, 060, 150, 217
Korean War 567
Kristallnacht 037, 141, 305,
   402, 434, 456
Ku Klux Klan 544, 545, 548
Lebensborn 363
Le Chambon-sur-Lignon 232,
   304, 356, 404
Lidice 400
Lodz Ghetto 009, 107, 297
Manzanar 580, 583
March of the Living 164, 410,
   415
Martyrs and Heroes
   Remembrance Act 296, 360
Medical Experiments 088
Mengele, Josef 088, 372,
   381, 403
Middle Passage 526, 529, 535
Militia Movement 542, 550
Native Americans 595, 596,
   597, 598, 599
Nazism 342, 354, 359, 367,
   371, 383, 390, 399, 417,
   420, 421, 423, 429, 447
Neo-Nazis 236, 545, 546
Niemoller, Martin 445

Nuremburg War Crimes
   Tribunal 147, 311, 320,
   403, 408, 470
Persian Gulf War 577
Plaszow 087
Pot, Pol 522
Pran, Dith 521, 522
Prejudice 547, 549, 551, 552,
   553, 554, 555, 556
Propaganda 365
Ravensbruck 026, 093
Rescuers 015, 027, 049, 055,
   056, 070, 076, 079, 095,
   102, 106, 109, 163, 223,
   228, 231, 314, 341, 346,
   368, 418, 419, 438
Resistance Movements 021,
   034, 036, 048, 061, 069,
   105, 109, 119, 133, 159,
   163, 176, 188, 203, 217,
   219, 227, 231, 269, 271,
   272, 273, 288, 291, 292,
   295, 304, 322, 332, 341,
   395, 397, 400, 424, 429,
   431, 438, 442, 563
Righteous Gentiles 027, 052,
   058, 072, 078, 081, 101,
   116, 117, 130, 211, 233,
   307, 317, 346, 356, 386,
   404
Schindlerjuden 098, 135, 211,
   317
Schindler, Oskar 101, 135,
   211, 317, 394
Senesh (Szenes), Hannah
   016, 105, 109, 145, 152,
   478
Shtetl 308
Simon Wiesenthal Center 378
Slave Narratives 527, 528,
   529, 530, 533
Slave Rebellions 528, 532

Sobibor 401
Spanish Inquisition 172
St. Louis 305
Streicher, Julius 403
Survivors 007, 017, 043, 045,
  050, 055, 056, 062, 063,
  064, 068, 069, 071, 073,
  074, 075, 076, 077, 079,
  080, 083, 089, 091, 094,
  097, 098, 102, 105, 113,
  115, 123, 128, 129, 132,
  136, 137, 155, 157, 169,
  171, 175, 185, 190, 194,
  198, 216, 224, 226, 230,
  254, 280, 283, 287, 288,
  299, 300, 317, 327, 336,
  337, 340, 344, 347, 357,
  377, 382, 407, 409, 413,
  422, 423, 433, 444, 446,
  450, 454, 459, 461, 465
Teenagers 014, 015, 040, 046,
  057, 085, 087, 107, 135,
  136, 137, 155, 171, 224,
  232, 233, 240, 245, 288,
  316, 344, 410, 415, 432
Theresienstadt (Terezin) 039,
  102, 328, 337, 349, 400,
  477
Third Reich 311, 331, 339,
  342, 351, 354, 371, 383,
  399, 416, 417, 418, 420,
  421, 441
Treblinka 025, 060, 129, 150,
  153, 276, 429, 451
Uncle Misha's Partisans 268,
  272
Underground (see Resistance
  Movements)
United States Holocaust
  Memorial Museum 229,
  302, 309, 378, 380

Vichy France 033, 144, 235,
  404
Vietnam War 566, 571
Waldheim, Kurt 372
Wallenberg, Raoul 027, 072,
  078, 081
War Criminals (German) 086,
  147, 151, 214, 315, 320,
  372, 381, 389, 403, 418,
  440, 470
War Criminals (Japanese) 389
Warsaw Ghetto 010, 022, 023,
  025, 060, 100, 150, 153,
  171, 216, 217, 243, 244,
  245, 276, 279, 318, 361,
  400, 428, 443
Warsaw Ghetto Uprising 070,
  205, 275, 304, 370, 373,
  379, 439, 442
Westerbork 236, 379
White Supremacists 545, 548,
  550
Wiesel, Elie 055, 113, 127,
  395
Wiesenthal, Simon 086, 440
World War I 586, 573, 574
World War II 564, 570, 575,
  576, 578
Yad Vashem 297

Title Index

The numbers refer to entries, not pages.

Address Unknown 274
Adem's Cross 538
After the War 227
Against All Hope: Resistance
   in Nazi Concentration
   Camps, 1938-1945 376
Ajeemah and His Son 525
Alan and Naomi 222
All Quiet on the Western Front
   573
Alicia: My Story 014
Along the Tracks 165
Amsterdam 414
An Album of Nazism 367
and God Cried...: The
   Holocaust Remembered
   378
And I Am Afraid of My Dreams
   093
And the Violins Stopped
Playing: A Story of the
   Gypsy Holocaust 250
Angry Harvest 183
Anna Is Still Here 284
Anne Frank (Admur) 012
Anne Frank (Epstein) 042
Anne Frank (Tames) 114
Anne Frank (Tyler) 118
Anne Frank: A Portrait in
   Courage 104
Anne Frank: Beyond the Diary
   437
Anne Frank, Beyond the
Diary: A Photographic

Remembrance 122
Anne Frank: Child of the
   Holocaust 031
Anne Frank: Life in Hiding
   059
Anne Frank Remembered: The
   Story of the Woman Who
   Helped to Hide the Frank
   Family 052
Anne Frank's Tales from the
   Secret Annex 343
Anthology of Holocaust
   Literature 002
Anti-Semitism 330
Anti-Semitism: The Road to the
   Holocaust and Beyond 393
Anton the Dove Fancier and
   Other Tales of the
   Holocaust 200
Approaches to Auschwitz: The
   Holocaust and Its Legacy
   412
The Armenian Genocide in
   Perspective 517
Art from the Ashes: A
   Holocaust Anthology 005
Arthur Miller's Playing for
   Time: A Full-Length Stage
   Play 142
The Art of Jewish Children:
   Germany, 1936-1941 388
Art of the Holocaust 313
   245
Assignment Rescue: An

Autobiography 049

The Assisi Underground: The Priests Who Rescued Jews 095

As the Waltz Was Ending 033

At the Crossroads 507

Auschwitz 088

Auschwitz: True Tales from a Grotesque Land 391

Avenue of the Righteous: Portraits in Uncommon Courage of Christians and the Jews They Saved from Hitler 360

Bad Times, Good Friends: A Personal Memoir 120

A Backward Look: Germans Remember 375

A Bag of Marbles 064

Bearing Witness: Stories of the Holocaust 006

The Beautiful Days of My Youth: My Six Months in Auschwitz and Plaszow 087

Becky's Horse 226

Behind Barbed Wire: The Imprisonment of Japanese Americans During World War II 581

Behind the Secret Window: A Memoir of Hidden Childhood During World War II 117

Behind the Bedroom Wall 290

Benny 174

The Berlin Stories 207

Between Two Worlds 501

Beyond Imagination: Canadians Write About the Holocaust 003

Beyond the High White Wall 504

Beyond the Killing Fields: Voices of Nine Cambodian Survivors in America 524

Beyond These Shores, 1934- 1940: Poems and Diary of a Jewish Girl Who Escaped from Nazi Germany 471

The Big Lie: A True Story 073

The Bird Has Wings: Letters of Peter Schweifert 106

Black Dog of Fate: A Memoir 515

Blood to Remember: American Poets on the Holocaust 458

The Book of the Just: The Unsung Heroes Who Rescued Jews from Hitler 419

The Book of Jewish Knowledge: 613 Basic Facts About Judaism 589

Born Guilty: Children of Nazi Families 418

The Borrowed House 281

The Boy from Over There 166

The Boys: The Untold Story of 732 Young Concentration Camp Survivors 347

The Boy Who Saved the Children 019

The Bracelet 587

The Bravest Battle: The Twenty-Eight Days of the Warsaw Ghetto Uprising 370

Breaking the Chains: African- American Slave Resistance

528
Briar Rose 293
*Bright Candles: A Novel of
  the Danish Resistance* 163
Broken Glass 143
The Broken Mirror: A Novella
  180
Brother Enemy 225
*Bullwhip Days: The Slaves
  Remember* 533
*Burned Child Seeks the Fire: A
  Memoir* 039
*Bury My Heart at Wounded
  Knee* 595
But Can the Phoenix Sing?
  216

The Cage 107
A Cambodian Odyssey 521
The Camera of My Family
  392
*Caught in the Crossfire:
  Growing Up in a War Zone*
  572
Ceremony of Innocence 188
A Certain Magic 241
Chase Me, Catch Nobody!
  203
Chernowitz! 160
Childhood: A Remembrance
  089
A Child in Prison Camp 585
*Child of the Holocaust: A True
  Story* 071
A Child of the Warsaw Ghetto
  010
*Children in the Holocaust and
  World War II: Their
  Secret Diaries* 004
Children of Bach 179
*Children of Cambodia's
  Killing Fields* 522
The Children of Mapu Street

239
*Children of the Holocaust:
  Conversations with Sons
  and Daughters of Survivors*
  337
Children of the Resistance 322
Children of the Swastika 362
*Children of Topaz: The Story
  of a Japanese-American
  Internment Camp* 586
The Children We Remember
  296
*A Child's War: World War II
  Through the Eyes of
  Children* 324
*The Choice: A Play in Two
  Acts* 145
The Chosen 593
*Christmas in the Big House,
  Christmas in the Quarters*
  531
*The Cigarette Sellers of Three
  Crosses Square* 443
Clara's Story 062
Code Name Kris 228
Code: Polonaise 291
*The Courage to Care:
  Rescuers of Jews During
  the Holocaust* 404
*Crystal Night: 9-10 November
  1938* 434
Crystal Nights 237
Cry, the Beloved Country 511

*Damned Strong Love: The
  True Story of Wiili G. and
  Stefan K.* 280
*Dancing on the Bridge of
  Avignon* 285
The Dangerous Game 176
Daniel's Story 229
Dark Hour of Noon 273

Darkness Casts No Shadow
    224
Darkness Over the Land 270
David and Jonathan 283
David and Max 249
Dawn 287
*A Day of Pleasure: Stories of a
    Boy Growing Up in
    Warsaw* 110
*Days of Judgement: The World
    War II War Crimes Trials*
    389
*Dear Unknown Friend,
    Children's Letters from
    Sarajevo* 539
The Deputy 141
The Devil in Vienna 242
The Devil's Arithmetic 294
The Diary of Anne Frank
    (Play) 140
*The Diary of a Young Girl:
    The Definitive Edition*
    047
*The Diary of David
    Sierakowiak: Five
    Notebooks from the Lodz
    Ghetto* 009
*Dictionary of the Holocaust:
    Biography, Geography, and
    Terminology* 492
*Different Voices: Women of
    the Holocaust* 405
*Discrimination: Prejudice in
    Action* 547
Displaced Persons 169
Dobryd 173
*Doctor Korczak and the
    Children* 150
Don't Forget 450
Don't Say a Word 195
*Don't They Know the World
    Stopped Breathing?:
    Reminiscences of a French*

*Child During the
    Holocaust Years* 044
The Drowned and the Saved
    079
*Dry Tears: The Story of a Lost
    Childhood* 115

18 Lives 594
The Eighth Sin 209
*Elli: Coming of Age in the
    Holocaust* 028
*Elie Wiesel: Messenger from
    the Holocaust* 055
Elie Wiesel: Witness for Life
    113
The Empty Moat 265
Encyclopedia of the Holocaust
    482
*Encyclopedia of the Third
    Reich* 493
*The Endless Steppe: Growing
    Up in Siberia* 498
Erika: Poems of the Holocaust
    462
Escape from Auschwitz 124
Escape from Sobibor 401
Escape from the Holocaust
    256
*Escape or Die: True Stories of
    Young People Who
    Survived the Holocaust* 344
*Europa, Europa: A Memoir of
    World War II* 091
*Eva's Story: A Survivor's Tale
    by Step-Sister of Anne
    Frank* 103
Eyewtiness Auschwitz 084
Exodus 278

*The Face of the Third Reich:
    Portraits of the Nazi
    Leadership* 339
Faithful Elephants: A True

Story of Animals, People, and War 575

Fallen Angels 571

Farewell to Manzanar 583

Far From the Place We Call Home 259

Father of the Orphans: The Story of Janusz Korczak 025

The Feather-Bed Journey 446

A Field of Buttercups 060

The Final Journey 248

Final Journey: The Fate of the Jews in Nazi Europe 348

Finding My Way 549

Five Chimneys 077

Flowers on the Wall 451

Flying Against the Wind: The Story of a Young Woman Who Defied the Nazis 048

For Every Sin: A Novel 157

For You Who Died I Must Live On. . . : Reflections on the March of the Living: Contemporary Jewish Youth Confront the Holocaust 410

Four Perfect Pebbles: A Holocaust Story 092

Fragments: Memories of a Childhood, 1939-1948 128

Fragments of Isabella: A Memoir of Auschwitz to Freedom 074

Friedrich 252

From a Ruined Garden: The Memorial Books of Polish Jewry 369

From Slave Ship to Freedom Road 529

A Frost in the Night 161

The Garden 230

The Gates of the Forest: A Novel 288

Genocide: The Systematic Killing of a People 541

Gentlehands 214

Ghosts of the Holocaust: An Anthology of Poetry by the Second Generation 459

Gideon: A Novel 153

A Girl Called Judith Strick 036

The Golden Tradition: Jewish Life and Thought in Eastern Europe 590

Grace in the Wilderness: After the Liberation, 1945-1948 267

Greater Than Angels 232

The Grey-Striped Suit: How Grandma and Grandpa Survived the Holocaust 208

Growing Up Latino: Memoirs and Stories 543

Gulf 577

Guns and Barbed Wire: A Child Survives the Holocaust 051

Habibi 553

Hannah Senesh: Her Life and Diary 109

Hannah Szenes: A Song of Light 105

Hasidic Tales of the Holocaust: The First Original Hasidic Tales in a Century 334

Haven: The Unknown Story of 1,000 World War II Refugees 353

Hear O Israel: A Story of the Warsaw Ghetto 276

A Hidden Childhood: A Jewish Girl's Sanctuary in a French Convent 125
The Hidden Children 352
Hidden Children: Forgotten Survivors of the Holocaust 425
Hide and Seek 123
Hiding from the Nazis 298
The Hiding Place 116
Hiding to Survive: Stories of Jewish Children Rescued from the Holocaust 407
Hiroshima (Hersey) 559
Hiroshima (Yep) 562
Hiroshima No Pika 560
Historical Atlas of the Holocaust 494
A History of the Holocaust 306
History of the Holocaust: A Handbbook and Dictionary 480
A History of the Jews in Europe during the Second World War 345
Hitler 082
Hitler and the Germans 351
Hitler and the Nazis: The Evil That Men Do 411
Hitler and Nazism 420
The Hitler File: A Social History of Germany and the Nazis 354
Hitler: From Power to Ruin 013
Hitler's Third Reich: A Documentary History 421
Hitler's War Against the Jews 301
Hitler Youth 426
Holocaust 470
Holocaust (series) 483

The Holocaust 427
The Holocaust: A Golier Student Library 495
The Holocaust: A History of Courage and Resistance 424
The Holocaust Lady 413
Holocaust Poetry 474
Holocaust Project: From Darkness Into Light 319
A Holocaust Reader 325
The Holocaust: The Fire That Raged 408
Holocaust Testimonies: The Ruins of Memory 377
The Holocaust: Society on Trial 314
The Holocaust: The World and the Jews, 1939-1945 405
The Holocaust: Understanding and Remembering 430
Horses of Anger 189
Hostage to War: A True Story 576
The House of Four Winds 282
The House on Prague Street 178
How Democracy Failed 432
How We Danced While We Burned: Followed by La justice, or, The Cock that Crew: Two Plays 135
Howl Like the Wolves: Growing Up in Nazi Germany 121

I Am an American: A True Story of Japanese Internment 584
I Am a Star: Child of the Holocaust 017
I Am Fifteen and I Don't Want

to Die 015
I Am Rosemarie 236
I Didn't Say Goodbye:
    Interviews with Children of
    the Holocaust 435
I Dream of Peace: Images of
    War by Children of Former
    Yugoslavia 540
If I Should Die Before I Wake
    240
I Have Lived a Thousand
    Years: Growing Up in
    the Holocaust 029
I Keep Recalling: The
    Holocaust Poems of Jacob
    Glatstein 459
Image Before My Eyes: A
Photographic History of
    Jewish Life in Poland
Before the Holocaust 329
Imagining Hitler 146
The Importance of Adolf Hitler
    018
The Importance of Oskar
    Schindler 101
Incident at Vichy 144
I Never Saw Another Butterfly:
    Children's Drawings
    and Poems from Terezin
    Concentration
    Camp, 1942-1944 477
In Evidence: Poems of the
    Liberation of Nazi
    Concentration Camps 463
In Kindling Flame: The Story
    of Hannah Senesh 016
In Memories Kitchen: A
    Legacy from the Women of
    Terezin 328
In My Father's Court 111
In the Camps 358
In the Face of Danger 210
In the Mouth of the Wolf 132

In the Shade of the Chestnut
    Tree 275
The Investigation 151
I Promised I Would Tell 126
Isabella: From Auschwitz to
    Freedom 075
I Shall Live 090
The Island on Bird Street 243
I Was There 253

Jacob's Rescue: A Holocaust
    Story 181
Jafta: The Homecoming 508
The Jewish-Americans: A
    History in Their Own
    Words, 1650-1950 384
The Jewish Holocaust for
    Beginners 366
The Jewish Resistance: The
    History of the Jewish
    Partisans in Lithuania and
    White Russia
    During the Nazi
    Occupation, 1940-1945
    332
The Jewish Wife and Other
    Short Plays 138
Johnny Got His Gun 574
Joseph and Me: In the Days of
    the Holocaust 058
The Journey 184
The Journey Back 097
The Joruney: Japanese
    Americans, Racism, and
    Rewewal 582
Journey of Conscience: Young
    People Respond to the
    Holocaust 400
Journey to America 220
Journey to Topaz: A Story of
    Japanese-American
    Evacuation 588
Justice at Nurmeberg 320

Kaffir Boy: The True Story of a Black Youth's Coming of Age in Apartheid South Africa 509
Kindertransport 037
A Kind of Secret Weapon 159
Kristallnacht: The Nazi Night of Terror 402
The Ku Klux Klan: America's Recurring Nightmare 544

The Land and People of South Africa 512
The Last of the Just 262
The Last Mission 233
The Last Seven Months of Anne Frank 379
The Lead Soldiers 244
Last Traces: The Lost Art of Auschwitz 323
Leon's Story 555
Lest Innocent Blood Be Shed: The Story of Le Chambon and How Goodness Happened There 356
Lest We Forget: The Passage from Africa to Slavery and Emancipation 535
Letters from Rifka 499
Let the Celebrations Begin! 454
Liberating the Ghosts: Photographs and Texts From the March of the Living Including Excerpts from the Writings of Participants 415
Life in the Shtetl: Scenes and Recollections 308
Light From a Yellow Star: A Lesson of Love from the Holocaust 045

Light One Candle: A Survivor's Tale from Lithuania to Jerusalem 050
Liliana's Journal: Warsaw, 1939-1945 134
The Lily Cupboard 452
Lisa's War 231
The Little Riders 266
The Living Witness: Art in the Concentration Camps and Ghettos 321
Lodz Ghetto: Inside a Community Under Siege 297
The Long Escape 286

The Macmillan Atlas of the Holocaust 349
The Man from the Other Side 245
The Man in the Box 234
The Man in the Glass Booth 147
Manya's Story 497
Maps and Photographs: A Record of the Destruction of Jewish Life in Europe During the Dark Years of Nazi Rule 350
Maus: A Survivor's Tale: Part I: My Father Bleeds History 422
Maus: A Survivor's Tale: Part II: And Here My Troubles Began 423
Memory Fields 030
Memories of Anne Frank: Reflections of a Childhood Friend 054
Memories of My Ghost Brother 567
The Middle Passage 526

Mila 18 279
The Militia Movement and
    Hate Groups in America
    550
The Militia Movement in
    America: Before and After
    Oklahoma City 542
The Miracle Tree 561
Miriam 269
Mischling, Second Degree 068
Monday in Odessa 505
Morning Is a Long Time
    Coming 201
Mottele: A Partisan Odyssey
    258
The Murderers Among Us: The
    Simon Wiesenthal Memoirs
    440
My Brother, My Enemy 190
My Brother's Keeper: The
    Holocaust Through the
    Eyes of an Artist 310
My Childhood in Nazi
    Germany 041
My Little Sister and Selected
    Poems, 1965-1985 466

Nazi Culture: Intellectual,
    Cultural, and Social in
    the Third Reich 390
Nazi Germany: The Origins
    and Collapse of the Third
    Reich 399
Nazi Hunter: Simon
    Wiesenthal 086
Nazi Hunting 381
The Nazis 371
Nazism 342
Nazi War Criminals (Landau)
    372
Nazi War Criminals (Rice)
    403
Neo-Nazis: A Growing Threat
    546
The Never-Ending Greenness
    453
Never to Be Forgotten: A
    Young Girl's Holocaust
    Memoir 083
Never To Forget: The Jews of
    the Holocaust 385
Night 127
The Night Crossing 154
Nightfather 194
Nightjohn 534
The Night Journey 500
The Nightmare in History: The
    Holocaust, 1933-1945 318
Night of the Broken Glass:
    Poems of the Holocaust
    456
No Hero for the Kaiser 568
North to Freedom 206
Notes from the Warsaw
    Ghetto: The Journal of
    Emmanuel Rigenblum 100
No Turning Back 510
The Number on My
    Grandfather's Arm 299
Number the Stars 223

Of Pure Blood 363
Odyssey 312
The Old Brown Suitcase: A
    Teenager's Story of War
    and Peace 171
On Both Sides of the Wall 230
100 Poems plus. . . 475
One Man's Valor: Leo Baeck
    and the Holocaust 085
One Yellow Daffodil: A
    Hanukah Story 444
On the Other Side of the Gate
    271
Oral History and the
    Holocaust: A Collection of

*Poems from Interviews with
Survivors of the
Holocaust* 461
*O the Chimneys: Selected
Poems* 472
Other People's Houses 263
*The Other Victims: First
Person Stories of Non-Jews
Persecuted by the Nazis*
345
The Other Way Round 212
*Outcast: A Jewish Girl in
Wartime Berlin* 035
*Out of the Whirlwind: A
Reader of Holocaust
Literature* 001

*Painful Echoes--Poems of the
Holocaust* 460
Parallel Journeys 303
The Parnas 496
A Passage to Ararat 514
*Peace and War: A Collection
of Poems* 460
*Pearls of Childhood: The
Poignant True Wartime
Story of a Young Girl
Growing Up in an Adopted
Land* 053
Petros's War 295
*Photomontages of the Nazi
Period* 359
*The Pictorial History of the
Holocaust* 479
*The Pink Triangle: The Nazi
War Against Homosexuals*
396
A Picture Book of Anne Frank
011
*A Place to Hide: True Stories
of Holocaust Rescuers* 394
Playing for Time 043
Plays of the Holocaust: An

International Anthology
139
Poems of the Holocaust
(Klein) 465
Poems of the Holocaust
(Melek) 467
*Polish Jews: A Pictorial
Record* 436
Posters of World War II 365
Prank 218
*Prejudice: Stories About Hate,
Ignorance, Revelation, and
Transformation* 552
*Preserving Memory: The
Struggle to Create
America's Holocaust
Museum* 380
*Promise of a New Spring: The
Holocaust and Renewal*
449

*Racial Prejudice: Why Can't
We Overcome?* 554
*The Racist Mind: Portraits of
American Neo-Nazis
And Klansmen* 545
*Raoul Wallenberg: Missing
Diplomat* 072
*Raoul Wallenberg: The Man
Who Stopped for Death*
081
*Rebels Against Slavery:
American Slave Revolts* 532
The Red Badge of Courage
565
The Red Magician 199
Refugee 255
*Remember Not to Forget: A
Memory of the Holocaust*
340
Rescue in Denmark 341
*Rescuers: Portraits of Moral
Courage in the Holocaust*

314
*Rescue: The Story of How
  Gentiles Saved the Jews in
  the Holocaust* 386
The Resistance 304
*Return to Auschwitz: The
  Remarkable Saga of a Girl
  Who Survived the
  Holocaust* 056
Reunion 277
*The Righteous Among the
  Nations* 307
*Righteous Gentile: The Story
  of Raoul Wallenberg* 027
*The Rise and Fall of Adolf
  Hitler* 416
*The Rise and Fall of the Third
  Reich* 417
*The Road from Home: The
  Story of an Armenian
  Girl* 518
*Rooftop Secrets and Other
  Stories of Anti-Semitism*
  172
Rose Blanche 448
*Routledge Atlas of the
  Holocaust* 481
*The Royal Resident: A
  Historical Tale* 502
Rumors and Stones: A Journey
  065

Sacred Shadows 261
Sadako 557
*Sadako and the Thousand
  Paper Cranes* 558
Sami and the Time of Troubles
  569
*Sarajevo Daily: A City and Its
  Newspaper Under Siege*
  537
*Saving the Fragments: From
  Auschwitz to New York*

076
Scent of the Snowflowers 067
*Schindler's Legacy: True
  Stories of the List
  Survivors* 317
Schindler's List 211
A Scrap of Time 185
*The Seamstress: A Memoir of
  Survival* 026
Season of Discovery 198
The Secret Ship 368
*The Secret Survivors of the
  Holocaust* 382
*Seder in Helrin and Other
  Stories for Girls* 215
*Seed of Sarah: Memoirs of a
  Survivor* 063
The Seeker and Other Poems
  473
*Sentenced to Live: A
  Survivor's Memoir* 066
*Seven Portholes in Hell:
  Poems of the Holocaust*
  476
The Shadow Children 260
The Shadow of the Wall 217
*Shadows of a Childhood: A
  Novel of War and
  Friendship* 196
*Shadows of the Holocaust:
  Plays, Readings and
  Program Resources* 149
The Shawl 247
Sheltering Rebecca 162
*Shielding the Flame: An
  Intimate Conversation with
  Dr. Marek Edelman, the
  Last Surviving Leader of
  the Warsaw Ghetto
  Uprising* 070
The Short Life of Sophie Scholl
  119
The Shrinking Circle:

Memories of Nazi Berlin,
1933-1939 131
The Sign in Mendel's Window
503
Silver Days 221
The Silver Sword 264
Sky: A True Story of
Resistance During World
War II 061
Slavery Time: When I Was
Chillun 527
Smoke and Ashes: The Story of
the Holocaust 406
So Far from the Sea 580
Some of Us Survived: The
Story of an Armenian Boy
516
Somehow Tenderness
Survives: Stories of
Southern Africa 513
So Much to Forget 112
So Young to Die: The Story of
Hannah Senesh.
Heroes, Heroines and
Holidays: Plays for Jewish
Youth 145
Sparks of Glory 398
Spyglass: An Autobiography
034
The Star Fisher 556
Star of Danger 219
Star of Fear, Star of Hope 447
Starring Sally J. Freedman as
Herself 170
Star Without a Sky 246
Stolen Years 136
The Stones Cry Out: A
Cambodian Childhood,
1975-1980 523
Stones in Water 238
The Story of Peter Cronheim
156
The Story of the Jews 592

Strange and Unexpected Love:
A Teenage Girl's
Holocaust Memoirs 057
Stranger to Her People 164
Struggle 137
Summer of My German Soldier
202
The Sunflower 289
Survival in Auschwitz 080
Surviving Treblinka 129
The Survivor of the Holocaust
040
The Survivor 191
Survivors Speak Out 007
Survivors: An Oral History of
the Armenian Genocide
519
The Swastika on the
Synagogue Door 254
Swastika Over Paris: The Fate
of the Jews in France 364

"Take Care of Josette": A
Memoir in Defense of
Occupied France 130
Taking a Stand Against Racism
551
Tales from a Child of the
Enemy 457
The Tattooed Torah 197
Tell No One Who You Are: The
Hidden Children of Regine
Miller 032
Tell Them We Remember: The
Story of the Holocaust 305
Terrible Things 445
The Testing of Hannah Senesh
(Play) 152
The Testing of Hannah Senesh
(Poetry) 478
Thanks to My Mother 094
That Denmark Might Live: The
Saga of the Danish

Resistance in World War II 438

The Theatre of the Holocaust 148

Their Brother's Keepers: The Christian Heroes and Heroines who Helped the Oppressed Escape the Nazi Terror 346

Theodore Herzl, the Road to Israel 591

They Called Me Frau Anna 020

They Called Me Leni 167

They Fought Back: The Story of the Jewish Resistance in Nazi Europe 431

They Thought They Were Free: The Germans, 1933-1945 383

The Third Reich (Berwick) 311

The Third Reich (Williamson) 441

Through Our Eyes: Children Witness the Holocaust 433

A Time of Fire 578

A Time to Choose 563

A Time to Fight Back: True Stories of Wartime Resistance 395

To Be a Slave 530

To Cross a Line 251

To Destroy You is No Loss: The Odyssey of a Cambodian Family 520

To Fight in Silence 292

To Life 108

Touch Wood: A Girlhood in Occupied France 257

To Vanquish the Dragon 024

Tracking the Holocaust 355

Traces 186

The Traitors 192

Treblinka 429

The Triumphant Spirit: Portraits and Stories of Holocaust Survivors. . . Their Messages of Hope and Compassion 327

Truth and Lamentation: Stories and Poems of the Holocaust 008

Tug of War 570

Tunes for Bears to Dance To 175

Twenty and Ten 168

The Twins 187

Tzili: The Story of a Life 158

Uncle Misha's Partisans 272

Under the Domim Tree 155

The United States Holocaust Memorial Museum: America Keeps the Memory Alive 302

Upon the Head of a Goat: A Childhood in Hungary, 1939-1944 268

The Uprising in the Warsaw Ghetto, November 1940- May 1943 439

The Upstairs Room 098

The Vapor 021

Variable Directions: The Selected Poetry of Don Pagis 469

Victory in Europe: The Fall of Hitler's Germany 331

The Visit 177

Voices from the Camps: Internment of Japanese Americans During World

War II 579
*A Voice from the Forest:
  Memoirs of a Jewish
  Partisan* 069
Voices from the Holocaust
  409
Voices from Vietnam 566
*A Voice in the Chorus: Life as
  a Teenager in the
  Holocaust* 135
The Voyage of the Ulua 336

Waiting for Anya 236
Waiting for the Rain 506
The Wall 205
*Wallenberg: The Man in the
  Iron Web* 078
*Walls: Resisting the Third
  Reich-- One Woman's
  Story* 133
*Wanted! The Search for Nazis
  in America* 315
*The War Against the Jews,
  1933-1945* 326
Warsaw Ghetto 428
*The Warsaw Ghetto: A
  Christian's Testimony* 022
*The Warsaw Ghetto: A
  Photographic Record,
  1941-1944* 361
The Warsaw Ghetto Uprising
  (Landau) 373
The Warsaw Ghetto Uprising
  (Zeinert) 442
*We Are Here: Songs of the
  Holocaust* 468
*We Are Witnesses: Five
  Diaries of Teenagers Who
  Died in the Holocaust* 316
Welcome Tomorrow 099
*We're Alive and Life Goes On:
  A Theresienstadt Diary* 102
We Remember the Holocaust
  300
We Survived the Holocaust
  374
*We Were Children Just Like
  You* 335
What About Me? 182
*What Did You Do in the War
  Daddy?: Growing Up
  German* 096
When Hitler Stole Pink Rabbit
  213
The White Crow 193
*The White Power Movement:
  America's Racist Hate
  Groups* 548
*Winter in the Morning: A
  Young Girl's Life in the
  Warsaw Ghetto and
  Beyond, 1939-1945* 023
With a Camera in the Ghetto
  351
*Witness and Legacy:
  Contemporary Art about
  the Holocaust* 338
Witness to the Holocaust 333
*The World Must Know: The
  History of the Holocaust
  as Told in the United States
  Holocaust Memorial
  Museum* 309
*The World of Our Fathers: The
  Jews of Eastern Europe*
  387
Worlds Torn Asunder 038
*World War II Resistance
  Stories* 397

The Yanov Torah 204
*The Year of Impossible
  Goodbyes* 564
*Yes, We Sang! Songs of the
  Ghettos and Concentration
  Camps* 464

*Young Moshe's Diary: The
    Spiritual Torment of a
    Jewish Boy in Nazi Europe*
    046
*Young People Speak:
    Surviving the Holocaust in
    Hungary* 357
*Young Voices from the Ghetto:
    A Collection of Children
    and Young People's Poetry
    Written in the Ghettos of
    World War II* 455

*Zlata's Diary: A Child's Life
    in Sarajevo* 536

About the Author

Ed Sullivan received his B.A. in English from Glassboro State College, an M.A. in English Literature from Memphis State University, and a M.S. in Library and Information Sciences from The University of Tennessee, Knoxville. He presently works as a Senior Project Librarian for The New York Public Library's Connecting Libraries and Schools Project (CLASP), an outreach program to K-8 students, and their parents and teachers. Previously, Ed worked as a Young Adult Librarian for NYPL's Staten Island branches. Prior to becoming a librarian, Ed taught high school English in Mississippi and courses in composition and literature at Memphis State University. An active member of the American Library Association, Ed serves on committees in the children's, young adult, and public library divisions. Ed has written articles, bibliographies, and reviews for *The ALAN Review*, *Book Links*, *Public Libraries*, *School Library Journal*, and *VOYA*. This is his first book. Ed lives in New Jersey with his wife Judy and their three cats.